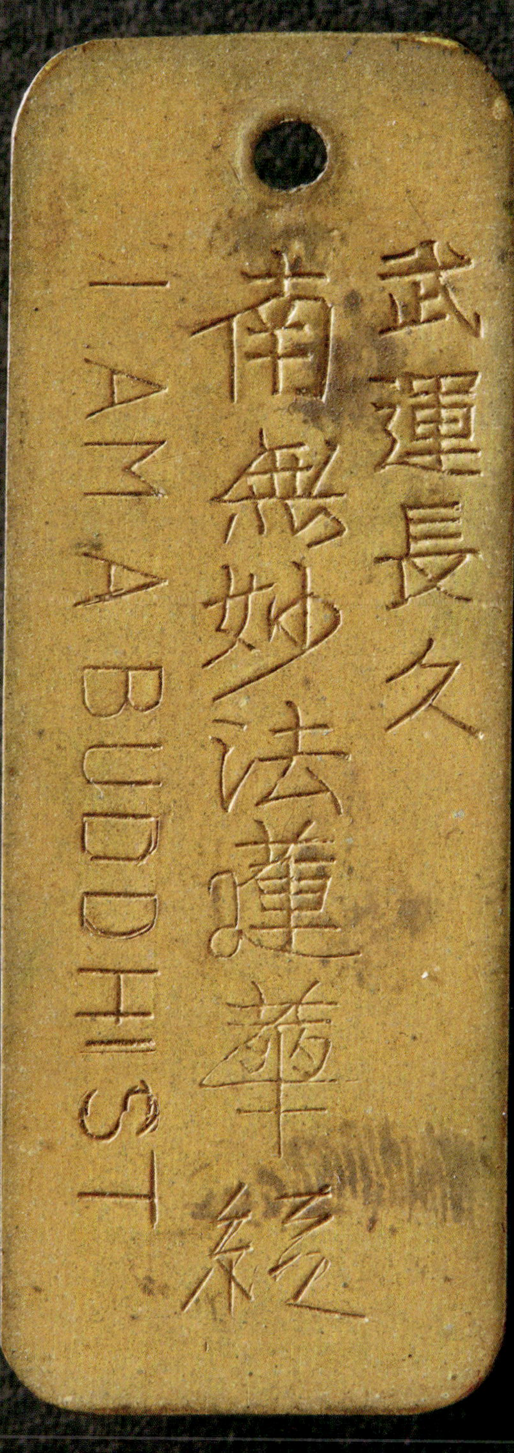

武運長久
南無妙法蓮華経
I AM A BUDDHIST

AF479626

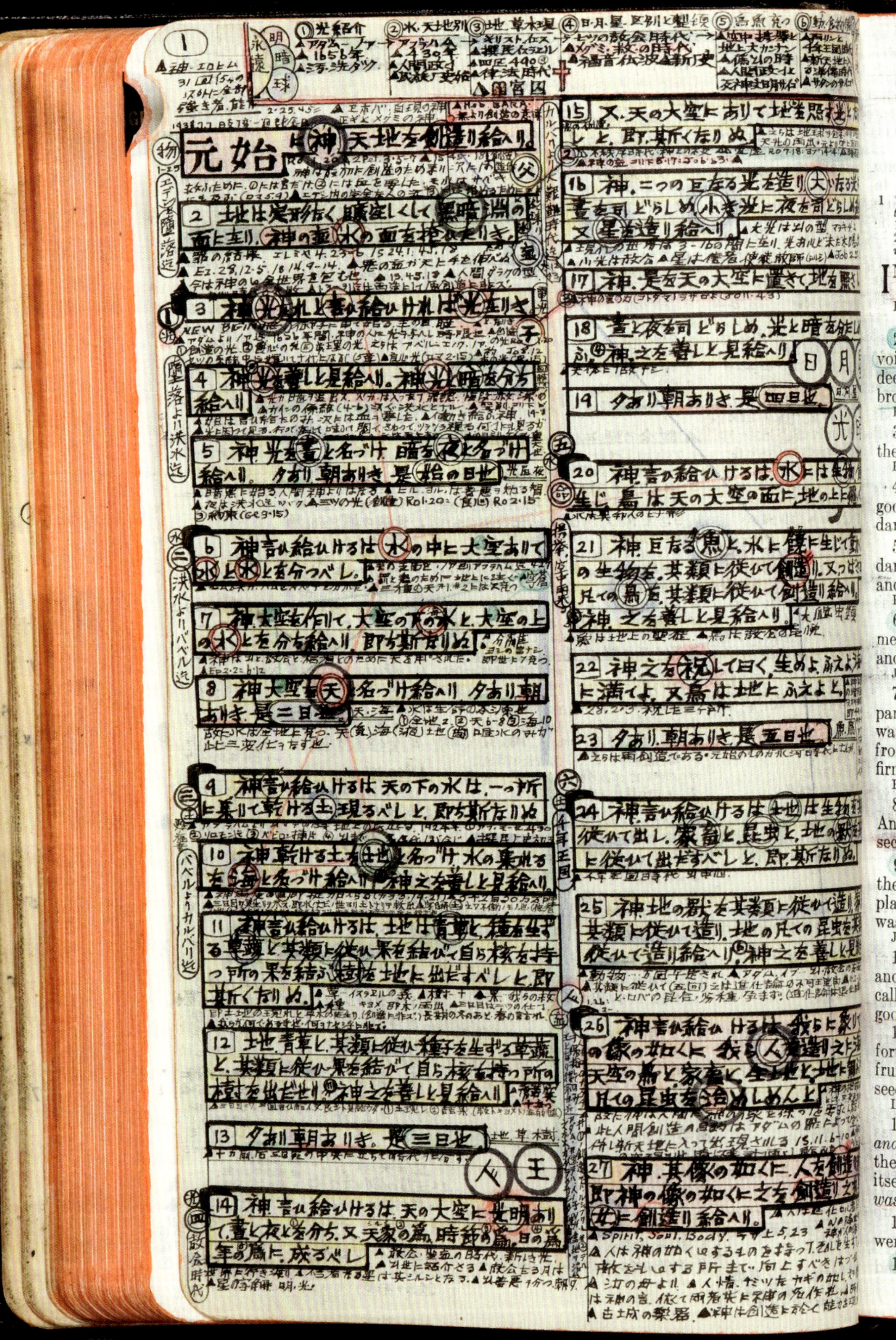

1 The creation o
the firmament,
11 and made f
20 of fish and
in the image of

IN the begi
and the e
Ps. 8.3; Pr.
Ac. 14.15;

2 And the
void; and dar
deep. And t
brooding] up
Ps. 33.6; Is. 4

3 And Goo
there was lig
Ps. 33.9; 2 Co

4 And Goo
good: and G
darkness.

5 And Goo
darkness he c
and the morr
Ps. 74.16; 104

6 ¶ And G
ment [expans
and let it divi
Job 37.18; Ps.

7 And Goo
panse above
waters whic
from the wa
firmament: a
Ps. 148.4; Pr.

8 And Goo
And the even
second day.

9 ¶ And G
the heaven b
place, and let
was so.
Job 26.10; 38.

10 And Go
and the gath
called he Sea
good.

11 And Go
forth grass, t
fruit tree yiel
seed is in itself
Lu. 6.44; He.

12 And th
and herb yiel
the tree yield
itself, after h
was good.

13 And th
were the thir

14 ¶ And

SUTRA AND BIBLE

Faith and the Japanese American
World War II Incarceration

Duncan Ryuken Williams and
Emily Anderson, editors

KAYA PRESS

USC SHINSO
ITO CENTER
FOR JAPANESE
RELIGIONS
AND CULTURE

JAPANESE
AMERICAN
NATIONAL
MUSEUM

Published by Ito Center Editions,
an imprint of Kaya Press
kaya.com

Ito Center Editions Editor: Duncan Ryuken Williams
Book design: The Royal Academy of Nuts + Bolts
Project photographer: John Tonai

Sutra and Bible: Faith and the Japanese American
World War II Incarceration
Co-edited by
Duncan Ryuken Williams and Emily Anderson
ISBN 978-1-885030-79-5
Library of Congress Control Number: 2021951857

First Edition

Printed in Canada by Prolific Group, Inc.
Distributed by D.A.P. / Distributed Art Publishers
artbook.com / (800) 388-BOOK

25 24 23 22 21 5 4 3 2 1

This publication is the companion book to the 2022
exhibition by the same name co-sponsored by the
Japanese American National Museum and the USC
Shinso Ito Center for Japanese Religions and Culture.

This material is based upon work assisted by a grant
from the U.S. Department of the Interior, National
Park Service. Any opinions, findings, and conclusions
or recommendations expressed in this material are
those of the author(s) and do not necessarily reflect
the views of the U.S. Department of the Interior.

This material received Federal financial assistance
for the preservation and interpretation of U.S.
confinement sites where Japanese Americans
were detained during World War II. Under Title VI
of the Civil Rights Act of 1964, Section 504
of the Rehabilitation Act of 1973, and the Age
Discrimination Act of 1975, as amended, the U.S.
Department of the Interior prohibits discrimination
on the basis of race, color, national origin, disability
or age in its federally funded assisted projects. If you
believe you have been discriminated against in any
program, activity, or facility as described above, or if
you desire further information, please write to:

Office of Equal Opportunity
National Park Service
1849 C Street, NW
Washington, DC 20240

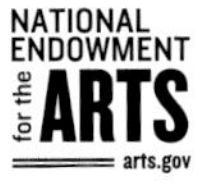
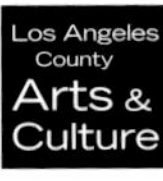
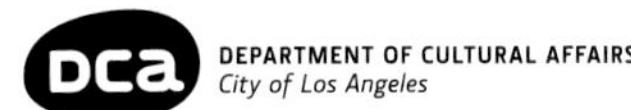

Kaya Press is also supported in part by the
National Endowment for the Arts, the Los Angeles
County Board of Supervisors through the Los
Angeles County Arts Commission, and the City of
Los Angeles Department of Cultural Affairs.

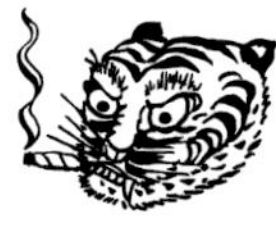
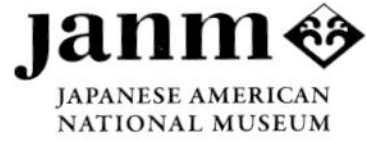

Page 1: Handmade US Army
dog tag made by Buddhist
soldier during World War II.

Page 2: Genesis 1 from
Bible annotated and
illustrated by Captain
Masuo Kitaji and completed
in Poston concentration
camp, Arizona, 1944.

CONTENTS

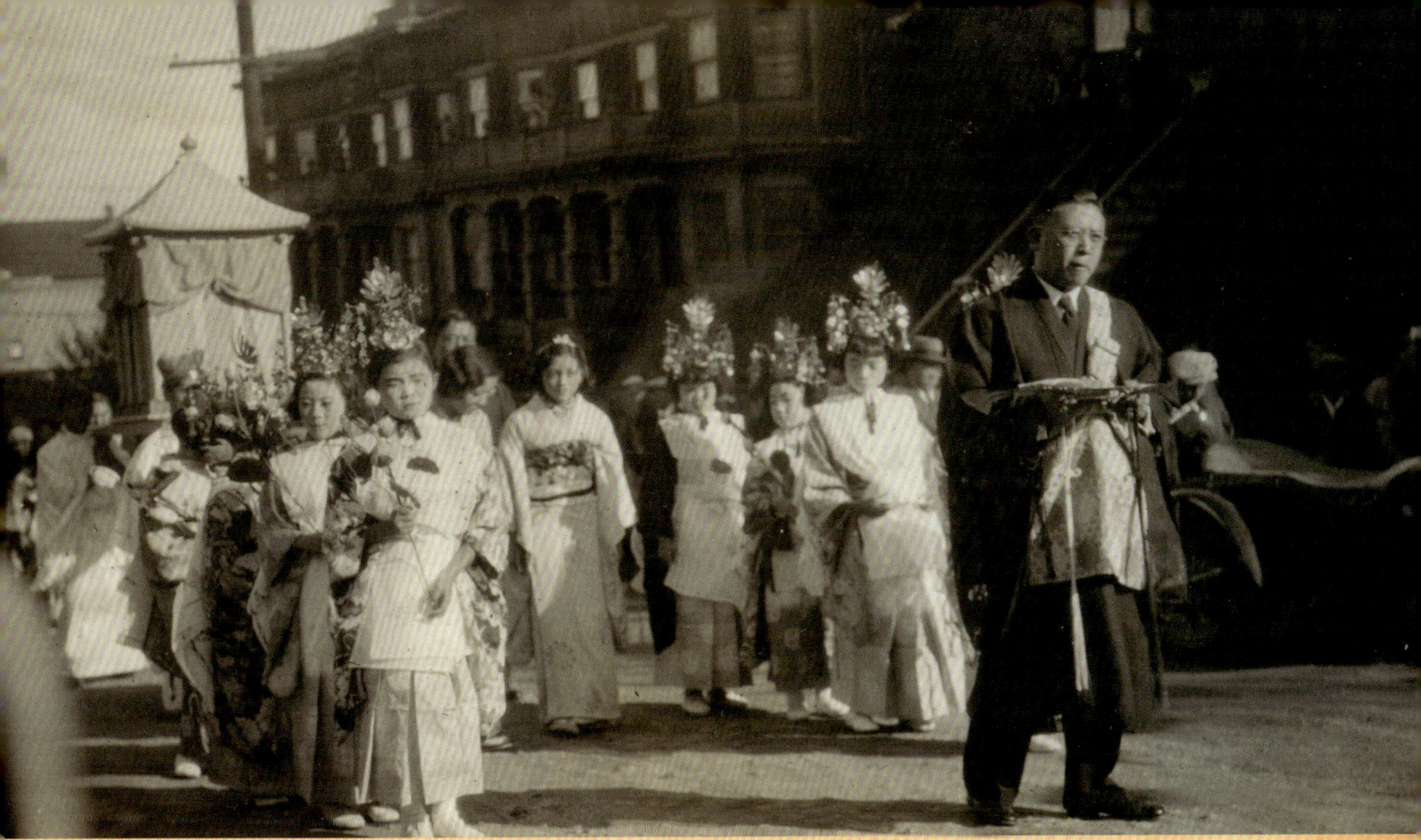

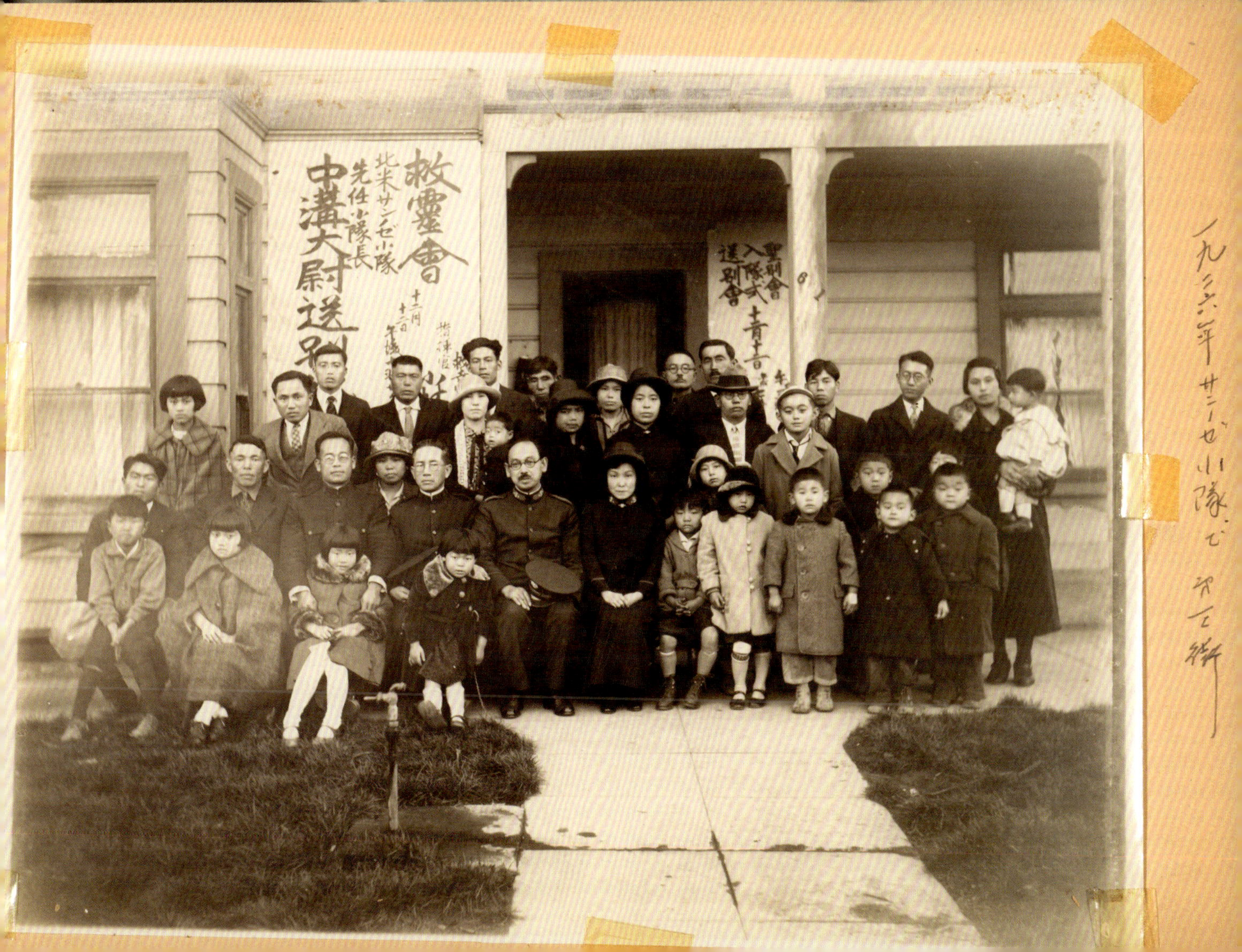

救靈會
北米サンゼ小隊
先任小隊長
中溝大尉送別
十二月
十三日

入隊式
送別會
青十二年

一九三六年サンゼ小隊で　弥七郎

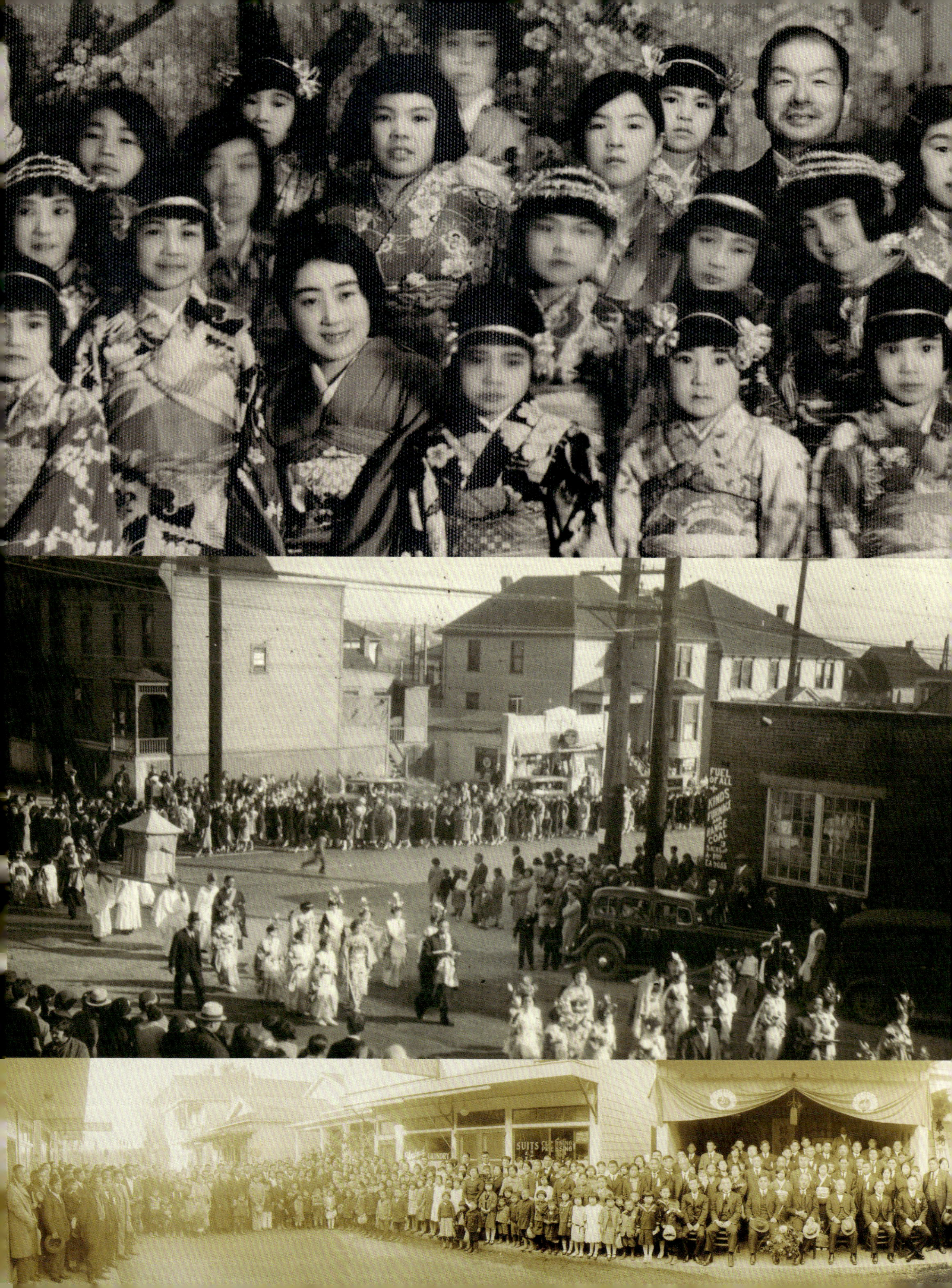

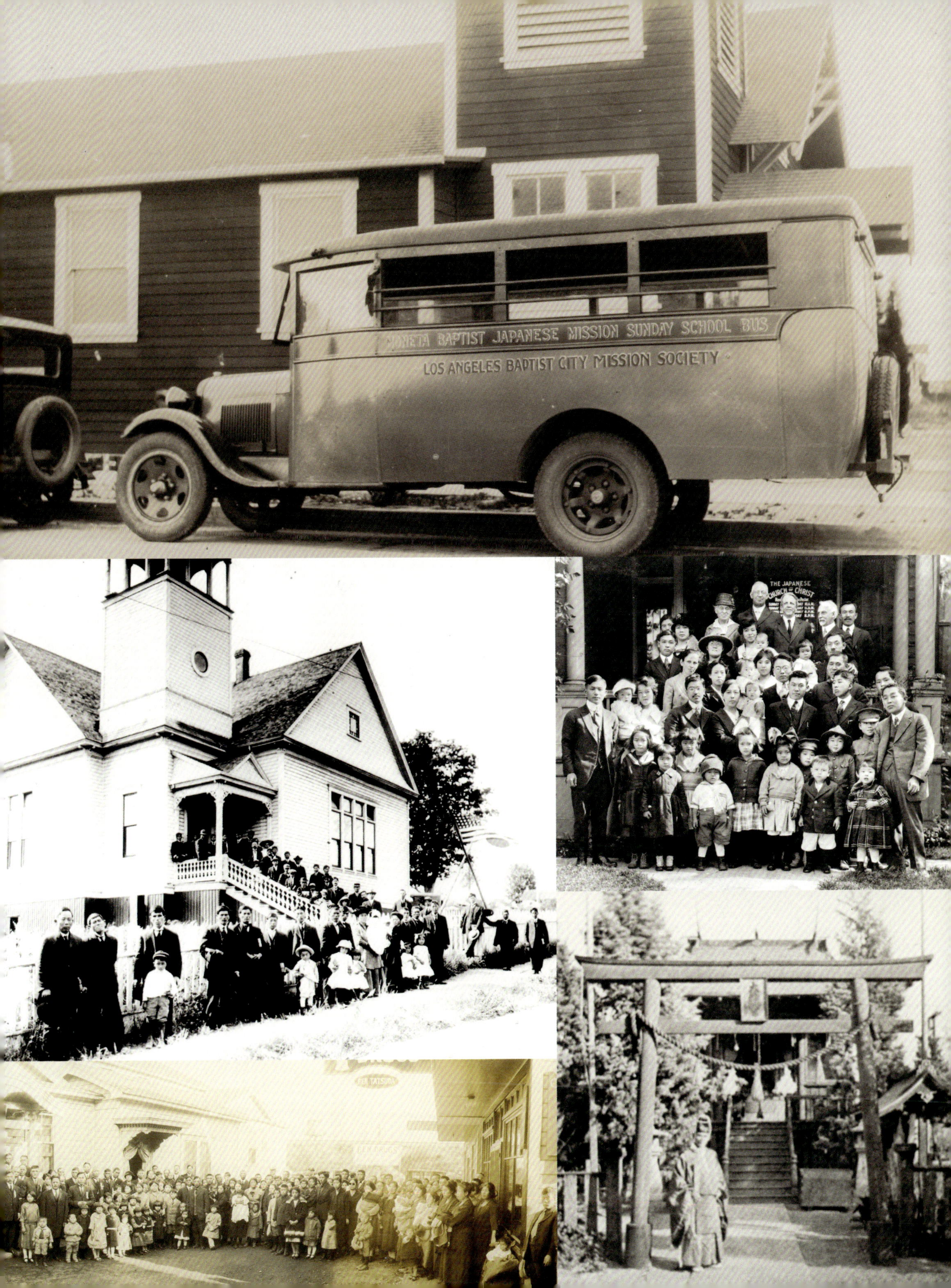
MONETA BAPTIST JAPANESE MISSION SUNDAY SCHOOL BUS
LOS ANGELES BAPTIST CITY MISSION SOCIETY
THE JAPANESE
CHURCH OF CHRIST

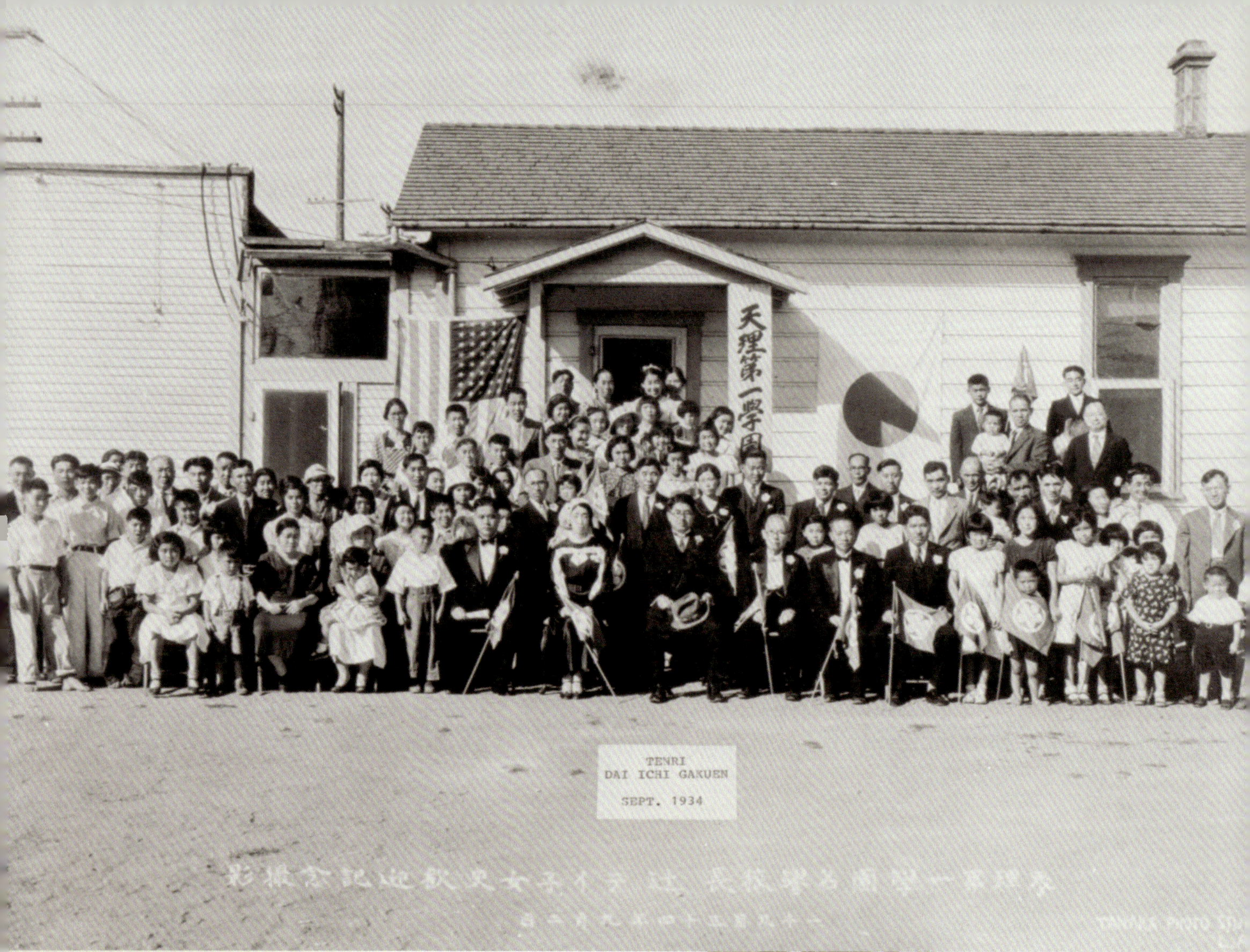

天理第一學園
TENRI
DAI ICHI GAKUEN
SEPT. 1934
天理第一學園々長板ハテイ女史歓迎記念撮影
TANAKA PHOTO STUDIO

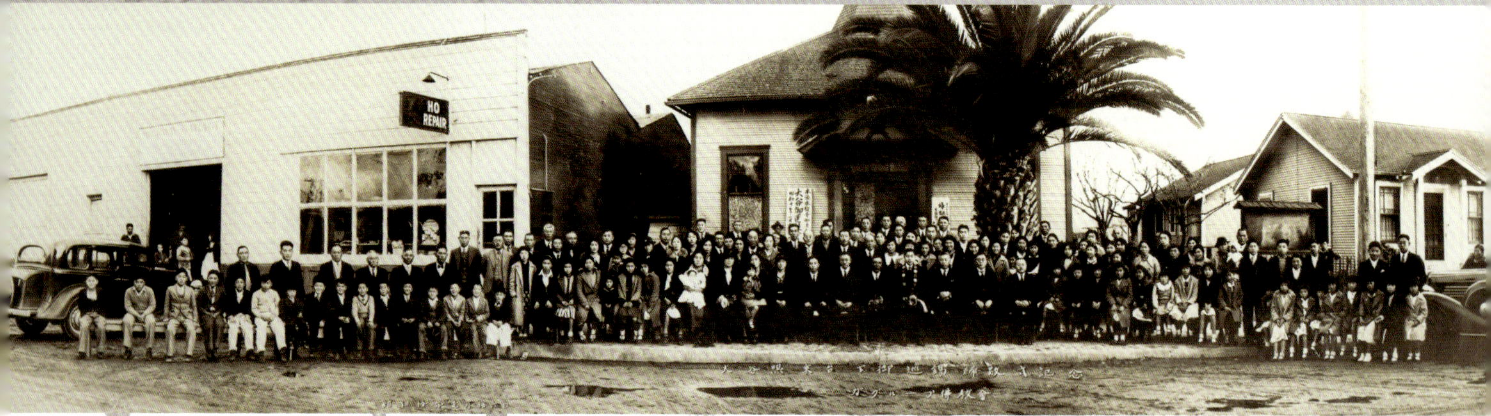

HO
REPAIR

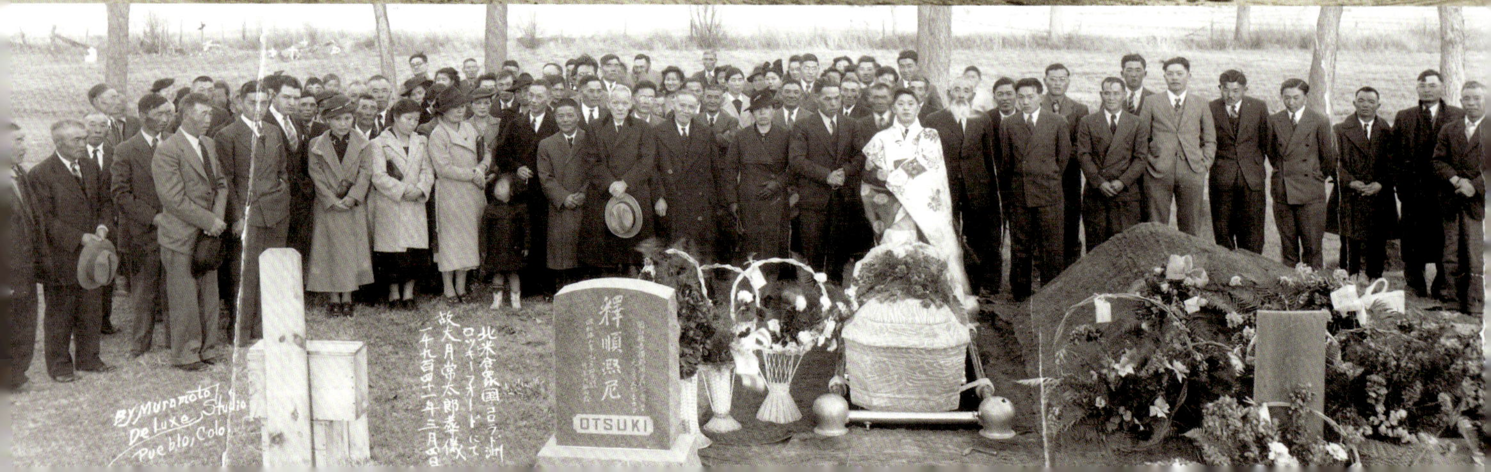

釋順照尼
OTSUKI
故大月常太郎葬儀
北米合衆国コロラド州
プエブロオードにて
一千九百四十二年三月四日
By Muramoto
De Luxe Studio
Pueblo, Colo.

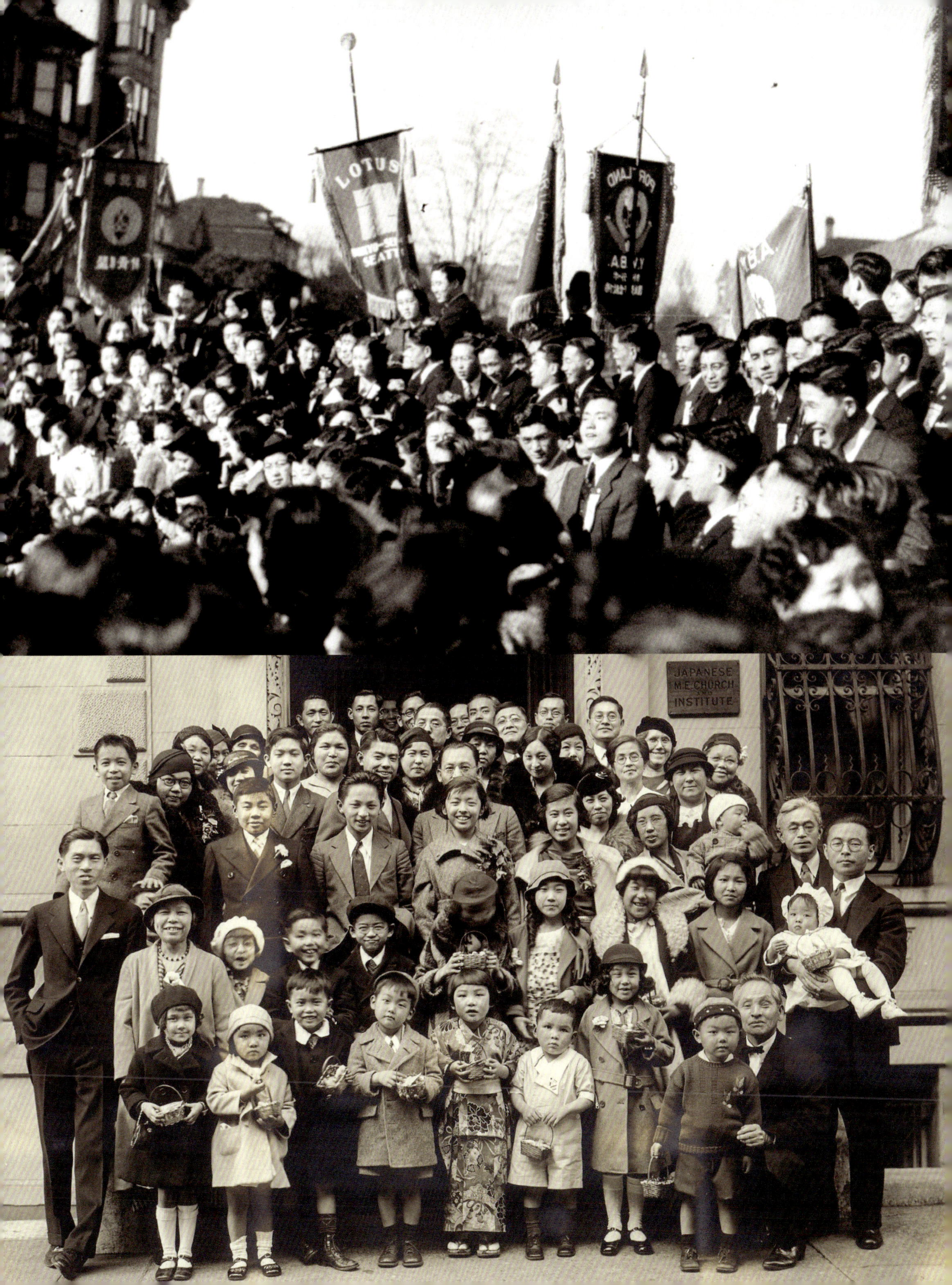
LOTUS
PORTLAND
Y.M.B.A.
JAPANESE
M.E. CHURCH
INSTITUTE

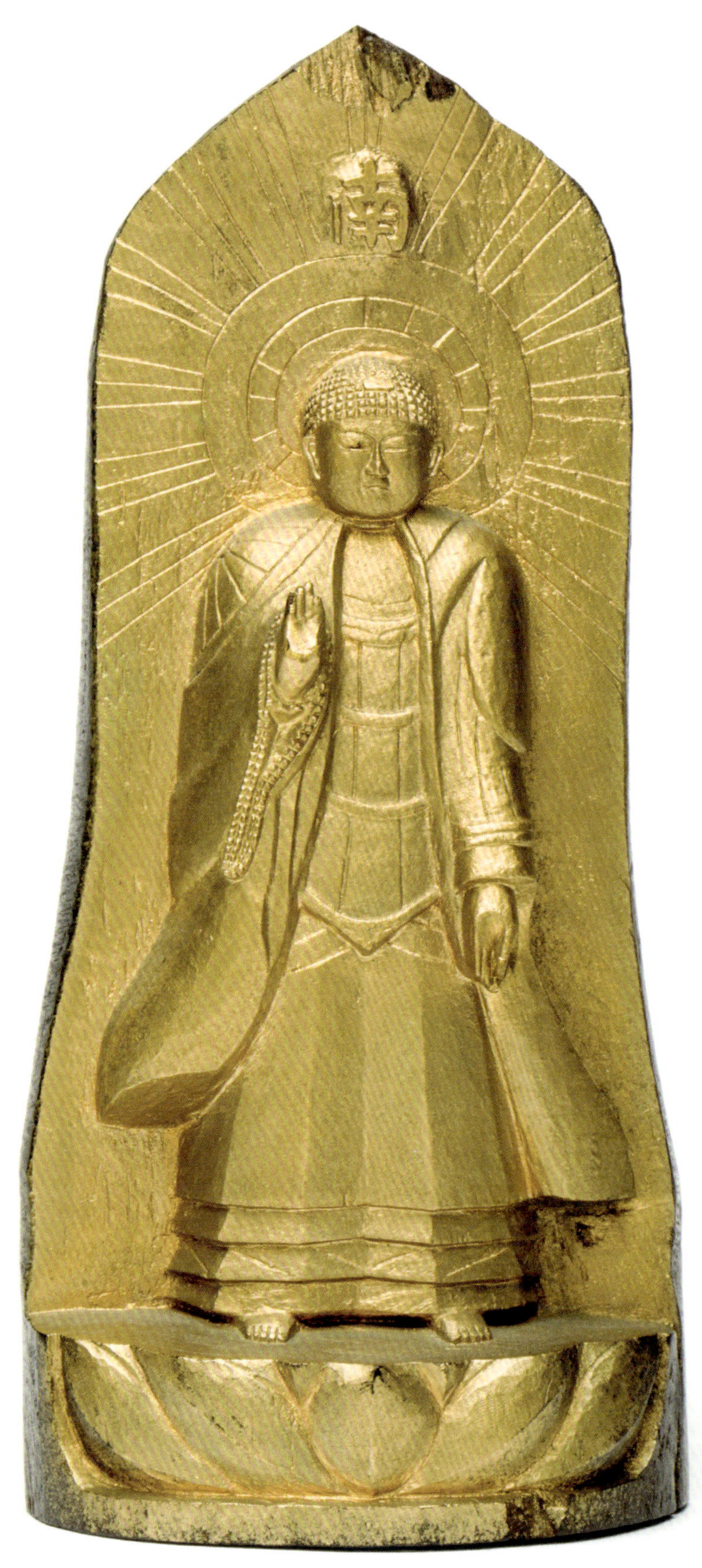

Prologue:
Relocating Religion

Religion at its best is a way of orienting oneself in the universe—a map that provides guideposts for navigating the terrain of one's journey through life. In an ever-changing world, it can help locate enduring truths about who we are by providing us with rituals that connect us to a realm beyond the everyday and values that help us connect with one another.

Religion can thus be instrumental in helping to create a sense of belonging. This is especially true for immigrants. Japanese immigrants who arrived in Hawai'i and the continental United States starting in the late 19th century longed for social and moral anchors as their dreams of making quick fortunes and then returning to Japan transformed into a determination to put down roots in a new land. For them, religion was something that could help create a true sense of home in a place that was otherwise utterly foreign. Religion was often at the heart of the communities they built as they adapted to a new social, political, and cultural landscape.

And yet the centrality of religious life has been overlooked in most accounts of Japanese immigration to the United States and the subsequent generations of Japanese Americans that followed. Looking at the role of religion in the forced removal and incarceration of Japanese Americans during World War II allows us to see a fuller and more complete picture of how they survived behind barbed wire, under martial law, and on the battlefield. It also reveals the extent to which religion has always been intertwined with policies of racial exclusion in the United States.

By drawing on sacred scriptures, ritual practices, and each other, Japanese Americans were able to find a degree of freedom even when their civil liberties were taken away. Told that they were a threat to national security, they insisted on a claim to American belonging. Faith made it possible to imagine a nation composed of people of many national origins, creeds, and races, mapping an alternative to a singular and supremacist vision of the United States.

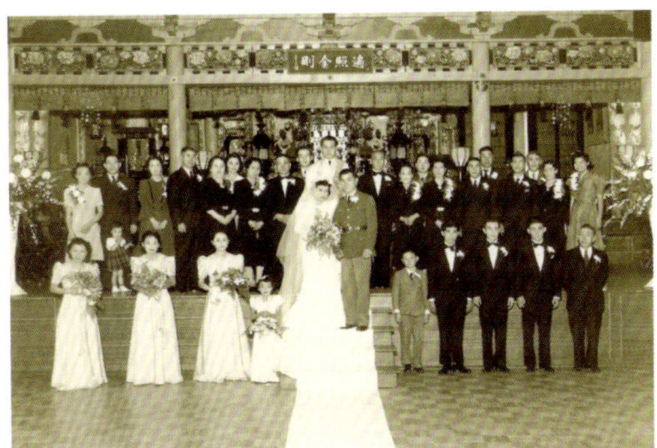

Opposite: Buddha statue handcrafted in Manzanar concentration camp, 1943.

Left: Tsuyoshi Akazawa and Kiyomi Mizote were the first couple to be married in the newly completed Los Angeles Koyasan Beikoku Betsuin sanctuary, September 20, 1941.

The First Dislocation:
Finding Refuge in a New Land

Starting in the late 19th century, hundreds of thousands of Japanese immigrants, over ninety percent of them Buddhist, crossed the Pacific to find work on the plantations of Hawai'i or in the canneries, railroads, mines, and farms of the American West. There, the earliest 19th century Japanese labor migrants faced stark realities: backbreaking work, illness, injury, or even death.

The first Japanese clergy of various religious traditions to arrive in Hawai'i and the continental US were brought over to perform funerary and memorial services for the predominantly male laborers. They also shared religious teachings that spoke to the loneliness, illness, and other hardships. Houses of worship—Buddhist temples, Christian churches, and Shinto shrines—thus became a focal point for the Japanese American community, functioning as both places to gather and sanctuaries from the widespread animus directed toward them.

Eventually, as women became more numerous and children, known as Nisei, rapidly increased in numbers, Japanese American religious institutions began to conduct regular baptisms, weddings, oratorical contests, and even

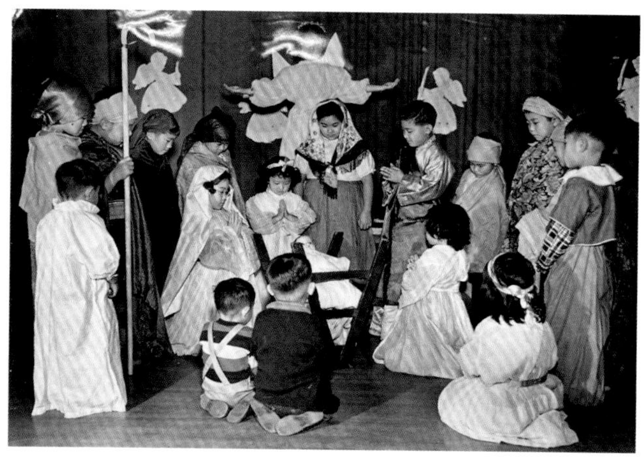

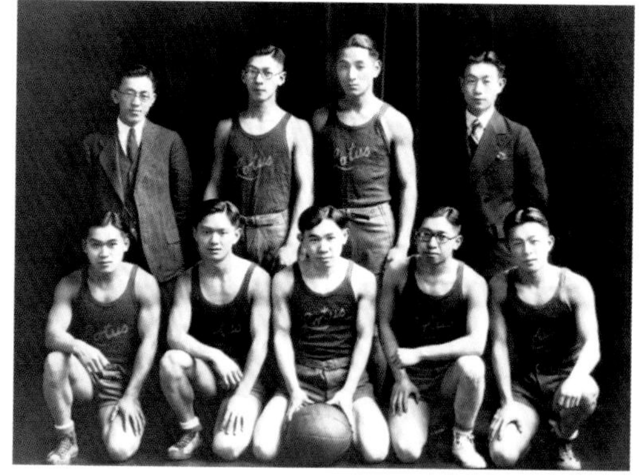

Above: Maryknoll School students perform in a Christmas play at St. Francis Xavier Church, Los Angeles, California, ca. 1935.

Above, right: Lotus basketball team affiliated with Seattle Buddhist Church, ca. 1935.

beauty pageants. Celebrations of holidays ranging from Hanamatsuri (the Buddha's Birthday) to Christmas punctuated the religious calendar.

The vast majority of Japanese Americans in the 1930s—between seventy to seventy-five percent—were Buddhist. Taken together, they comprised the largest group of Buddhists in America at the time. By way of contrast, roughly twenty-five percent of the community claimed affiliation with various Christian denominations, and only about one percent identified as exclusively Shinto.

This religiously diverse community, two-thirds of whom were born and brought up as US citizens, had worked hard to establish themselves as Americans. Despite xenophobic laws and racially stratified wage structures, Japanese Americans had built flourishing communities, established thriving businesses, and enjoyed a full complement of religious and social activities. Few could have foreseen the mass denial of due process that would lead to their incarceration and change their lives forever in the aftermath of Japan's attack on Pearl Harbor.

Page 7, top: Seattle Buddhist Church members parade through the neighborhood, Seattle, Washington, 1933.

Page 7, bottom: Japanese branch of the Salvation Army, San Jose, California, 1936.

Page 8, top: Girls' Day celebration at Terminal Island Baptist Church, California, ca. 1935. This community was not able to return to this neighborhood after the war.

Page 8, middle: Seattle Buddhist Church members parade through the neighborhood, Seattle, Washington, 1933.

Pages 8 & 9, bottom: Congregation gathers in front of the Walnut Grove Buddhist Temple, Walnut Grove, California, ca. 1925.

Page 9, top: Gardena Valley Baptist Church used this bus to pick up children for Sunday School, Gardena, California, ca. 1930.

Page 9, middle left: Congregation gathers at Eagle Harbor Congregational Church to celebrate Japanese emperor's birthday, Bainbridge Island, Washington, ca. 1920.

Page 9, middle right: Congregation gathers in front of the Japanese Church of Christ, Salt Lake City, Utah, 1924.

Page 9, bottom: Rev. Shinkichi Miyoshi stands outside San Pedro Daijingu, a Shinto shrine, on Terminal Island, California, no date. In keeping with the common Shinto practice of honoring locally significant figures as deities, Miyoshi enshrined George Washington and Abraham Lincoln in the shrine.

Page 10, top: Tenrikyo Daiichi Gakuen, a Japanese language school, opens in the Boyle Heights neighborhood of Los Angeles, California, 1924.

Page 10, middle: Congregation gathers in front of the Guadalupe Buddhist Church, Guadalupe, California, ca. 1930.

Page 10, bottom: Japanese Buddhist community welcomes Buddhist priest from Tri-State Buddhist Temple to conduct funeral, Pueblo, Colorado, 1941.

Page 11, top: Young Buddhist Association Conference attendees, Tacoma, Washington, ca. 1930.

Page 11, bottom: Congregation gathers in front of Japanese Methodist Church and Christian Institute for Easter, New York, 1934.

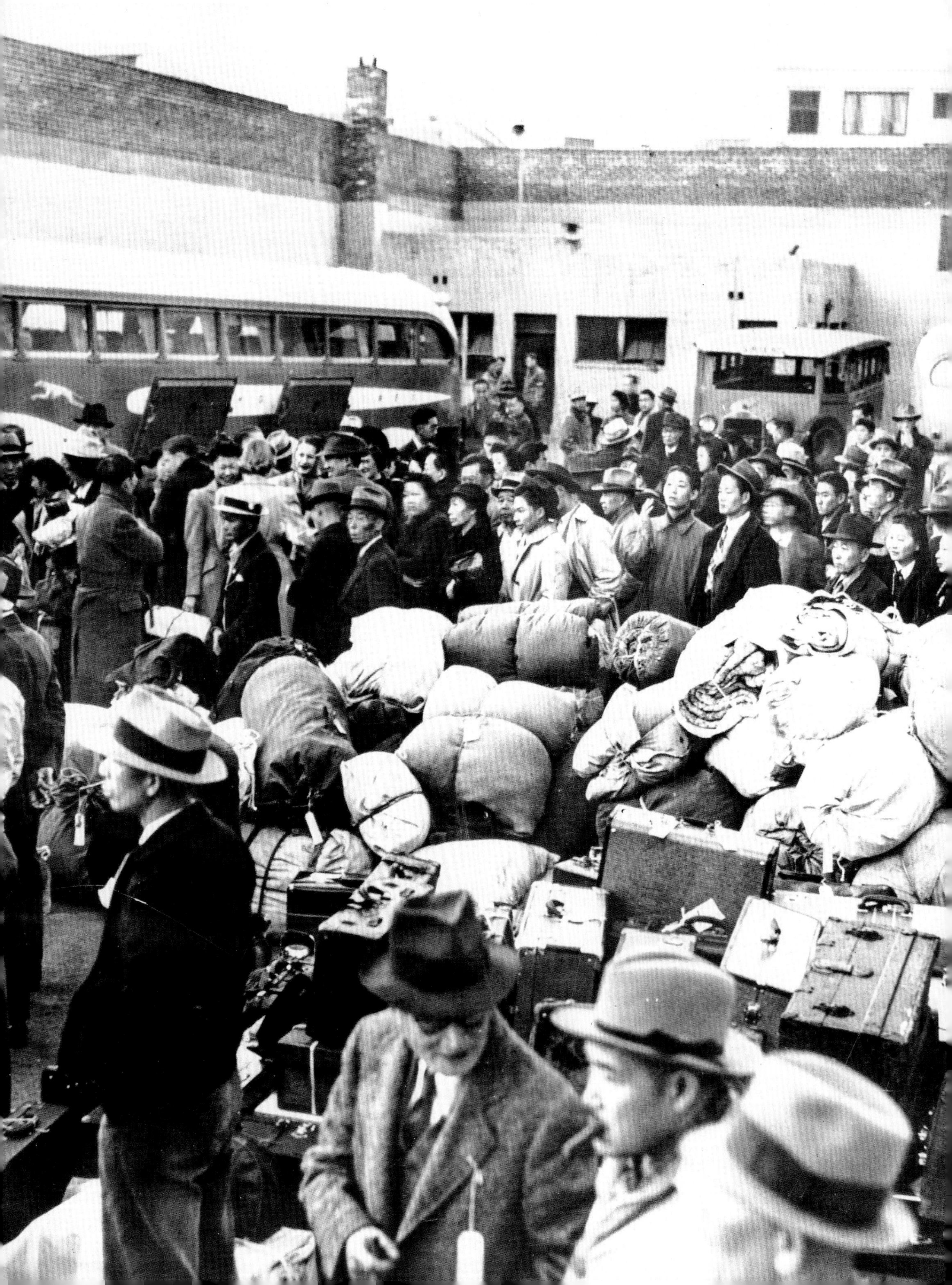

1

THE SECOND DISLOCATION

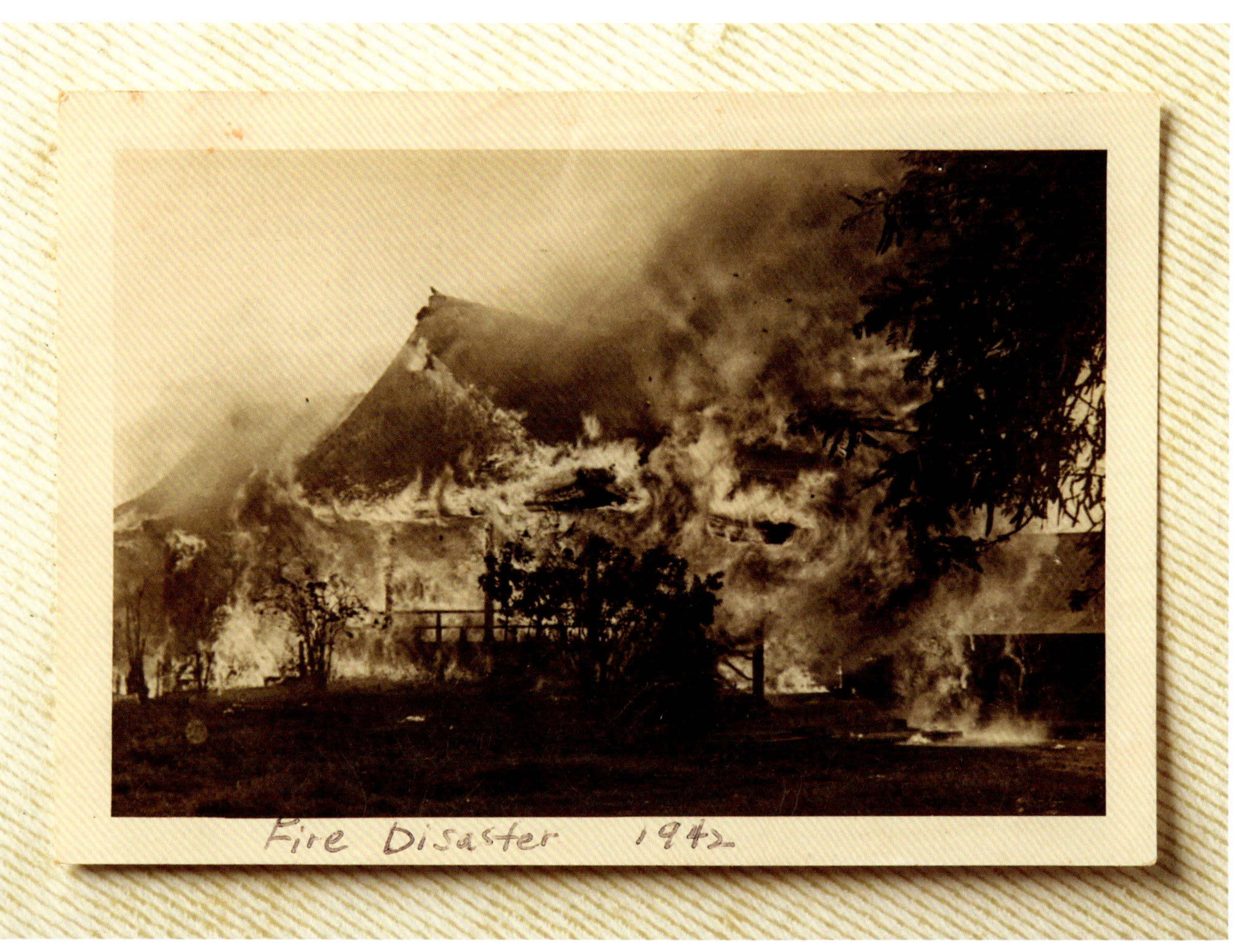
Fire Disaster   1942

Despite deteriorating diplomatic relations between the US and Japan throughout the 1930s, Japan's invasion of Pearl Harbor on December 7, 1941 came as a huge shock to Japanese American communities both in Hawaiʻi and on the continental US. The attack happened on a Sunday; this meant that Japanese Americans were listening to morning services at their temples, churches, and shrines when they learned of the attack. In the ensuing battle, two temples in Honolulu were shelled, both by friendly fire; at one of them, children attending Buddhist Sunday school were killed.

In the months that followed, nationwide discussions about how much of a threat Japanese American communities might pose to national security helped fan suspicions about Japanese Americans and their religious affiliations. Temples and churches became the targets of vandalism and worse.

The forced removal decreed in 1942 by Executive Order 9066 meant a second involuntary rupture for Japanese Americans. During this time of uncertainty, religion would continue to provide spiritual guidance as well as the resolve to bear and even fight the injustice being done to them.

Opposite: Pahala Hongwanji Mission on fire due to suspected arson, Pahala, Hawaiʻi, 1942.

Page 16: The Maryknoll School and St. Francis Xavier Church were used by the US Army as one of the registration and departure points in the Little Tokyo neighborhood of Los Angeles, California, 1942.

Internment of Community Religious Leaders

Because people of Japanese descent constituted more than a third of the population in Hawai'i, the wholesale removal and incarceration of Japanese Americans living there was considered impractical. Instead, the territorial government declared martial law. Thirty minutes before this was enacted — before the smoke from the attack on Pearl Harbor had even cleared — the FBI arrested Reverend Gikyo Kuchiba, the head Buddhist priest at the Honpa Hongwanji Hawaii Mission, Honolulu's largest Buddhist temple.

Intelligence agencies began creating registries of prominent Japanese Americans to arrest in case of war long before the invasion of Pearl Harbor. Reports that have now been declassified describe non-Christians as "un-American" and non-Christian clergy as "dangerous and likely to encourage sedition, espionage, and subversion." Reverend Kuchiba may have been the first community leader picked up for detention, but in the weeks that followed, three-quarters of all Buddhist priests and every single Shinto priest in Hawai'i and on the continental US were rounded up. By way of contrast, just seventeen percent of Japanese Christian ministers were detained.

Shutting down Shinto shrines and Buddhist temples became another priority under martial law. The new Office of the Military Governor in Hawai'i decided to "discourage Japanese religious activities other than Christian." This official policy would remain in place until April 1944.

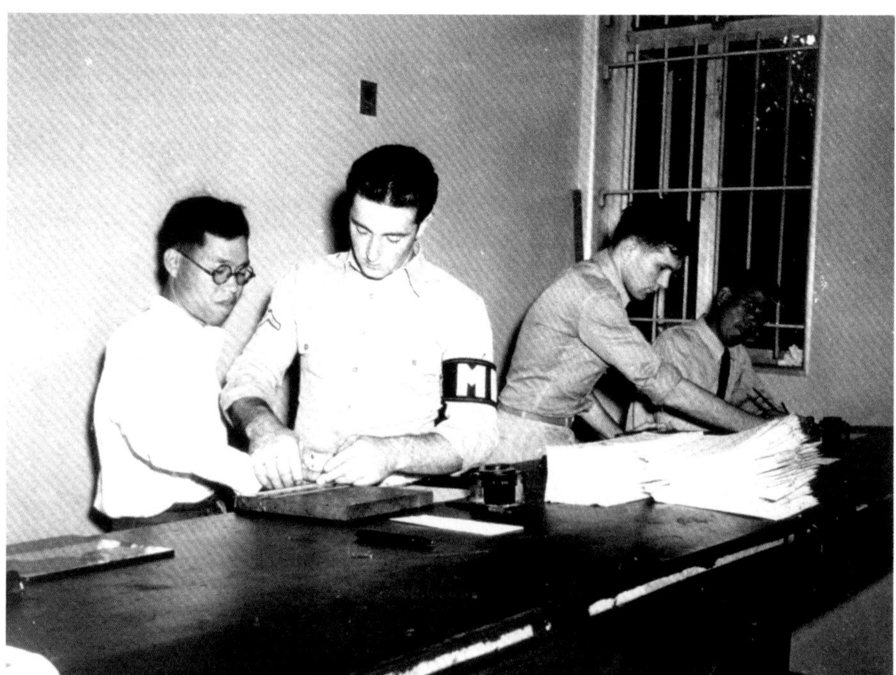

Rev. Horyu Asaeda of the Liliha Shingonji Mission is fingerprinted by MPs at the Honolulu immigration station soon after his arrest, 1941.

Public Sentiment Turns against Japanese Americans

Between February and March 1942, the Tolan Committee, formally known as "The House Select Committee Investigating National Defense Migration," led a Congressional investigation into the necessity of removing people of Japanese ancestry from the West Coast. Headed by John H. Tolan (D-CA), the committee went to four cities — Seattle, Portland, San Francisco, and Los Angeles — to hear testimony from the general population as well as business and government leaders about the issue. Almost all of those who testified supported partial or complete exclusion of people of Japanese ancestry from the West Coast, citing religion alongside race as the reasons why Japanese Americans could not be trusted during a time of war.

Japanese Buddhist teachers were brought in ... [and] the Japanese indoctrination of American-born Japanese occurred.... [T]he Emperor of Japan not only is the head of a nation but likewise he is the head of the church and the descendant of the Sun God.

— Robert H. Fouke (California Joint Immigration Committee)

[T]here is more potential danger among the group of Japanese who are born in this country than from the alien Japanese who were born in Japan.... [I]n some instances the children ... receive their religious instruction which ties up their religion with their Emperor, and they come back here imbued with the ideas and the policies of Imperial Japan.

— Earl Warren (CA Attorney General)

Gathering Before Exile

In the wake of the forced removal and mass incarceration that resulted from President Roosevelt's issuance of Executive Order 9066, religious institutions played a significant role in helping to coordinate the practical needs of a community suddenly confronting exile.

Churches and temples often served as gathering spots from which families and luggage were transported to temporary confinement sites euphemistically known as "assembly centers."

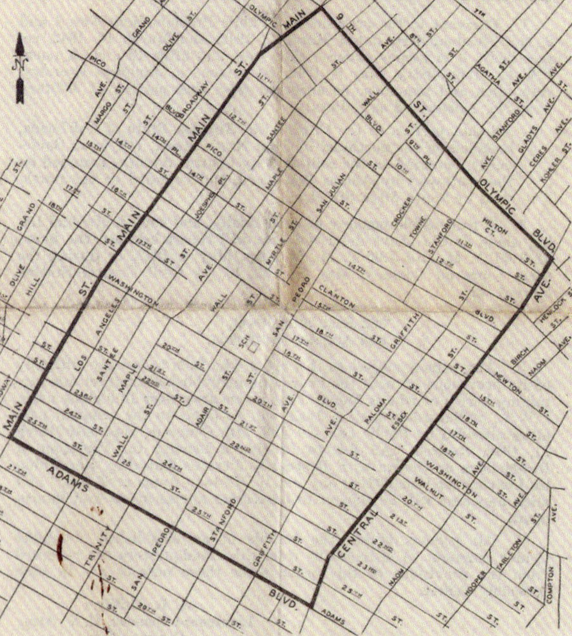

**WESTERN DEFENSE COMMAND AND FOURTH ARMY
WARTIME CIVIL CONTROL ADMINISTRATION
Presidio of San Francisco, California**

INSTRUCTIONS
TO ALL PERSONS OF
JAPANESE
ANCESTRY
LIVING IN THE FOLLOWING AREA:

All that portion of the City of Los Angeles, State of California, bounded on the northeast by East Ninth Street, (Olympic Boulevard), bounded on the southeast by Central Avenue, bounded on the southwest by Adams Boulevard, and bounded on the northwest by South Main Street.

Pursuant to the provisions of Civilian Exclusion Order No. 32, this Headquarters, dated May 3, 1942, all persons of Japanese ancestry, both alien and non-alien, will be evacuated from the above area by 12 o'clock noon, P.W.T., Saturday, May 9, 1942.

No Japanese person living in the above area will be permitted to change residence after 12 o'clock noon, P.W.T., Sunday, May 3, 1942, without obtaining special permission from the representative of the Commanding General, Southern California Sector, at the Civil Control Station located at:

> Japanese Christian Church,
> 822 East 20th Street,
> Los Angeles, California.

Such permits will only be granted for the purpose of uniting members of a family, or in cases of grave emergency.

The Civil Control Station is equipped to assist the Japanese population affected by this evacuation in the following ways:

1. Give advice and instructions on the evacuation.

2. Provide services with respect to the management, leasing, sale, storage or other disposition of most kinds of property, such as real estate, business and professional equipment, household goods, boats, automobiles and livestock.

3. Provide temporary residence elsewhere for all Japanese in family groups.

4. Transport persons and a limited amount of clothing and equipment to their new residence.

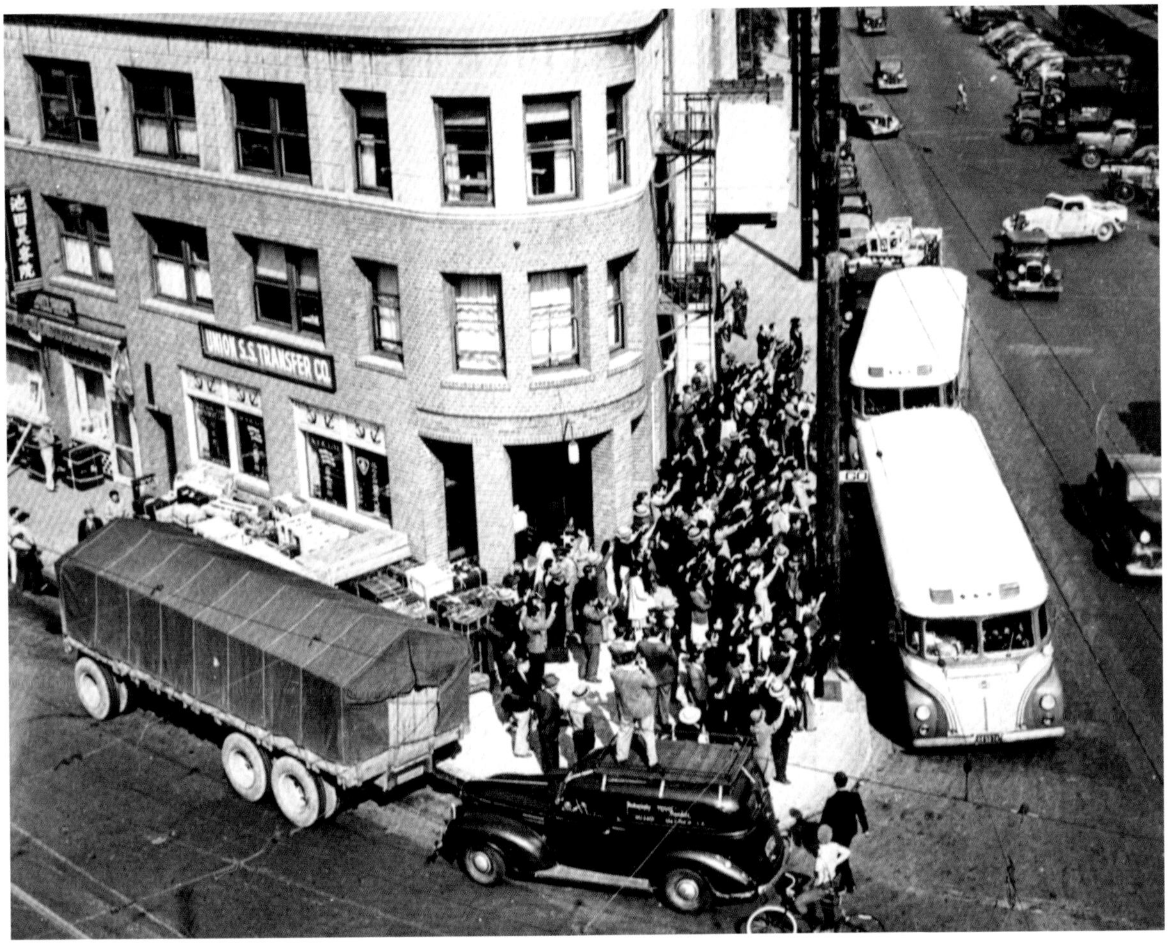

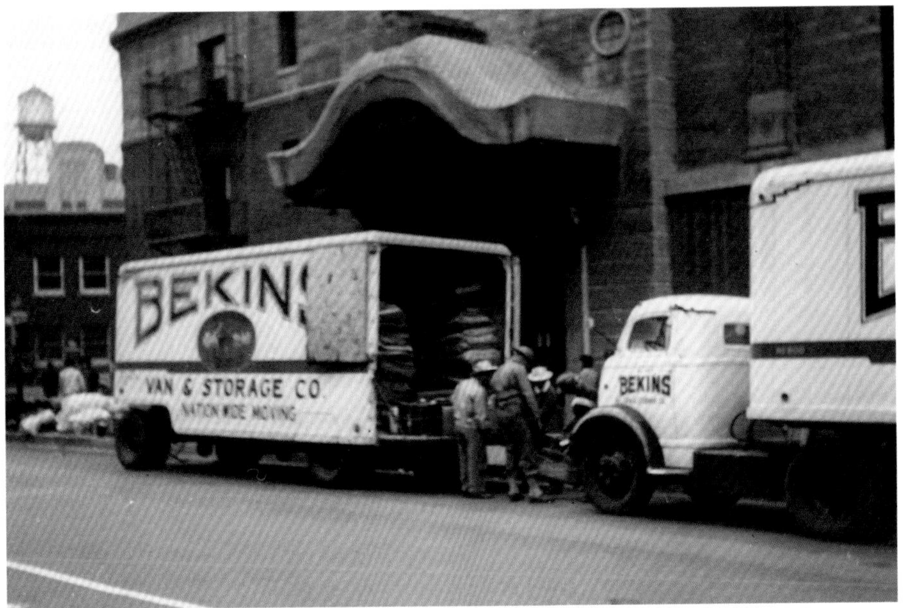

Opposite: Exclusion Order poster for the West Adams neighborhood in Los Angeles, with instructions for "All Persons of Japanese Ancestry" to meet at the Japanese Christian Church on 20th Street for transport to a so-called "Assembly Center."

Above: Japanese Americans gather in front of the Los Angeles Nishi Hongwanji Betsuin as they board buses bound for an assembly center, 1942.

Left: Moving vans are parked in front of the Los Angeles Nishi Hongwanji Betsuin as Japanese Americans prepare to be forcibly removed, 1942.

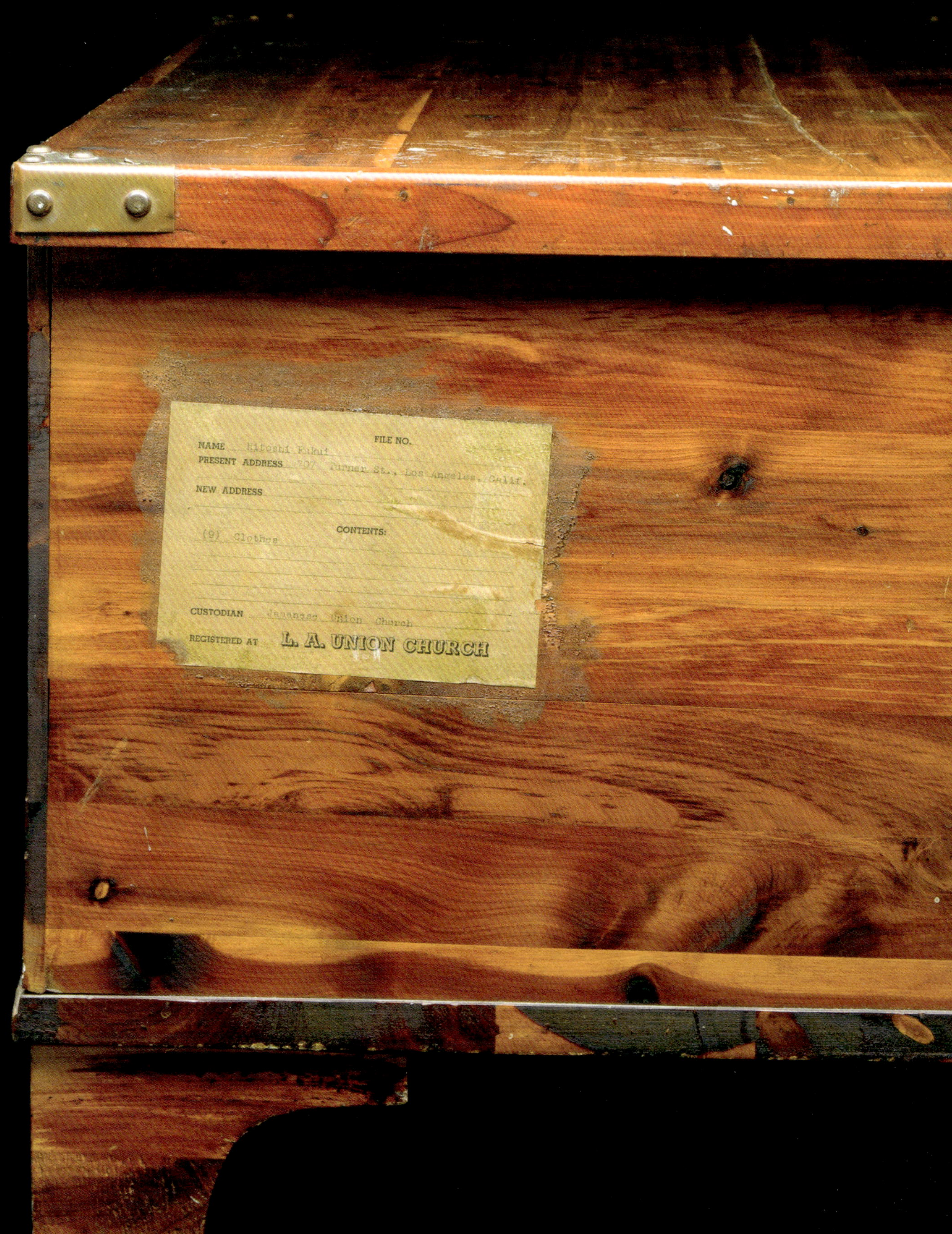

FILE NO.
NAME   Hitoshi Fukui
PRESENT ADDRESS   707 Turner St., Los Angeles, Calif.
NEW ADDRESS
CONTENTS:
(9) Clothes
CUSTODIAN   Japanese Union Church
REGISTERED AT   L. A. UNION CHURCH

Sanctuaries for Family Treasures

Faced with indefinite incarceration, Japanese American families turned to trusted institutions such as churches and temples as sites where they might safely store their family treasures. Extensive looting during and in the immediate aftermath of the war meant that many families returned to find their belongings stolen or destroyed through acts of vandalism.

The Chest
Timothy Wagner

I still remember the only time I saw my father cry. It was a gloomy winter morning at our home in Little Tokyo, and the fog was thicker than blood.

Thunk.

He let out a weary sigh as he set the chest down on our living room floor. My mother stood in the corner, her eyes anxiously scanning the room, fingers fidgeting at her sides. She was already calculating.

"What is it?" I asked innocently, staring at that mighty cedar chest. It was larger than I was, and it filled my youthful mind with wonder. "Another suitcase?"

My father shook his head slowly.

"No, we're not allowed another. This is different. The folks at the church offered it to… keep our things safe while we're gone." He forced a smile. I stared at him curiously.

"How long will we be gone?"

My father said nothing, his expression growing harder than stone.

"Come," my mother said quickly, taking me by the hand into the kitchen.

"But… we've already packed?" I asked, staring at the three pitiful suitcases by the front door. It was hardly enough space for more than a few sets of clothes for each of us.

"That's for the road. Now for everything else…"

Without another word, we began emptying the shelves and the cupboards, the garage and the bedrooms. We pulled down pictures and paintings, piling our belongings on the floor of the living room. And as we gathered heaps of precious memories and heirlooms, that great chest began to shrink. Tears streamed down my mother's face as she separated the precious from the priceless, desperate not to leave so much behind. It was an impossible task.

"They might as well have given us a matchbox," my father choked.

I glanced up at him, and he quickly wiped something from his eyes, putting on a brave, grim smile. He refused to cry again. Even on that fateful day, March 30th, 1942, as we watched the chest in front of Union Church shrink into the distance, and later as we approached our horse stall prison, his eyes were dry and his brow furrowed. It was not until years later, when I returned, to a house occupied by strangers in Little Tokyo, that I realized what my father meant. Compared to all that we had lost, that chest might as well have been nothing at all.

But when I opened it, I found a nostalgic scent lingering in my nostrils—of dust and precious memories, of a childhood lost overnight. And in that moment, that tiny cedar chest, filled with what little we could fit… it might as well have been the whole world.

Opposite: Wooden chest used by the Fukui family to store belongings at the Japanese Union Church, Los Angeles, California. Timothy Wagner is the grandson of Mitsuko (Fukui) Dyo, the daughter of Hitoshi Fukui, who stored the chest.

Spiritual Responses to the Impending Dislocation

Clergy from both traditions tried their best to offer perspective in sermons, speeches, and poems that used the impending dislocation to encourage deeper reflection. Many Christians drew on narratives of exodus and exile that presume dislocation as a precursor to freedom. Buddhists often described deepening one's commitment to the path of liberation as "leaving home" (Jpn. *shukke*).

L. E. Suzuki

<u>FACING EVACUATION</u> (last Sun. before evacuation.)

   Text: "But the God afl all grace , who hath called us unto his eternal glory by Christ Jesus, after that ye have suffered a while, make you perfect, stablish, steengthen, settle you". 1 Pet. 5: 10.
   Scripture: 1 Peter 1: 1-2; 2: 18-23; 4: 12-16: 5: 10.

   I. INTRODUCTION.

   Brethren, we are facing the eve of evacuation. We must evacuate our homes and churches and be taken to strange places, and we will not know what will happen to us. This is our Last Sunday on which we can worship in our own sanctuary. Most of you have cherished memories of this chapel and the other chapel. Many of you attended the Sunday School from your young days and have grown up in the church, and many of you were married in this chapel and in the other chapel. A good many of the older people remember this church from the days when it was merely a mission church down on Georgia St., meeting in just a residence house, and they have seen this church grow into this large beautiful church, with two plants. This Wesley Chapel is only a year old, and it is the first chapel built for the sole purpose of taking care of the religious services of in the U.S.
the Niseis, and it is all yours. You paid for the pews, the altar, and you contributed to the building of it. But now you must vacate it, not knowing whether you will be able to use it again.

The Sunday Before:
Japanese American Christians Prepare for Exile

For many Christian congregations, preparations for departure coincided with the celebration of Easter. Sympathetic non-Japanese Christians—Allan A. Hunter, the pastor of Mt. Hollywood Congregational Church, and Gurney and Elizabeth Binford, a Quaker couple—sought to show solidarity by gathering "sermons by Pacific Coast pastors of the Japanese race on the Sunday before Evacuation."

Drawing on Bible verses that recounted experiences of exile, loss, and faith in a time of uncertainty, these sermons acknowledged the trauma of the moment while exhorting congregants to recognize their own trials as part of a longer Biblical history of loss and struggle.

In 1945, the American Friends Service Committee published these collected sermons under the title *The Sunday Before*. They carefully explained their reasons for doing so: "First, as a continuation of the 11th chapter of Hebrews showing the victory of faith by those who went out not knowing whether they went nor why they were required to go; and [S]econdly, this witness brings to Christians the knowledge and understanding which will help American churches to welcome Japanese Christians into their church fellowship."

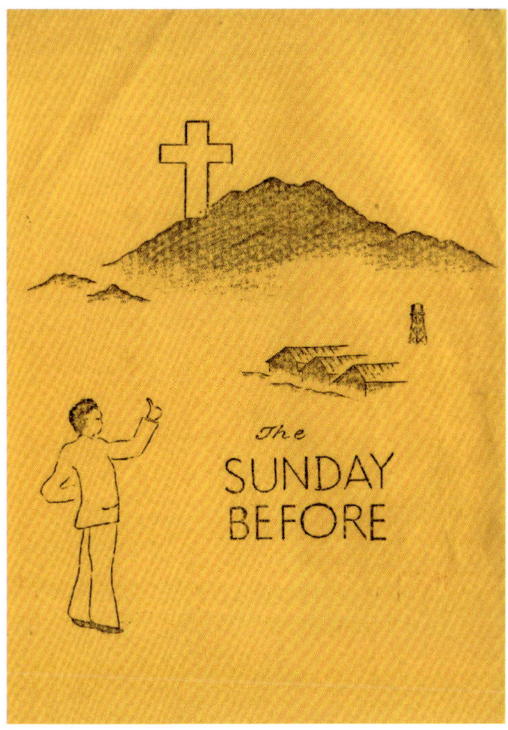

Opposite: First page of Lester Suzuki's last sermon before camp titled "Facing Evacuation," given at the Los Angeles Japanese Methodist Church, 1942.

Left: Exterior cover of *The Sunday Before*, 1945.

Righteous Rage
Naomi Hirahara

I chose the second Easter weekend during the coronavirus pandemic to read the last sermons preached by Japanese American Christian ministers to their congregations before their wholesale ouster from their homes and communities along the Pacific Coast. I searched for anything that might offer comfort during a season of great discomfort, a life completely upended by global shutdowns and a racial reckoning for our nation. I was a bit disappointed. Faced with the question of how to reconcile their government's unjust action with the need to sustain and guide their flock, these ministers encouraged their congregants to look upon their impending incarceration as a challenge to their faith, evoking the calling of Abraham in the Book of Genesis to leave his home for an unknown land that would become his people's new nation. Could the exodus of Japanese Americans from the West Coast be God's calling?

Hawai'i-born Reverend Royden Susu-Mago was the only minister in this collection of sermons, collected during the war as a testament to faith-based teachings in a time of direst need, to make direct connections between what was happening to the Japanese Americans and the plight of Black Americans. In words spoken more than twenty-five years before the civil rights movement of the late 1960s, he said: "You would think the Negroes would jump at the opportunity of crying 'Japs' and [join] the nation in oppressing us, but they have not done it. They understand how it hurts to be segregated and denied civil rights." Continuing, Susu-Mago called for his congregants at the Japanese Independent Church of Hollywood to be free of "resentment and bitterness."

These sermons reveal the tension within Christianity in America. How do we approach systemic racial injustice, particularly when victimized by it? Do we internalize it and wonder if we are somehow responsible for what has befallen us? Do we consider it a test that we must overcome to spread the good news? What do we do with righteous rage?

In the sermon he gave the Sunday before being incarcerated, Issei minister Reverend Sohei Kowta of Wintersburg Presbyterian Church preached: "In this critical hour, the spiritual anguish of the Japanese people is undescribable [sic], their mental perplexity unsoluble [sic], their economic loss inestimable. The mighty economic structure which the Issei have constructed with their sweat and blood during the past several decades is fast crumbling down to its foundation." Like the other Japanese American clergy in these sermons, he instructed his people to be inspired by the actions of Abraham during his exodus. But he also evoked the three principles of Christianity: faith, hope, and love.

In my Christian faith circles, lamentation as a religious practice has been embraced after George Floyd was killed at the hands of Minneapolis police. Pasadena Union Church's Reverend Kengo Tajima ended the sermon he gave that second Easter Sunday of the pandemic with these words: "…the only effective fight we can put up against war now is love." Love, sometimes mysterious and confounding in its manifestations, pulls us through the wilderness, whether it be during World War II or today. Without this love, righteous rage can only do so much.

THE
SUNDAY BEFORE

(Sermons by Pacific Coast Pastors of the Japanese race on the Sunday before Evacuation to Assembly centers in the late spring of 1942.)

Edited by
ALLAN A. HUNTER
4609 Prospect Avenue
Los Angeles 27, Calif.
and
GURNEY BINFORD
4230 Budlong Avenue
Los Angeles 37, Calif.

SPONSORED
BY

SOUTHERN CALIFORNIA BRANCH
AMERICAN FRIENDS SERVICE COMMITTEE

Buddhists Answer the Call

Japanese American Buddhists often found themselves struggling to prove that they could be fully American and fully Buddhist at the same time. Subsequent to the arrest of Issei Buddhist leaders throughout the US and Hawai'i, some Buddhist organizations turned to English-speaking, American-born priests to coordinate an appropriate response. Nisei priests such as Reverend Kenryo Kumata sent out regular bulletins from the San Francisco headquarters of the Buddhist Mission of North America (later renamed Buddhist Churches of America). These missives repeatedly called on temples to continue operating to serve their temple membership and urged their tens of thousands of affiliated individuals to demonstrate their patriotism through such initiatives as the purchase of defense bonds and blood donation drives.

BUDDHIST MISSION OF AMERICA
HEADQUARTERS
1881 Pine Street, San Francisco, California

January 13, 1942

Buddhist Churches in the
United States of America

YOUR RED CROSS NEEDS YOU

Gentlemen:

This is to notify you on the importance of the following:

1. Buddhists must have unswerving faith and find true spiritual comfort in the Teachings of the Buddha.
2. Buddhists in this war must answer the call of the United States of America with unreserved loyalty that must be shown with action motivated by spiritual strength.
3. Buddhists must realize the importance of industry and agriculture: utilize every moment to increase productiveness usefulness.
4. Buddhists must be healthy, thrifty and saving: afford adequate protection to children; attentive to the education of the young; alert to cooperate with the Red Cross; and especially willing to buy Defense Saving Stamps and Bonds.
5. Buddhists must be calm in crisis; cool-headed in decisions and positive in action in the defense of the Stars and Stripes.

May it be suggested that Buddhist Churches make provisions, where possible, for the care of the children. Open a nursery and kindergarten so that the parents and elders may give their full attention to increased industrial and agricultural production.

Keep the Buddhist churches open to the public as a spiritual haven. Keep up your church program as heretofore or, even better, increase your activities and maintain a high standard of morale.

The First Line of Defense of the United States lies in the religious conviction, character and high morale of the citizens and residents.

With the Blessings of the Buddha,

THE BUDDHIST MISSION OF AMERICA

No.7
m/k

Opposite: Interior title page for *The Sunday Before*, 1945.

Left: A bulletin about ways for Buddhists to contribute to national defense issued by the headquarters of the Buddhist Mission of North America, January 13, 1942.

A Principled Stance against Injustice

Best known for the US Supreme Court case that bears his name, *Hirabayashi v. United States* (1943), Gordon K. Hirabayashi was one of three individuals who openly defied the government's forced removal and incarceration. His Christian beliefs were central to his justification for refusing to comply with government orders. For his efforts, he was sentenced to time in a federal prison.

**Gordon K. Hirabayashi and
the Sustaining Influence of Faith**
Jay Hirabayashi

My grandfather, Shungo Hirabayashi, was born in Hotaka (Nagano Prefecture) in the Japanese Alps. As a young man, he converted to Christianity after hearing Kikenji Iguchi talk about the Bible. Iguchi was a disciple of Kanzo Uchimura, who was the founder of Mukyokai, an unusual non-church movement that emphasized a personal experience with God and a morality based on truth, hard work, and responsibility to others. While studying in the US in 1884, Uchimura visited with Quakers in Pennsylvania, and by the time he went back to Japan, his theological perspectives had been deeply influenced by their example.

Iguchi, Uchimura's disciple, was the principal of Kensei Academy, where my grandfather studied the Bible, English, ethics, the Chinese language, Confucius, Mencius, and public policy. At the time, the Japanese government was encouraging young Japanese to emigrate to other countries to earn money. Iguchi, by way of contrast, encouraged his students to "Have good ambition. Don't go to the USA just to make money. Don't be a slave to materialism; go to build God's kingdom. Live a courageous life. Be a good citizen. The meaning of Christianity is to love people—love other people as you love yourself. If you can hold fast to that spirit, nothing in this world can trouble you." These words guided my grandfather's spirit when, in 1907, he immigrated to Seattle, Washington.

My father, Gordon Kiyoshi Hirabayashi, was born in 1918 and raised in Thomas, a small farming community to the south of Seattle, where four Issei families from Nagano Prefecture had formed a Christian cooperative called White River Garden.

While growing up, he would regularly attend Mukyokai-style gatherings where, in lieu of a minister, each family patriarch would take turns speaking of their own spiritual thoughts and experiences.

In 1937, my father started part-time studies at the University of Washington while living at the campus YMCA. He visited different churches in the district before deciding that he felt most comfortable at the Society of Friends Quaker meetings. The similarity between these gatherings, where Friends would speak their own minds about their spiritual experiences, and the Mukyokai gatherings he had participated in at home, was undoubtedly a factor in giving him comfort.

In 1940, the YMCA sent my father to the President's Summer School in New York, where officers of the student Christian movement, the YMCA, and the YWCA were being trained. While there, he attended seminars with activists such as A. J. Muste, Frank Olmstead, and Dr. Evan Thomas, as well as Norman Thomas, a former Presbyterian minister and active Socialist, and Bayard Rustin, a Quaker Socialist and civil rights activist. All were members of the War Resisters League for Peace and Freedom. Later, when my father was awaiting trial in King County jail for refusing curfew and evacuation orders that he felt violated his constitutional rights as an American citizen, both Thomas and Rustin visited him, buoying his spirits.

Christian faith and faith in the United States Constitution gave my father perseverance and resolve. The Constitution, as it turned out, did not protect him—apparently it was a crime to be of Japanese ancestry. His belief in his fellow man, however, never wavered.

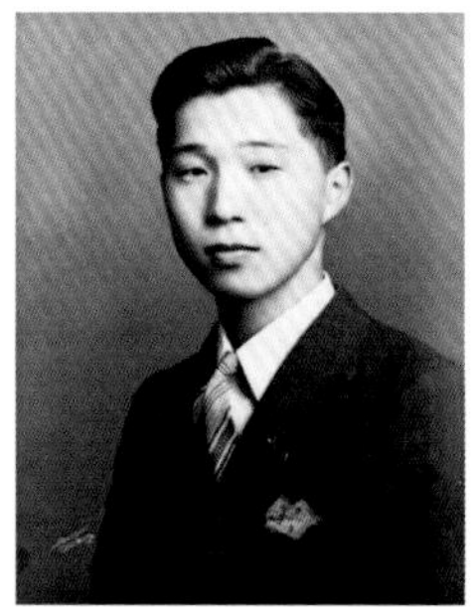

Gordon K. Hirabayashi,
ca. 1936.

Why I Refuse to Register for Evacuation

Over and above any man-made creed or law is the natural law of life—
the right of human individuals to live and to creatively express
themselves. No man was born with the right to limit that law. Nor,
do I believe, can anyone justifiably work himself to such a position.

Down through the ages, we have had various individuals doing
their bit to establish more securely these fundamental rights. They
have tried to help society see the necessity of understanding those
fundamental laws; some have succeeded to the extent of having their
natural laws recorded. Many have suffered unnatural deaths as a
result of their convictions. Yet, today, because of the efforts of
some of these individuals, we have recorded in the laws of our
nation certain rights for all men and certain additional rights for
citizens. These fundamental moral rights and civil liberties are
included in the Bill of Rights, US Constitution, and other legal
records. They guarantee that these fundamental rights shall not be
denied without due process of law.

The principles or the ideals are the things which give value to
a person's life. They are the qualities which give impetus and purpose toward meaningful experiences. The violation of human personal-
ity is the violation of the most sacred thing which man owns.

The order for the mass evacuation of all persons of Japanese
descent denies them the right to live. It forces thousands of ener-
getic law-abiding individuals to exist in a miserable psychological
and a horrible physical atmosphere. This order limits to almost the
full extent the creative expressions of those subjected. It kills
the desire for a higher life. Hope for the future is exterminated.
Human personalities are poisoned. The very qualities which are
essential to a peaceful creative community are being thrown out and
abused. Over 60 percent are American citizens, yet they are denied
on a wholesale scale without due process of law the civil liberties
which are theirs.

If I were to register and cooperate under those circumstances,
I would be giving helpless consent to the denial of practically
all of the things which give me incentive to live. I must maintain
my Christian principles. I consider it my duty to maintain the
democratic standards for which this nation lives. Therefore I must
refuse this order of evacuation.

Let me add, however, that in refusing to register, I am well
aware of the excellent qualities of the army and government person-
nel connected with the prosecution of this exclusion order. They are
men of the finest type, and I sincerely appreciate their sympathetic
and honest efforts. Nor do I intend to cast any shadow up the Japanese and the other Nisei who have registered for evacuation. They
have faced tragedy admirably. I am objecting to the principle of this
order, which denies the rights of human beings, including citizens.

— Gordon K. Hirabayashi, statement prepared and disseminated prior to arrest, May 12, 1942

Parting

Thus have I heard:
The army ordered
All Japanese faces to be evacuated
From the city of Los Angeles.
This homeless monk has nothing but a Japanese face.
He stayed here thirteen springs
Meditating with all faces
From all parts of the world,
And studied the teaching of Buddha with them.
Wherever he goes, he may form other groups
Inviting friends of all faces,
Beckoning them with the empty hands of Zen.

— Nyogen Senzaki

Leaving Santa Anita

A government must practice its policy without sentiment.
All Japanese faces will leave California to support
    their government.
This morning, the winding train, like a big black snake,
Takes us as far as Wyoming.
The current of Buddhist thought always runs eastward.
This policy may support the tendency of the teaching.
Who knows?

—Nyogen Senzaki

Dislocation as Practice

While some Buddhists used their faith to help organize their communities, others turned to the Buddhist teachings themselves to find their way through the impending displacement.

By the time the Rinzai Zen Buddhist priest Nyogen Senzaki penned the poems "Parting" and "Leaving Santa Anita" in the spring of 1942, he had already been in the US for close to four decades. Written on the eve of his departure from the community in Los Angeles he had worked so hard to build, he begins "Parting" with the classic opening words for a sutra or Buddhist teaching: "Thus have I heard." For Senzaki, the realization that the journey to the camps might be viewed as an opportunity to put Buddhist ideas into practice was itself a teaching. In his poem "Leaving Santa Anita," written as he was being taken from the horse stalls that housed Los Angeles residents prior to their removal to more permanent camps, he even went so far as to invoke "the eastward flow of Buddhism"—an idea originally used in Japan to refer to the Buddha's prophecy that the Dharma inevitably moves eastward, from India through China and Korea to Japan and beyond. Senzaki connects his impending journey to a Wyoming concentration camp to the fulfillment of Buddhism's eastward journey.

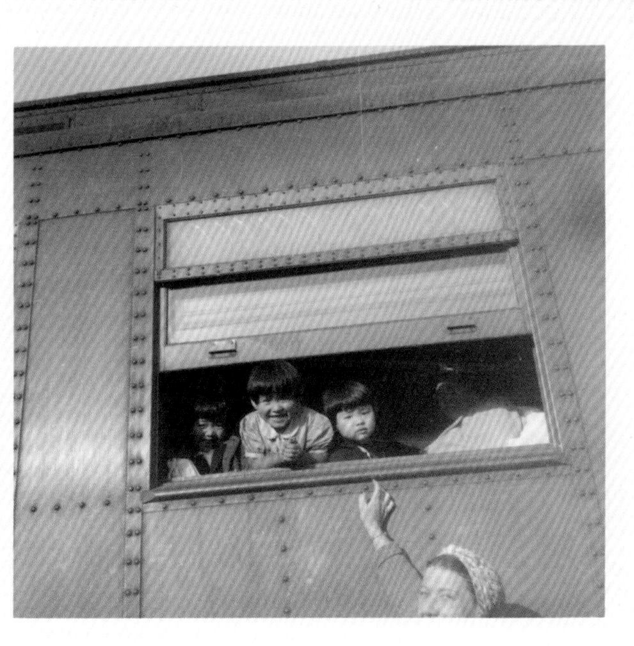

Children peer out of a train in the Boyle Heights neighborhood of Los Angeles while waiting to be transported to a camp due east, 1942.

The Empty Hands
for/after Nyogen Senzaki
Brandon Shimoda

I cannot help
but see
and yet struggle to see
in Nyogen Senzaki's poems

faces
floating

along the body
of a snake

black, winding away
from the spring flower
blooming in

America,

that is
the ritual effacement

of those whose faces
I cannot help
but see

in ours, in yours
in my own

floating along the body
of a silent, surreptitious snake

like scales, like sequins, shining
suns

like suns
shining into

the future
with the shades drawn

That is where we, the descendants, are
and where we will always be

Beckoning them
with the empty hands

of those from whom everything was taken

Faces
separated
from their bodies

bodies arrested, separated
into phases

that constitute what passes
for history

There is no such thing

There is teaching. There is learning
There is heaven, earth

but history? There is no such thing

if the light of a face
if the light of many thousands of faces
takes generations to reach us

and to be seen
clearly
and to not even be seen, clearly

but as a figurative concentration

there is no such thing

There is teaching, there is learning
that is heaven, *that* is earth

that is the endless reconstitution of faces
into the meaning and the order
of independence
in between

heaven and earth, *the empty hands*

open and introduce
their emptiness as sanctuary

but, as the scripture of a harder-won fate
will have it,

cannot be filled, cannot be taken
or even touched

by the lives—by the faces
rising off the winding body

and to which they are held out
to which they are conditioning
their beneficent and beautiful atmosphere
to hold

The empty hands
must remain

empty
or they are not

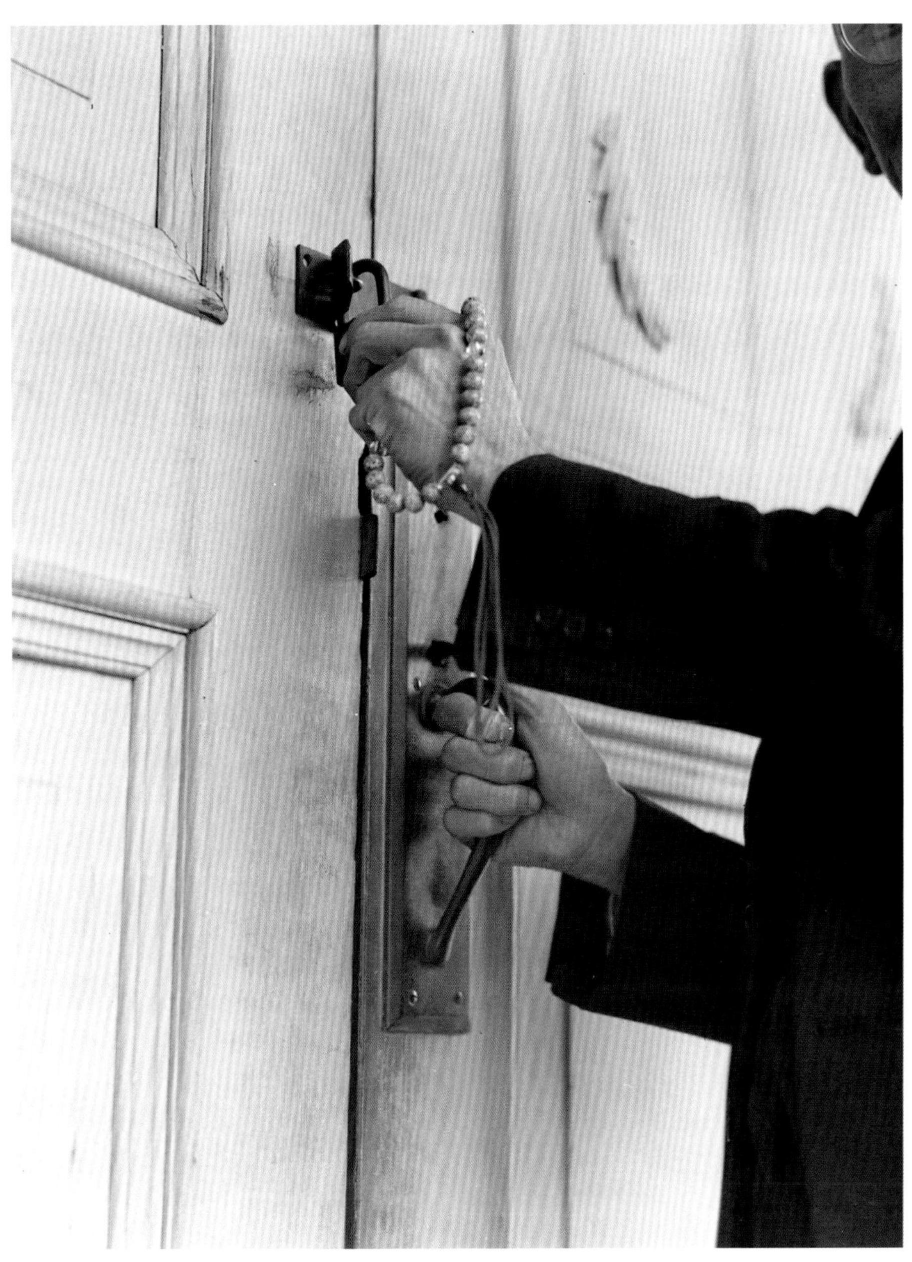

Rev. Naito closes the Florin
Buddhist Temple doors as
he is about to leave for an
assembly center, 1942.

Opening words of
Wyoming Zen-do

The evacuation cramped Japs by heads, into the units
of barracks.
Fortunately, the monk could stay with a Buddhist family.
He called his share of space E-kyō-an, a room of
Wisdom-mirror.

He suffered heat with the family in Santa Anita.
He suffered cold with the family in Heart Mountain.
He and the family and a number of Buddhist in the
two places
Meditated together, and recited Sutras and studied
Buddhism every morning.

America gave the monk the alms, a single room, to-day.
He now re-opens Po-Zen-Zen-kutsu, the meditation hall
of the east bound teaching

He had it twenty years in California
Inviting many Caucasian Buddhists from all parts
of world.

He has to wait exclusively the Japanese Zen-students
to come,
In this snow-covered desert of internment,
a Wyoming plateau
He has nothing to do with the trivialities of
the dusty world.

He rather prefers to sit alone, burning the lamp of Dhamma
Than to receive any insincere visitors and waste time.
Heart mountain Wyoming, Dec 20, 1942.
— Nyogen Senzaki

東漸禪窟開單
一簑煙雨辭去
惠鏡容庵再
開龕雲東漸
會議東漸
世俗風塵
渾不管
寒燈火獨耀
對老燈獨耀
曇雲
如幻

2

RESILIENCE

Ever since I became Buddha I have widely discoursed and taught with various karmic reasonings and various parables, and I have led living beings to the abandonment of all attachments with innumerable skillful means.

方便 – SKILLFUL MEANS – LOTUS SUTRA

It was by faith that he [Abraham] sojourned in the promised land, as in a foreign country, residing in tents, as did Isaac and Jacob who were co-heirs with him of the same promise; he was waiting for the city with its fixed foundations, whose builder and maker is God.

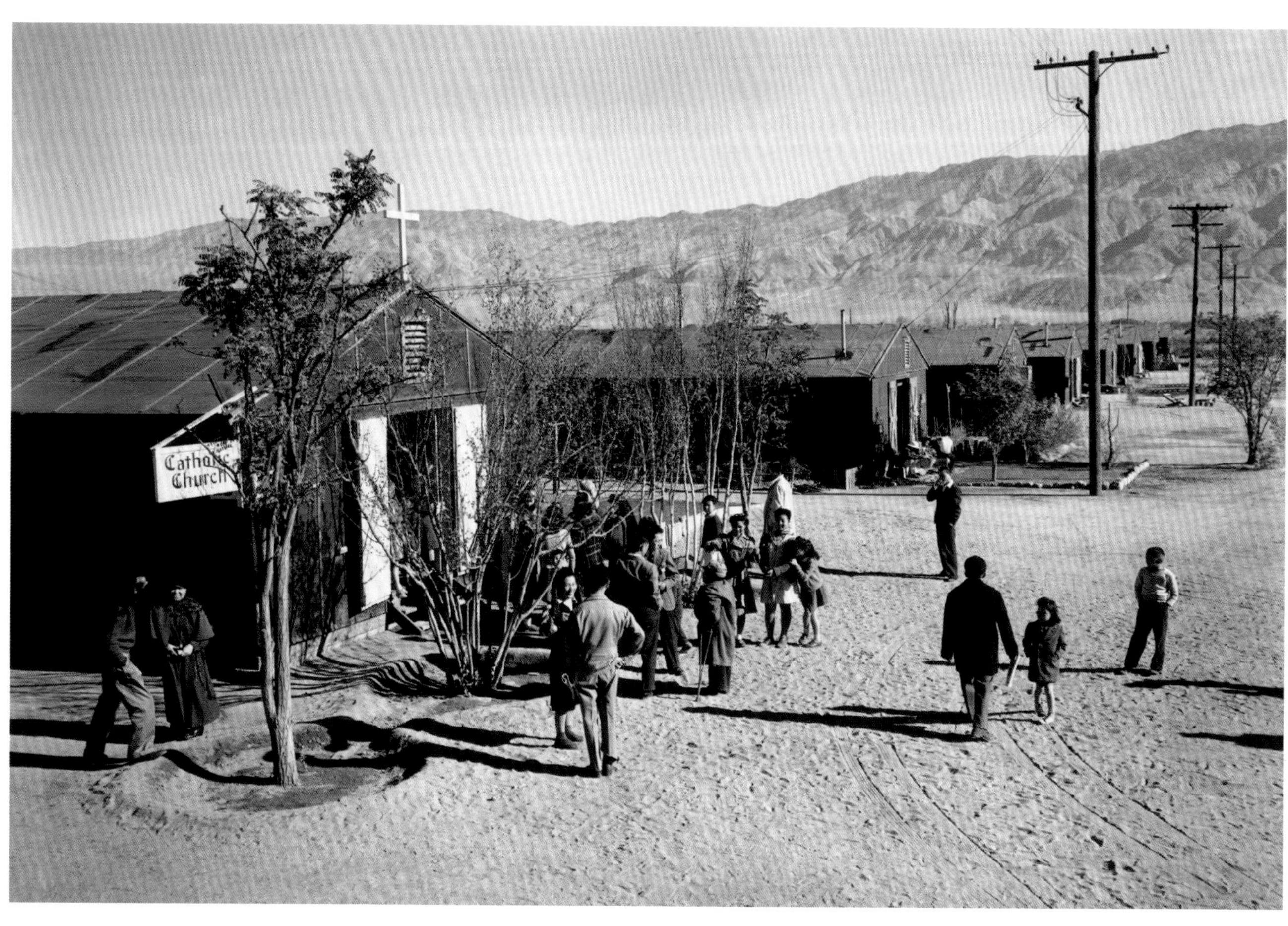

Catholic
Church

Resilience is the practice of skillfully adapting to a change-able and sometimes distressing world by grounding oneself in enduring truths. For a number of Japanese Americans, the true magnitude of what they had lost as a result of their forced relocation only began to sink in after their difficult journey to the remote camps. Many turned to their faith in this moment to regain a sense of normalcy as well as pur-pose. At times, their desire for spiritual guidance manifest-ed as private acts of devotion, at times as communal acts of fellowship. Whether creating space for prayer and worship, or marking time through religious holidays, or crafting reli-gious objects, Buddhists and Christians alike used creativ-ity to find their way through the difficult circumstances in which they found themselves.

Opposite: Catholic Church at Manzanar concentration camp, California, ca. 1943. Photo by Ansel Adams.

Page 36: Declaration of the opening of the Wyoming Zendo handwritten by Nyogen Senzaki, Heart Mountain concentration camp, Wyoming, 1942.

Sacred Space for Religious Gatherings

The demarcation of sacred space became an important means by which Japanese Americans sought to orient themselves and find some measure of meaning, purpose, and spiritual liberation in the midst of incarceration.

When the first Japanese Americans arrived at the camps, they found that little if any consideration had been given to providing dedicated structures for religious practice. Instead, they were forced to improvise using recreational halls and other camp buildings.

Many of the most vulnerable members of the community—the elderly, the infirm, and young children—did not survive that first year in camp. The wish to memorialize those who had died gave urgency to the push to build dedicated religious spaces. Non-Christians in particular had to petition the War Relocation Authority (WRA) for adequate space. Many camp administrators often favored Christianity, barely tolerated Buddhism, and banned Shinto rituals and worship entirely.

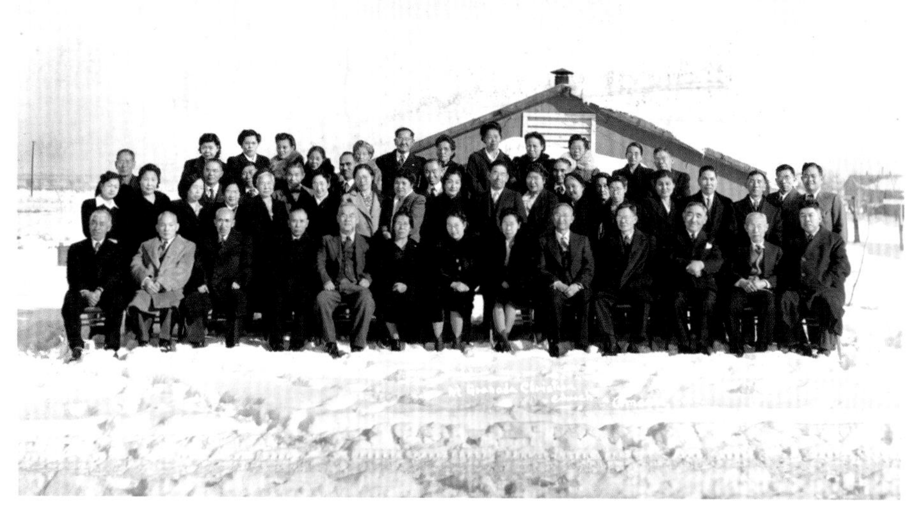

Right: Members gather in front of Amache Christian Church, Colorado, ca. 1945.

Opposite: Nyogen Senzaki preaches inside barracks apartment, Heart Mountain concentration camp, Wyoming, ca. 1943. Drawing by Estelle Ishigo.

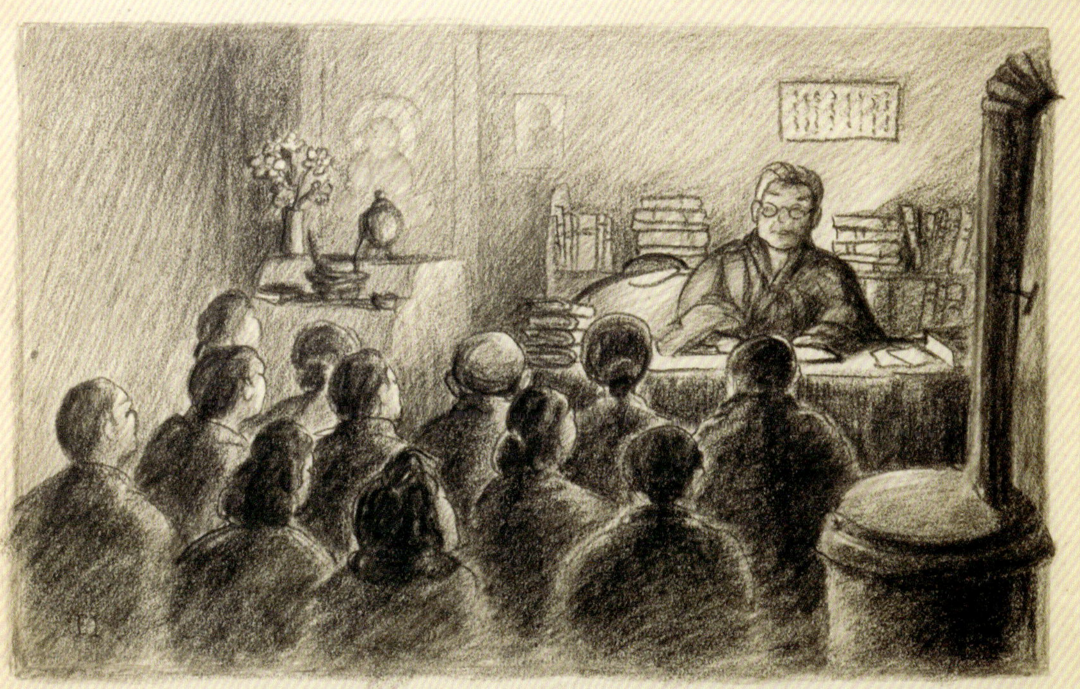

A monk teaching Buddhism

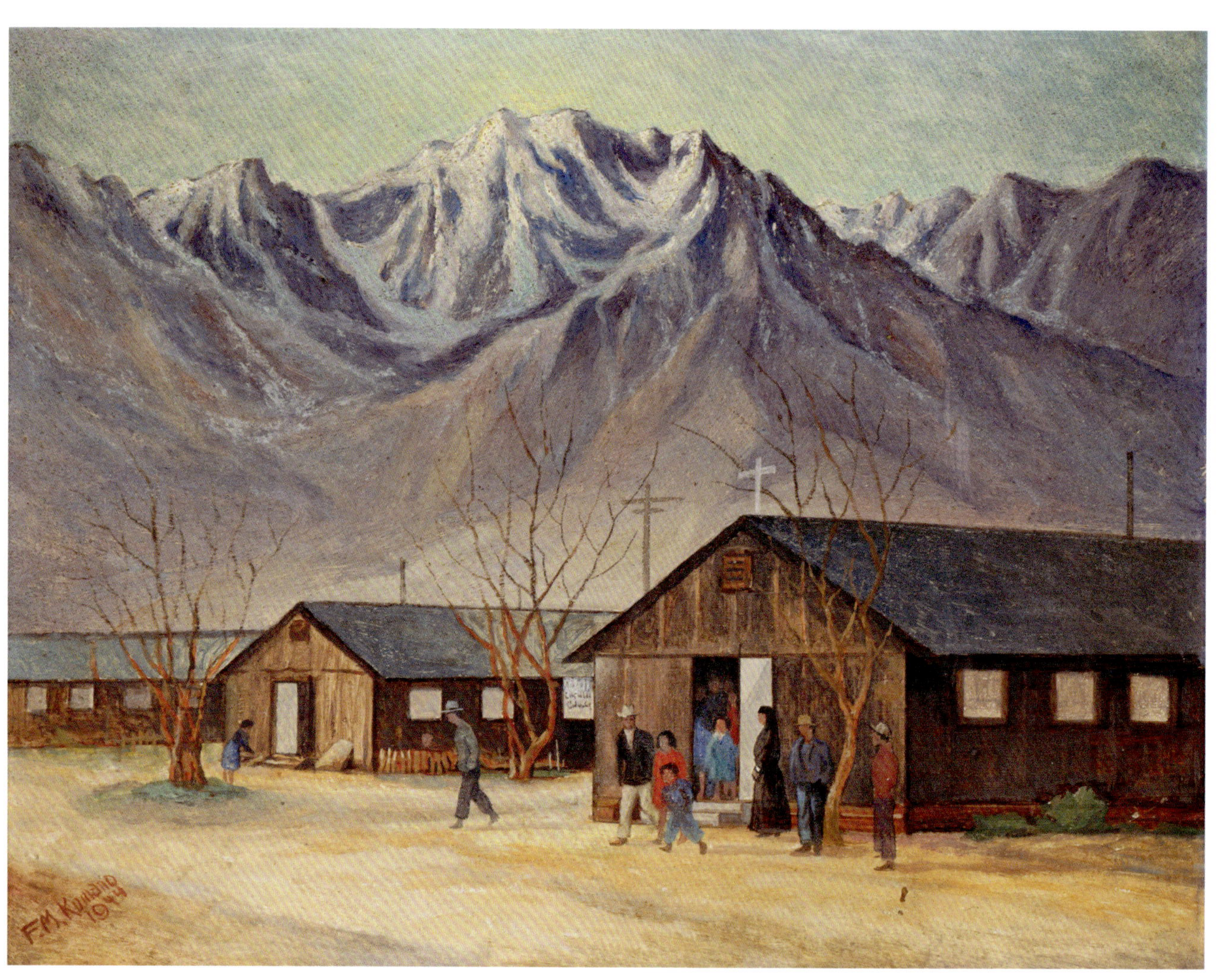

Above: Catholic Church at
Manzanar concentration
camp, California. Painting
by F.M. Kumano, 1944.

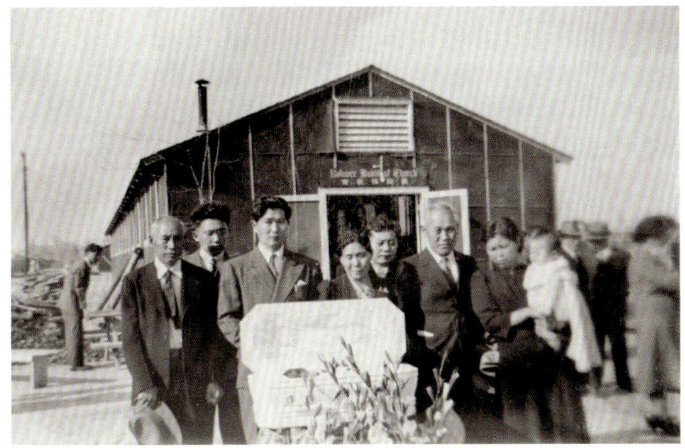

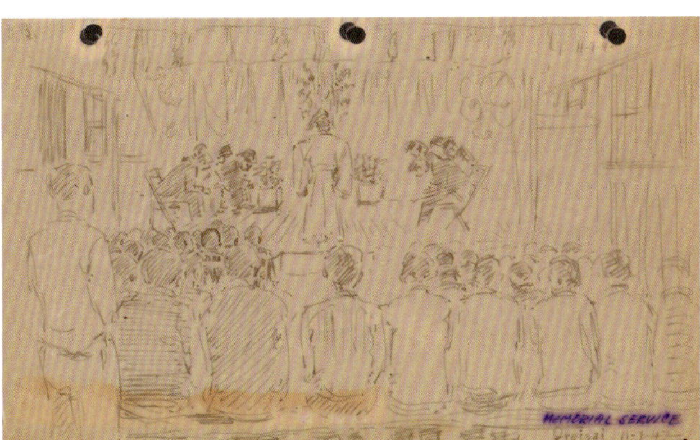

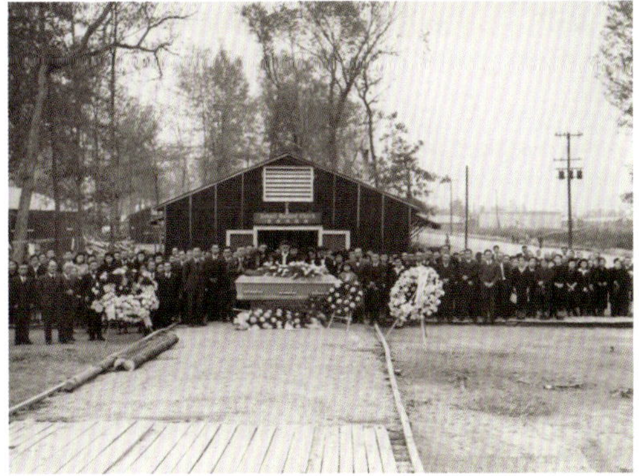

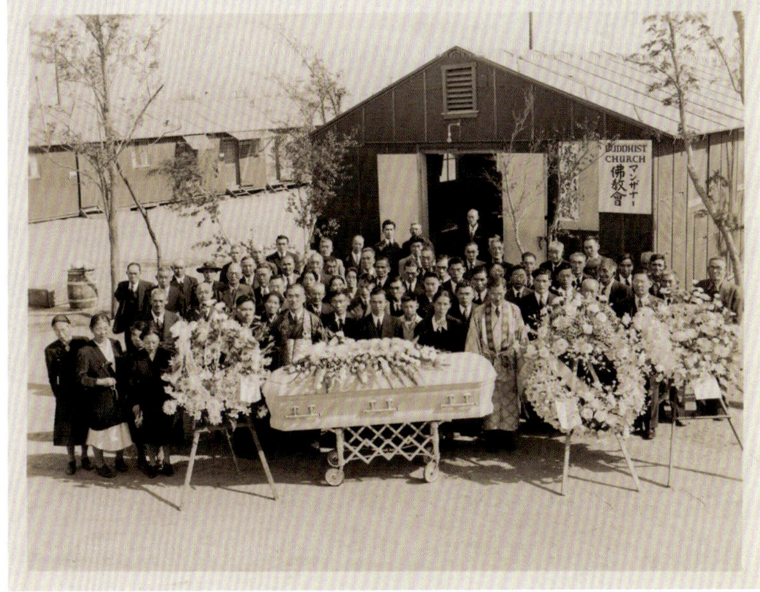

Left, top: Attendees at a funeral gather around a baby's coffin outside Buddhist church at Rohwer concentration camp, Arkansas, 1943. Photo by Walter Muramoto.

Left, bottom: Funeral in front of the Rohwer Buddhist Church, Rohwer concentration camp, Arkansas, ca. 1943.

Right, top: Memorial service held inside barracks, Lordsburg Internment Camp, New Mexico, 1942. Drawing by George Hoshida.

Right, bottom: Funeral officiated by Rev. Shinjo Nagatomi at the Manzanar Buddhist Church, Manzanar concentration camp, California, 1943.

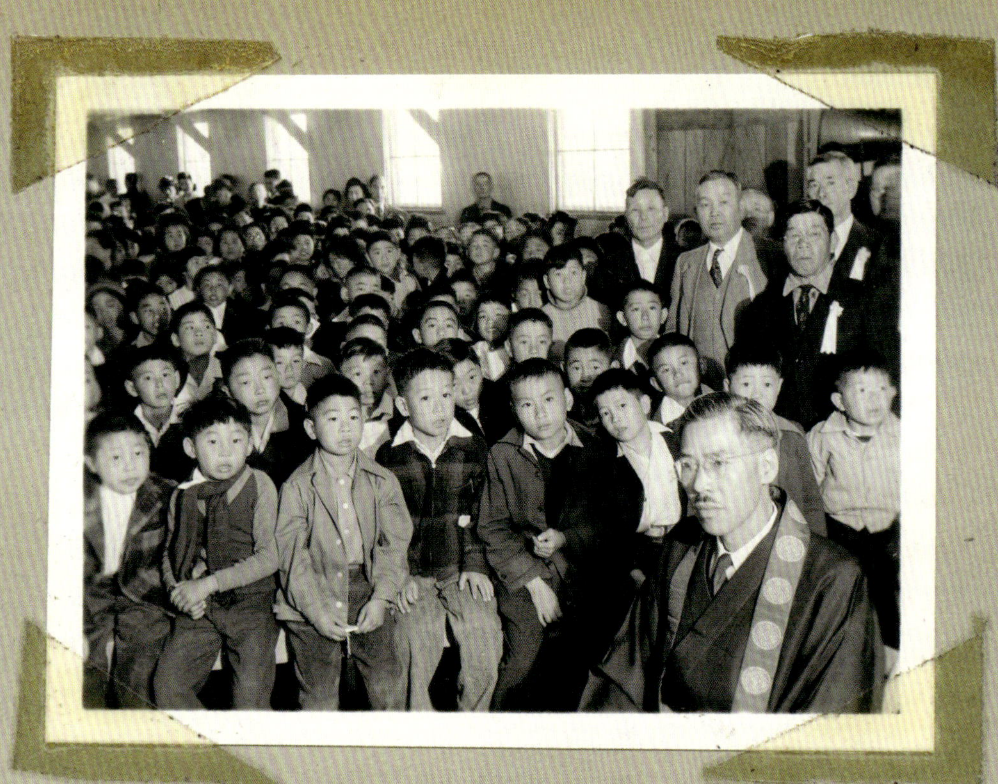

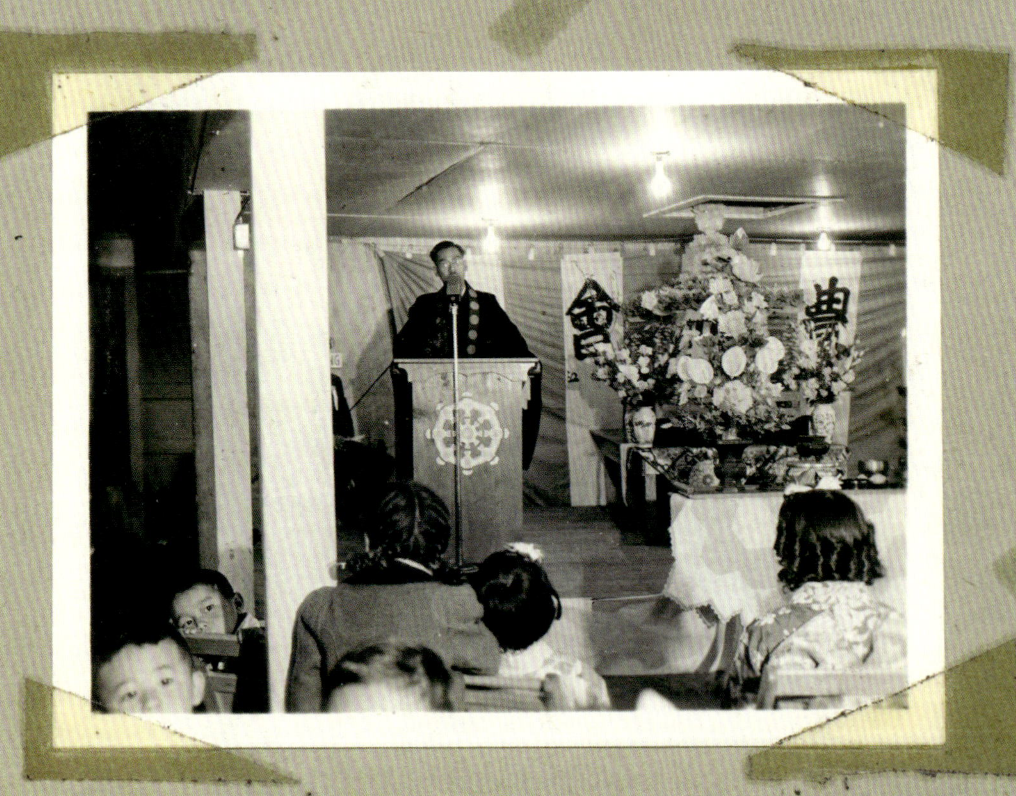
會
農

An Exile with No Clear Ending

Religious services and holidays that punctuated the days, weeks, and years helped create order in the camps by giving structure to the uncertainties of indefinite incarceration.

Dharma talks, chanting, scripture study, and fellowship provided weekly opportunities for Japanese Americans to connect with each other and something larger than themselves. Indeed, Buddhists and Christians often found their adult and youth gatherings on Sundays even better attended in camp than they had been before the war.

Similarly, celebrations for New Year's Day, Hanamatsuri, Easter, Obon, and Christmas became ways of reenacting the annual rhythms of prewar religious life.

Opposite, top: Rev. Shinjo Nagatomi with young Buddhist children at the Manzanar concentration camp, California, ca. 1943. Photo by Toyo Miyatake.

Opposite, bottom: Rev. Shinjo Nagatomi preaches at a podium with a Dharma wheel at the Manzanar concentration camp, California, ca. 1943. Photo by Toyo Miyatake.

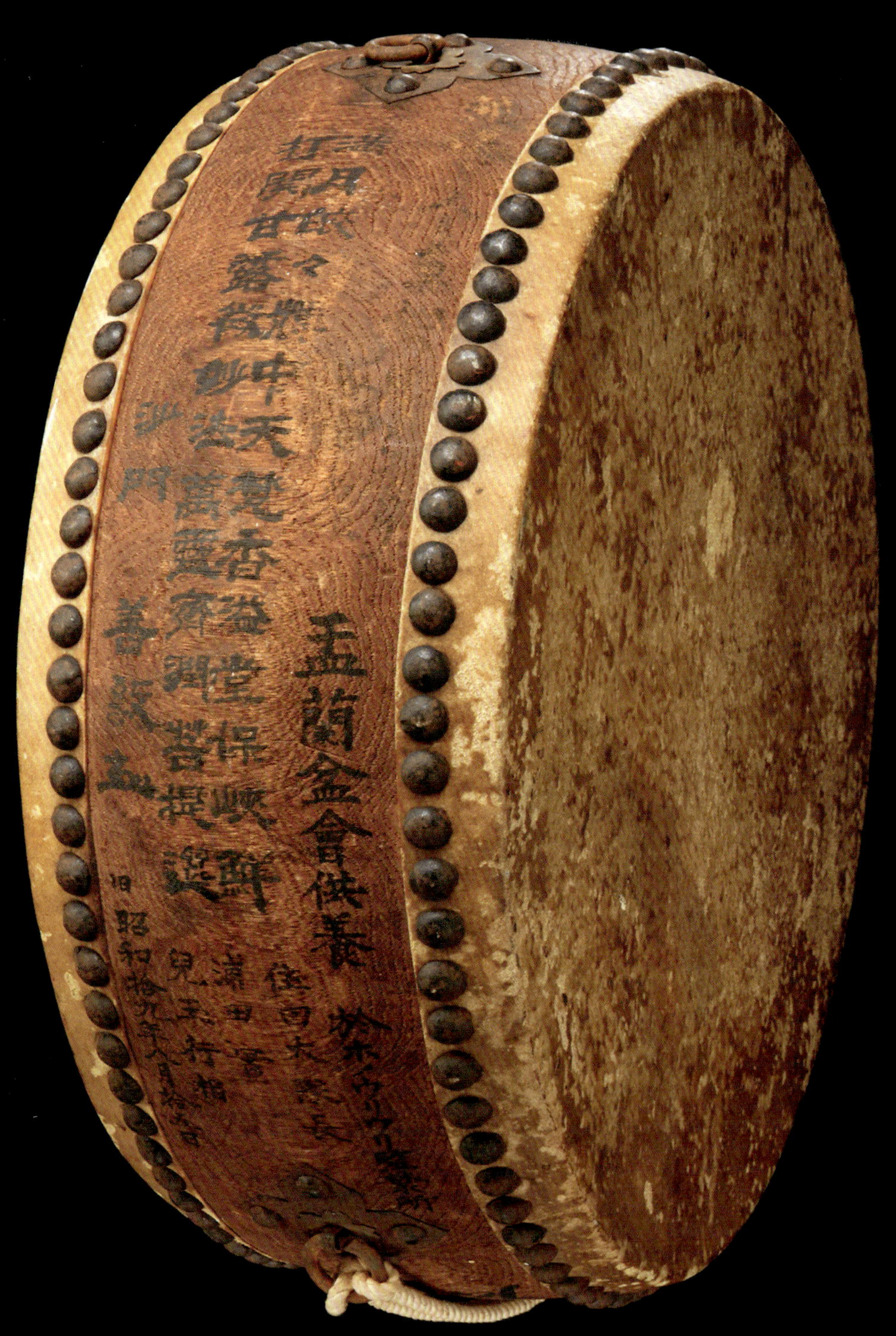
盂蘭盆會供養
昭和拾九年八月

Marking Sacred Time: Summer/Fall

By the summer of 1942, the forced removal of Japanese Americans from the West Coast was more or less complete. This meant that the first religious holiday to be celebrated in camp was the summer ritual of Obon, the Buddhist festival in which ancestors are honored. Despite the heat of the mid-summer season, Obon ceremonies and dances drew the biggest participation of any religious activity in the concentration camps, with families from both Buddhist and Christian backgrounds joining the dances and festivities.

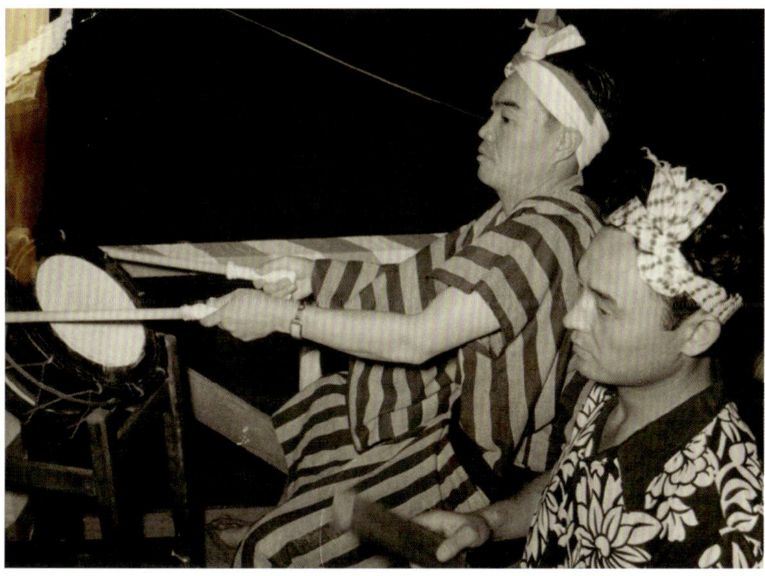

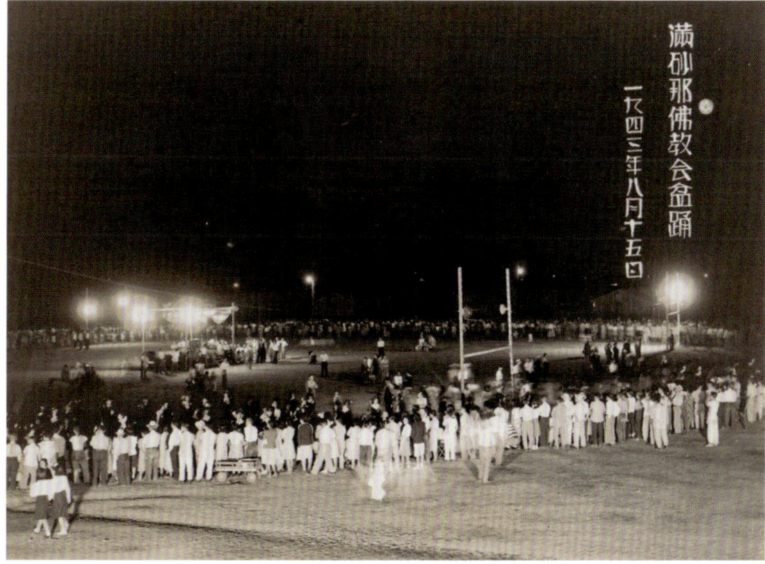

Opposite: Drum used during Obon ceremony at Honouliuli Internment Camp, Hawaiʻi, 1942.

Left, top: Obon in Amache concentration camp, Colorado, 1943.

Left: Nighttime Obon festivities in Manzanar concentration camp, California, 1943. Photo by Toyo Miyatake.

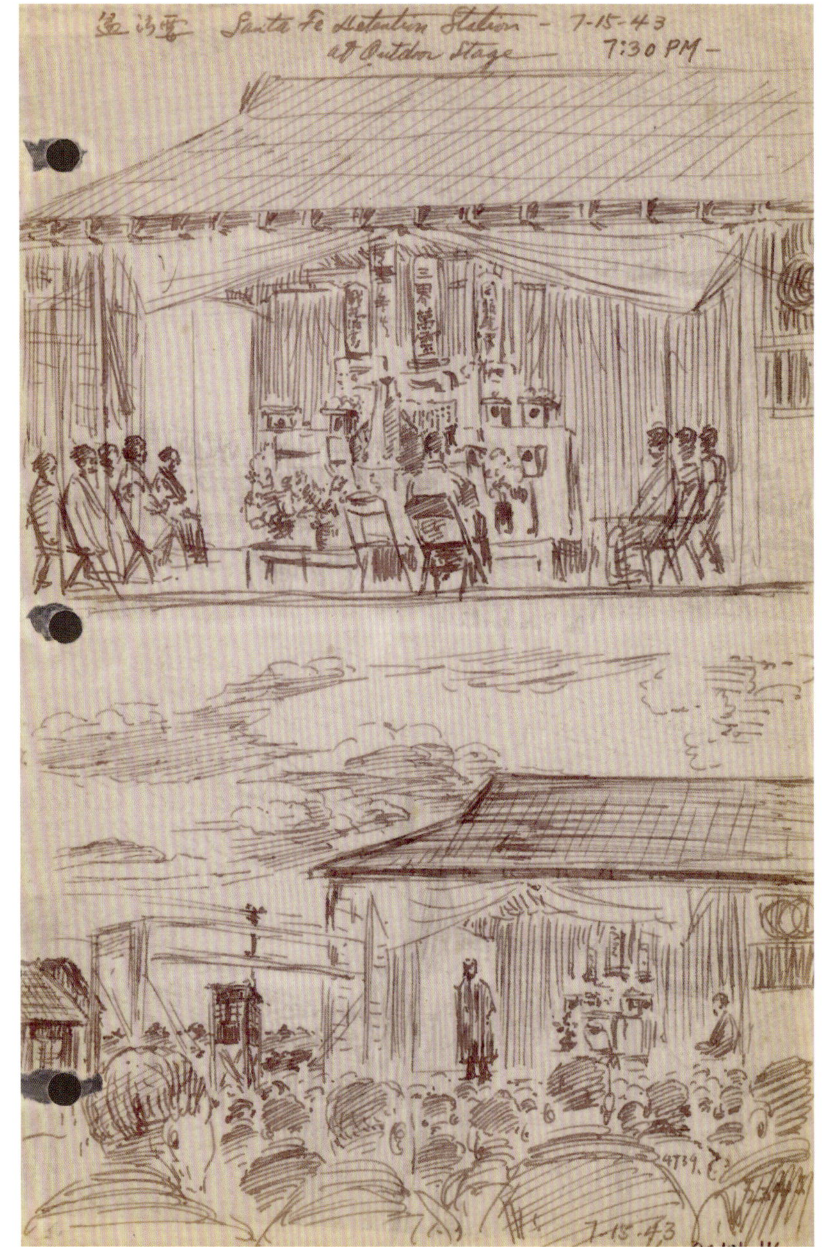

Right: Obon festivities at Santa Fe Internment Camp, New Mexico, July 1943. Drawing by George Hoshida.

Opposite: Japanese Americans in kimono participating in Obon dancing, Heart Mountain concentration camp, Wyoming, 1943. Photos by Bill Manbo.

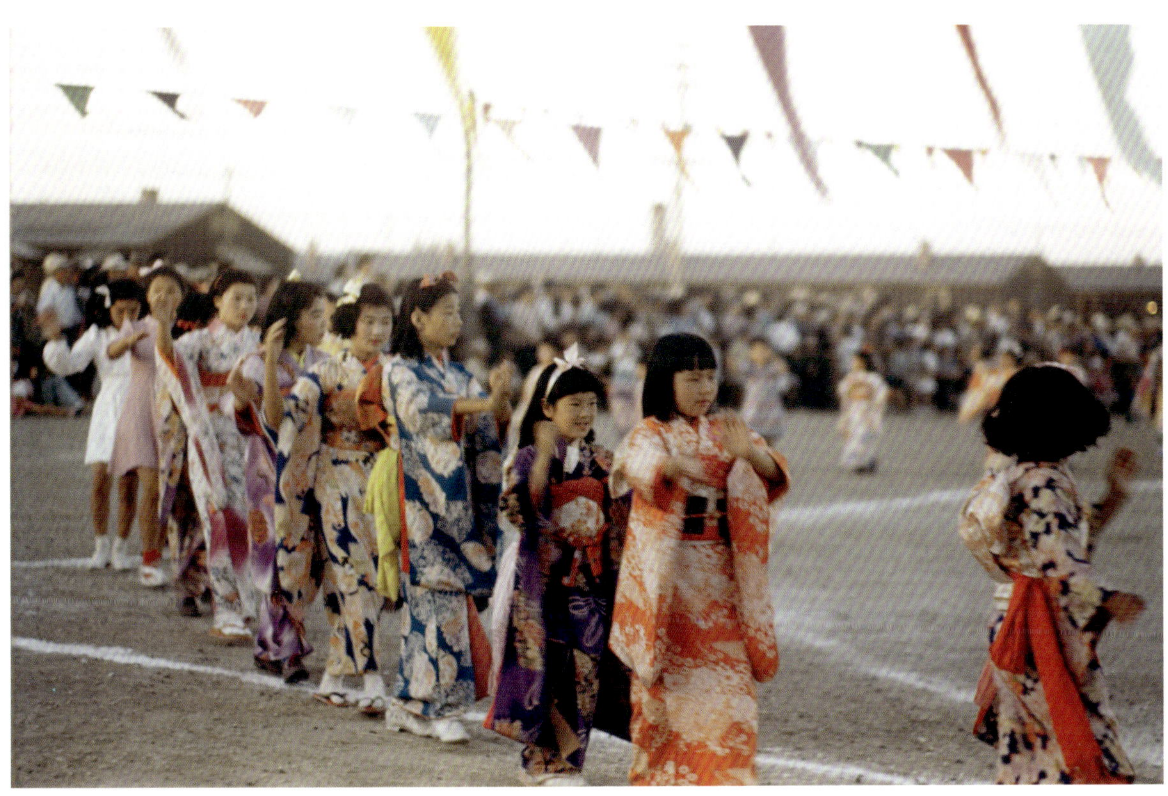

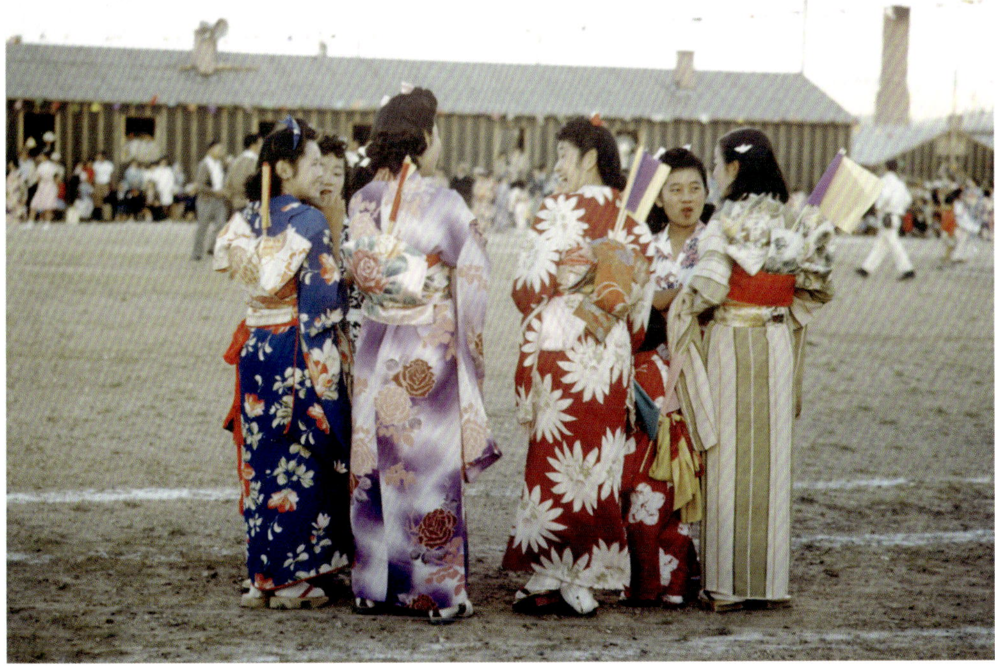

Marking Sacred Time: Winter

In 1942, a Protestant organization called the Home Missions Council proclaimed its wish to hold "America's Biggest Christmas Party" for the Japanese Americans in camp.

Working together with the Protestant Commission for Japanese Service, the Quaker-run American Friends Service Committee, the interdenominational Fellowship of Reconciliation, and the secular Japanese American Citizens League, it launched a project to bring Christmas gifts to all children in the WRA camps regardless of denomination or faith tradition. Throughout the war, Buddhists and Christians would often share Christmas cards and decorate the dining hall together during the winter holiday season.

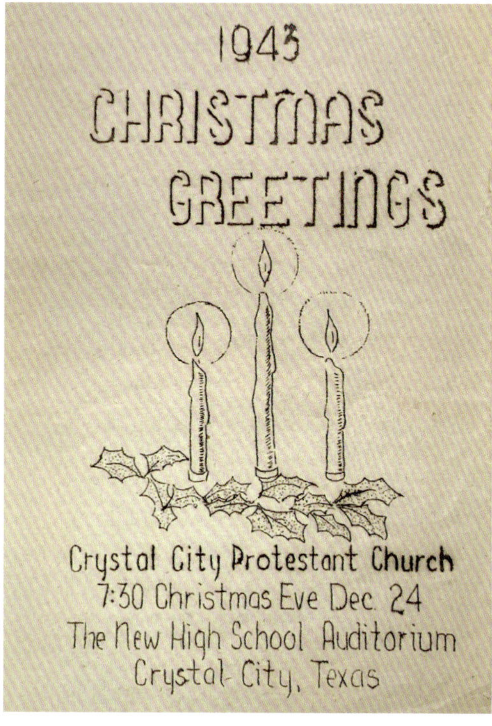

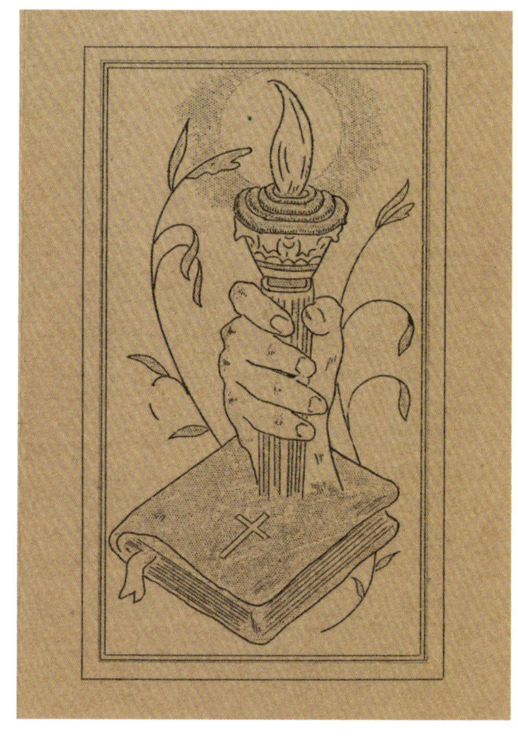

Right: Christmas service program of Christian church in Crystal City Internment Camp, Texas, 1943.

Far right: Santa Anita Assembly Center Federated Churches Christmas Service Program, California, 1942.

Opposite: Leaflet made to advertise Christmas parties and gift giveaways in camp, 1944.

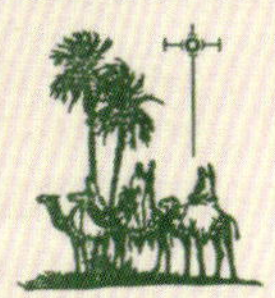

For Christmas Behind Barbed Wire

For the last two years, many churches and other organizations cooperated in sending Christmas gifts to boys and girls in War Relocation Projects. These American children, whose ancestors immigrated to this country from Japan, will this year have their third Christmas away from home, their third Christmas behind barbed wire.

Once again, the American Friends Service Committee wishes to help carry Christmas to these children. Because of the response to the project last year, the parents of these children are to be included in the 1944 Christmas program. Something either for their own personal use or for their small one roomed homes will bring joy and give faith in America to the older people.

Directions for sending gifts to residents in Relocation Centers:

1. Select a NEW gift for a person of any age.

2. Put your name and address on a Christmas card.

3. Tie the card to the gift.
   DO NOT WRAP THE GIFT. However, please send tissue paper and ribbon with the gift which will be wrapped at its destination.

4. Mail your gift to one of the A.F.S.C. receiving centers:

AFSC Storeroom **1515 Cherry Street** **Philadelphia 2, Pa.**	**AFSC Storeroom** **501 N. Raymond Ave.** **Pasadena 3, Cal.**
Friends Meeting House **2151 Vine Street** **Berkeley 7, Cal.**	**Friends Center** **3959 - 15th Ave.** **Seattle 5, Wash.**

5. Mail NOT LATER THAN NOVEMBER 15th so that the Committee may have time to pack it and get it to its destination (by freight) in plenty of time for Christmas.

You may send more than one gift if you wish.

Please do not send war toys. Christmas celebrates the birth of One who preached "Peace on Earth, Good Will to men."

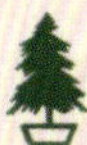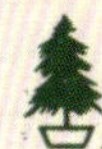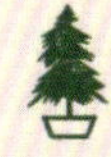

Marking Sacred Time: Spring

The Hanamatsuri festival commemorating the Buddha's birth and Easter both take place during the spring. Despite their clear associations with different faith traditions, both are seen as celebrations of new life and rebirth, and as such, were particularly poignant in the setting of the concentration camps.

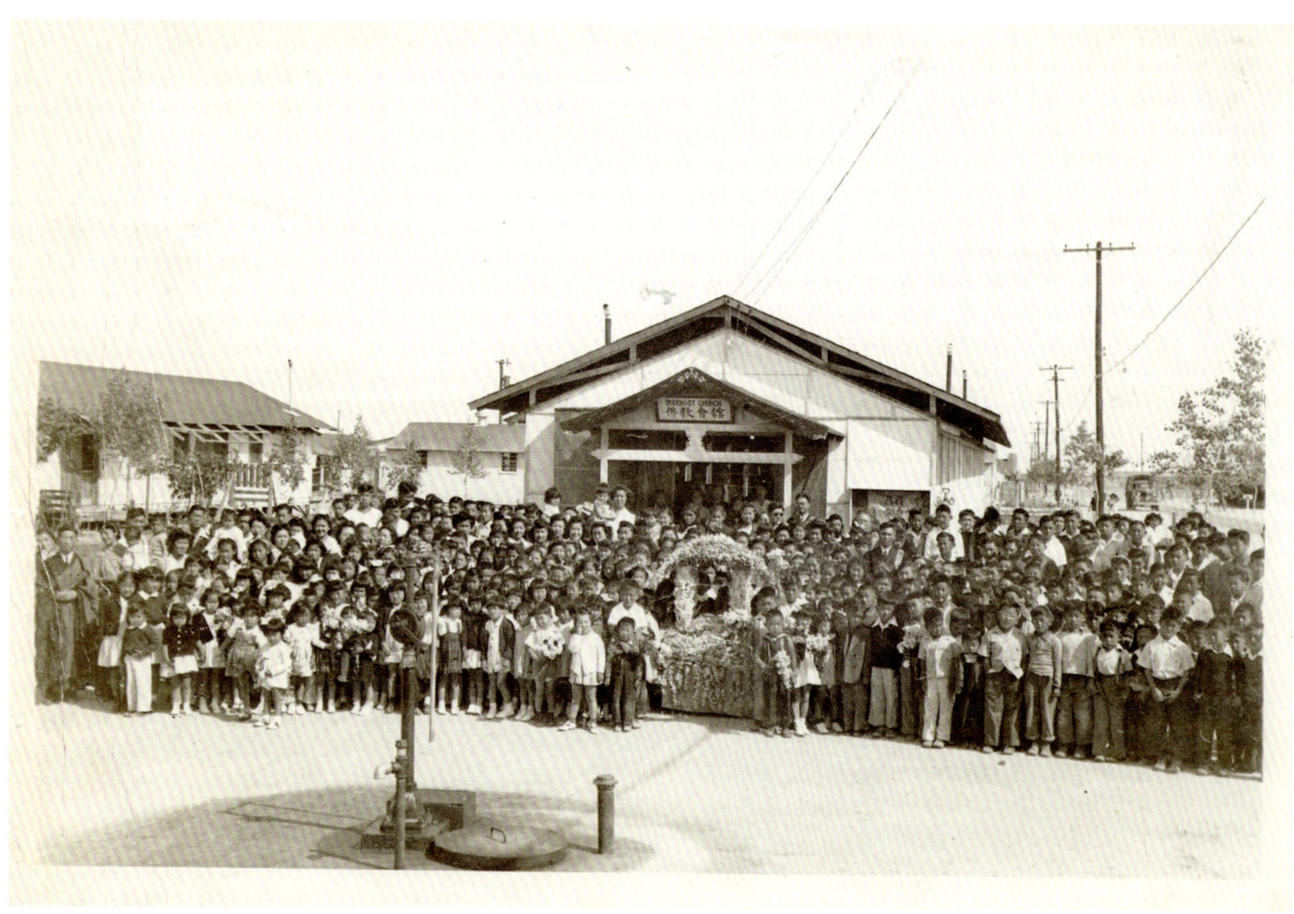

Above: Hanamatsuri, the celebration of the Buddha's birth, held at Gila River concentration camp, Arizona, 1944.

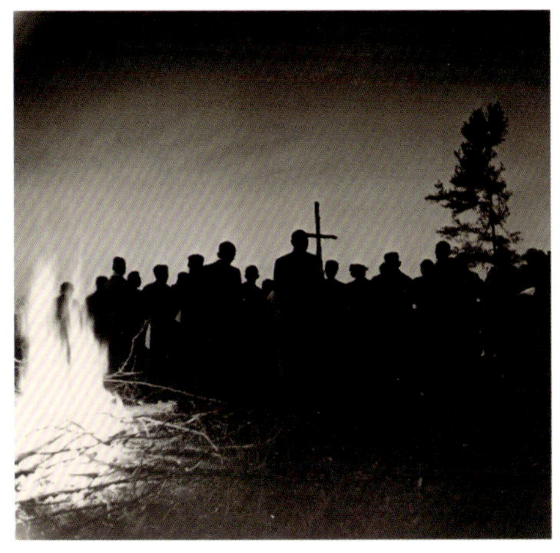

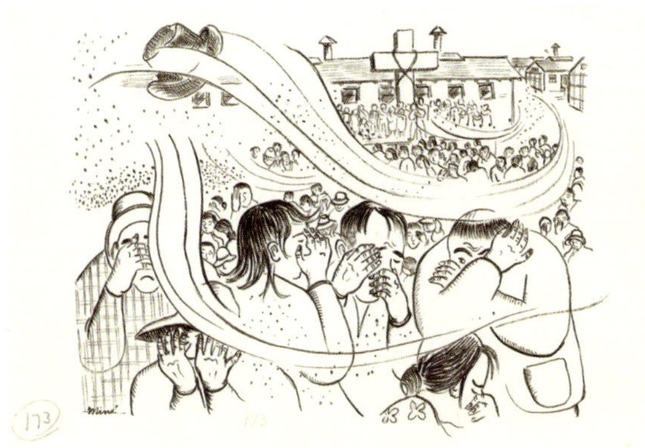

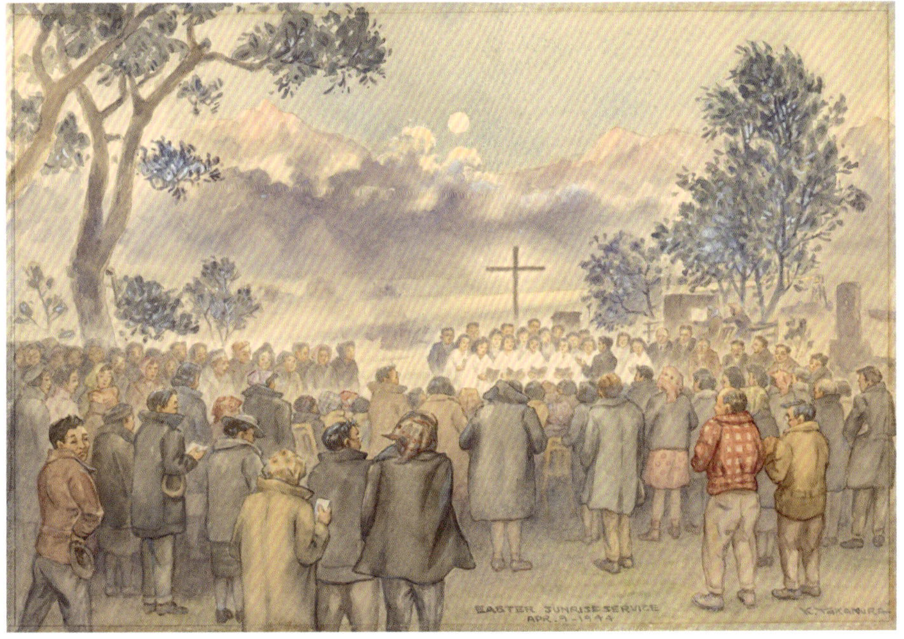

Top, left: Sunrise Easter service at Jerome concentration camp, Arkansas, 1943.

Top, right: "Easter in Topaz," illustration for *Citizen 13660*, by Mine Okubo, ca. 1945.

Left: "Easter Sunrise Service, April 9, 1944," Manzanar concentration camp, California, by Kango Takamura. The artist noted that it was "Cold and windy at sunrise, the moon still shone over Mt. Williamson."

Below: Crucifix, scapular, and saint cards taken to Manzanar concentration camp by Mary Naide Poon.

When Mary's mother passed away when she and her siblings were still children, her father placed his children in the Maryknoll Sister's Orphanage in the Boyle Heights neighborhood of Los Angeles. He was eventually hired on as the gardener so he could spend more time with his children. Mary contracted tuberculosis in Manzanar and was even given last rites, but eventually recovered. The small crucifix, scapular, and saint cards were a source of comfort and reassurance for her as she endured hardships, including incarceration.

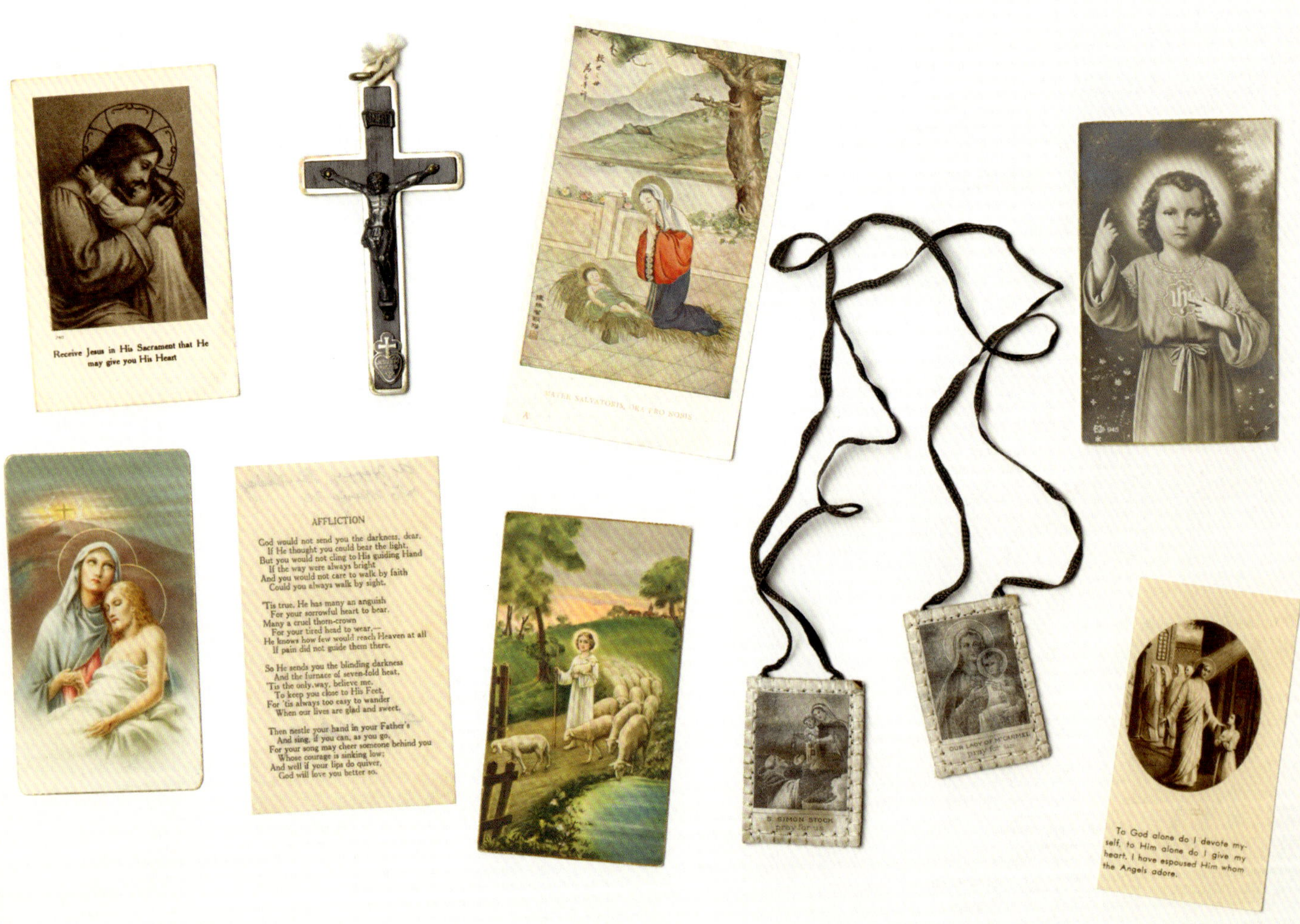

Sustaining Religious Life

Strict restrictions on how much and what people were able to bring with them to camp meant that items needed to help sustain religious life often had to be made by hand or secured from sympathetic friends on the outside. The altars, prayer beads, rosaries, service books, crosses, scriptures, statuary, and other implements of faith that were used or created in camp, many of them handcrafted, testify to the persistence and ingenuity of Japanese American faith in even the most difficult of circumstances.

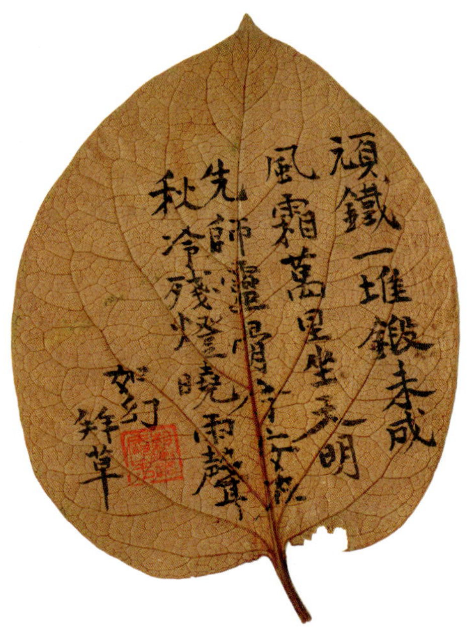

The work goes on
Hammering and forging
The steel of Zen.
Wherever a monk lives
The old process continues, time after time.
Here comes another autumn dawn!
The lamp still remains burning
While the morning rain patters at the window!
Let us pay homage to our Roshi, Soyen Shaku

—Nyogen Senzaki (translation of poem written on persimmon leaf)

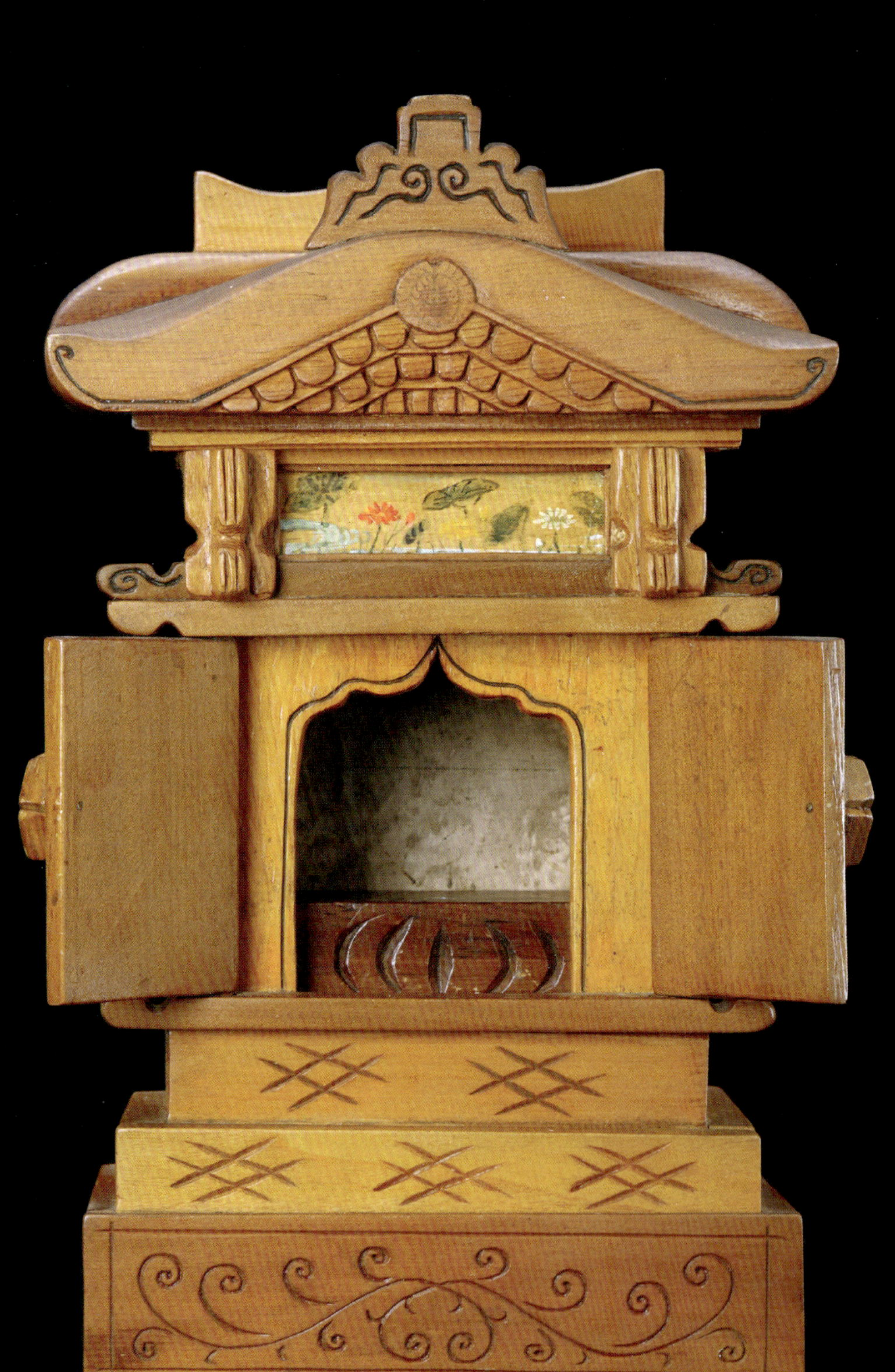

Crafting Ritual Implements

Many of the religious items used in camp tended to be ephemeral—paper flowers for memorials or celebrations, mimeographed orders of service programs, a statue of the Buddha made from a mess-hall carrot. But camp-made *butsudan* (also known as *obutsudan*), Buddhist home altars traditionally used to commemorate loved ones and ancestors, were so valued that many have survived to this day. Crafted from scavenged scraps of wood or metal or materials secured at great cost from the outside, they remain intimate and personalized testaments to a lineage of devotion, each carved line suffused with the soul of its maker.

Butsudan: Recreating Home and Family Practice in the Barracks
Jane Naomi Iwamura

To take refuge. To focus. To remember.

The *butsudan* or Buddhist home altar is the spiritual center of the Buddhist household, the place where the sacred values of enlightenment, impermanence, and gratitude are encapsulated, where space for prayer, reflection, and remembrance has been hallowed. As such, the *butsudan* is intimately linked to one's own life. Flanked by *ihai* (memorial tablets) or photos of deceased family members, the *butsudan* is a site for rituals such as offering the first rice of the day or sharing an edible gift from a neighbor. These small household rites constitute the spiritual rhythm and flow of life.

During World War II, however, and especially after Pearl Harbor, many Japanese American households feared that any connection to Japanese religion and culture could be viewed by the US government as a sign of allegiance to Japan, and so discarded or burned their altars. Others chose to store their *butsudan*, hoping to retrieve them when they returned home.

Many Japanese Americans were thus unable to continue home altar practice during their imprisonment. However, there were some who found ways to recreate their home shrines in the barracks. Crafting *butsudan* from found wood and objects scattered throughout the camps, they held fast to their Buddhist faith and traditions, an impulse that speaks to the spiritual resilience and creativity of the internees.

This practice of setting up home altars remained strong among Issei and Nisei during the postwar period. While subsequent generations of Japanese American Buddhists have increasingly abandoned the practice, the *butsudan* remains a powerful symbol of endurance, connection, and faith.

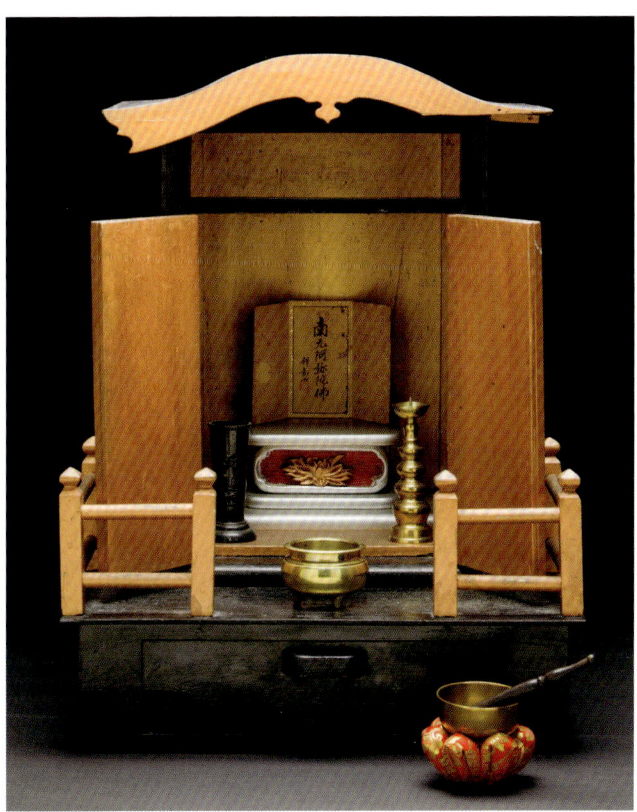

Above: Butsudan made from scrap wood found in a mess hall in Gila River concentration camp, Arizona.

Opposite: Butsudan made by Zenichi Yamashita in Santa Fe Internment Camp, New Mexico.

The Figure of Compassion

The Elsa Kannon, as this statue is colloquially referred to, is a beautiful wartime rendition of the bodhisattva of compassion, known as Avalokitesvara in Sanskrit, Guanyin in Chinese, and Kannon in Japanese. Two kanji characters make up the word "Kannon"—"Kan" (to see) and "On" (to hear)—reflecting the Buddhist concept of compassion as the ability to clearly see and hear the suffering in the world. The "Elsa" in the statue's name refers to the four letters etched in its back. Though the Elsa Kannon's exact provenance remains unknown, its very mystery is an invitation to look closer at what has been carved.

Remembering the Unknown
George Tanabe

Who is Elsa? That's the name inscribed on the back of a wooden carving of the Bodhi-sattva Kannon enshrined at the Daifukuji Soto Mission in Kona, Hawai'i. According to one story heard by a Soto Zen Buddhist minister, the Elsa Kannon was carved in an internment camp during World War II. Another minister remembers a story about an internee who carved the image of Kannon using tools made out of scrap metal. Yet another version has it that Elsa was the daughter of an artist interned at Crystal City. Though always linked to the internment experience, Elsa's identity is more conjecture than certainty.

Contrast that to the *toba*, or memorial tablets produced in wartime Hawai'i at around the same time. Made from wood veneer and inscribed with the names of Nisei soldiers killed in action, they give silent testament to the specifics of each casualty's life: who they were, where they came from, and the exact dates of their birth and death. This form of memorialization seems more familiar to us—it helps us to fix memory in place.

We tend to commemorate our war dead in cemeteries such as Arlington National Cemetery, where thousands of names are laid out in measured rows. But the most poignant gravesite in Arlington is the Tomb of the Unknown Soldier, where honor guards never rest, keeping alive the memory of an anonymous soldier who remains "known only to God." This is a fitting tribute to the depth of our moral memory, which can be measured by the value we accord to the unknown just as much as the known.

If the day should ever come when we can unravel the mystery of Elsa's identity, we will commit her history to the past. But until then, we have no choice but to keep the mystery of her existence alive by continuing to ask in the present tense: Who is Elsa?

Below: Inscription on the back of the "Elsa" Kannon.

Opposite: The "Elsa" Kannon, the bodhisattva of compassion, enshrined at the Kona Daifukuji Soto Mission, Hawai'i.

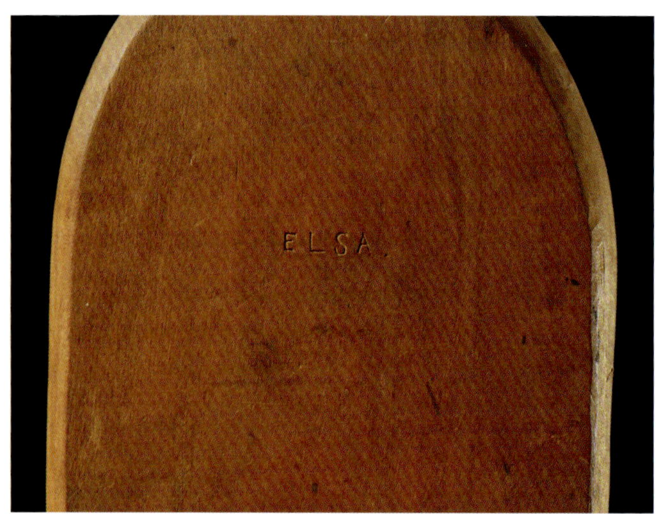

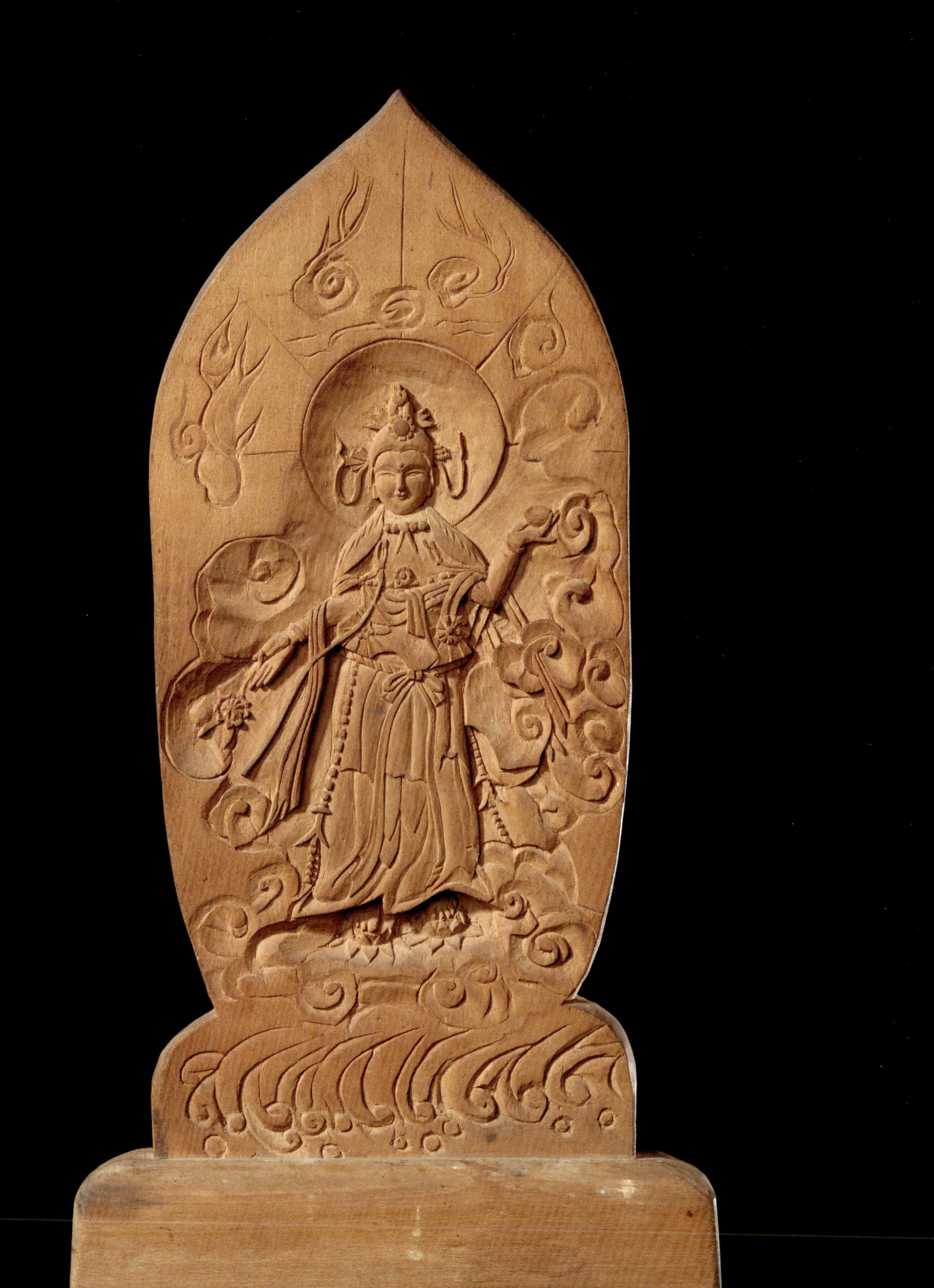

Anchoring Faith

The cross in Christianity has long served as a symbol of the salvific power of faith in the death and resurrection of Jesus Christ. When placed at the front of a room, this simple wooden cross, handmade by Reverend Tamasaku Watanabe in the Santa Fe Internment Camp, had the power to transform an ordinary barrack into a place for Christian fellowship. Despite being a distinct minority in the Department of Justice camps, small Christian congregations persevered, anchored around symbols of sacrifice and redemption such as this.

Remembering My Grandfather: Inklings and Revelations
Gail Y. Okawa

"About 65 brothers come every afternoon and we study in [sic] the Bible. I offer prayer[s]." — Reverend Tamasaku Watanabe

On December 7, 1941, a day of many infamies, my grandfather Reverend Tamasaku Watanabe was arrested at his parsonage at the ʻŌlaʻa Japanese Christian Church on Hawaiʻi Island, Territory of Hawaiʻi. Detained for being a community leader, he continued his ministry at first in Hawaiʻi, where he was initially imprisoned, and subsequently in the Lordsburg and Santa Fe Internment Camps in New Mexico, where he was exiled along with hundreds of other Hawaiʻi Japanese. He and his fellow Christian ministers continued to conduct prayer meetings as well as church and funeral services—even performing Christmas plays—throughout their imprisonment. His Christian mission remained central to his identity, life, and sense of purpose.

Born over a year after his arrest, I wasn't even aware that he was absent from my life, much less that he had been interned. My earliest and fondest memory of him stems from around when I was in the fifth grade and had to stay at home from school one day with a cold. He was on one of his once- or twice-a-year visits from Maui to Honolulu, and I remember making my favorite egg salad and Spam sandwiches for both of us for our lunch. A tall, thin, quiet man, he expressed his enjoyment of the simple meal I had prepared by smiling impishly and remarking in English that I should open a sandwich shop!

I didn't find out about my grandfather's internment on the mainland during the war until I was in high school, when I learned about it by chance from a family friend. Stunned, I questioned my parents, who confirmed that he had indeed been incarcerated. They commented without elaboration that he had returned a "changed man." I deeply regret now that I never asked further about this. Decades later, I found a single photo in a trunk that contained my grandfather's World War II documents and artifacts: it depicted a group of men in front of an adobe building with *vigas* (wooden beams) much like those I'd seen in New Mexico. The return addresses on letters he had written to my mother confirmed the location.

It wasn't until I embarked on a research project as a university professor years later that I began to look more carefully at the letters he sent from the Lordsburg and Santa Fe Internment Camps to my mother Sumi. These letters, which reveal he had received numerous baby pictures taken by my father, express an intimate involvement in my birth and growth about which I had no knowledge. In them, he approves of my Japanese middle name "Yukie," possibly after my grandmother Yuki, commenting in his halting English that "the sound is very nice as for a girl's name." After not receiving mail from my mother for several weeks in Lordsburg, he writes, "I am worried about your health and baby Yukie and all your family members. Please write to me how you are getting along." His anxiousness was a natural response for someone who had lost his youngest child in 1922 to a truck accident and was now isolated from his family. Through his comments on my baby pictures, I could appreciate how engaged

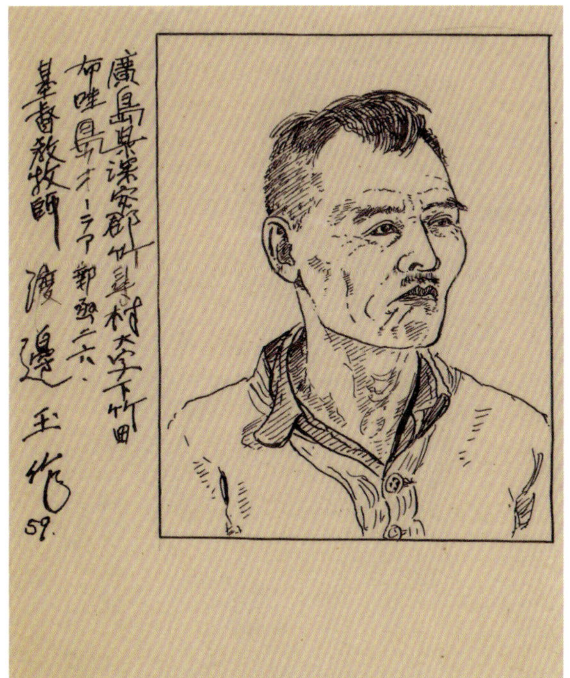

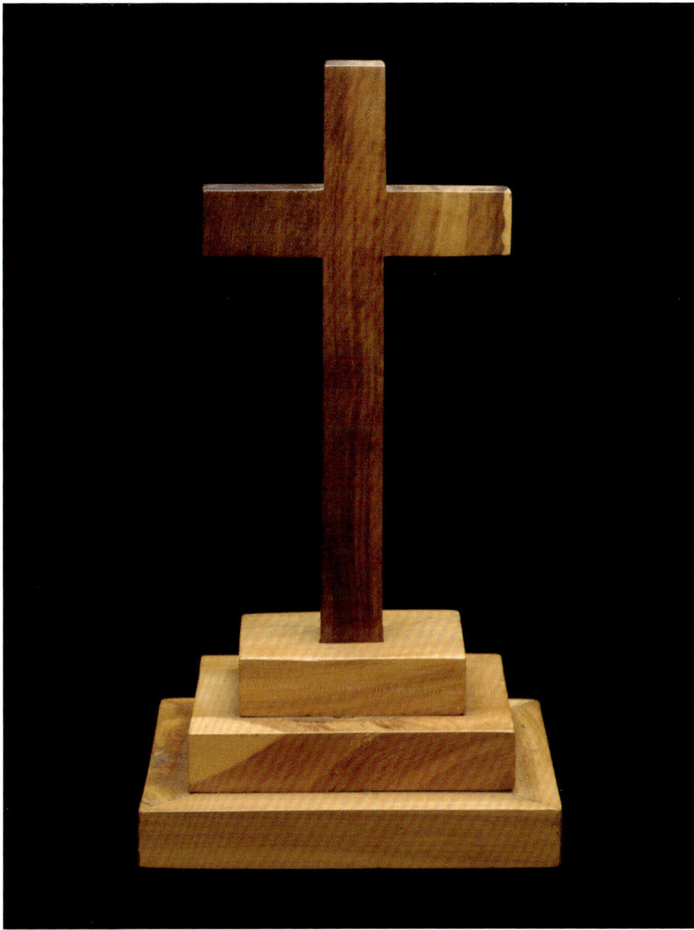

he had actually been in my earliest years: "I do not hear Yukie's voice, but I get used to see her picture [on] my desk. Her innocent face attracts me from the bottom of my heart. Now in my old age I feel I could understand more why Jesus loved a small child."

A few months later, writing from Santa Fe, he begins referring to me by my English name: "Gail is very happy to grow nicely day by day. I have now received eleven of her pictures. They show a good process of her growth." A few months after that, he writes: "Your writing [about] Gail is very interesting because I can see how lovely she is growing…. I hope she will grow without any mishap." A year later, he comments in Japanese on two more snapshots: "Gail has really grown, hasn't she? Just like the photo of Sumi taken in Stockton, Gail looks exactly like Sumi when you were little. I'm happy to know that she will be going to kindergarten in September."

Reading my grandfather's letters, I've come to realize that he hadn't been absent from my childhood at all despite the geographical distance and his unjust incarceration. Telling this Issei internment story in its myriad forms has become a lifelong commitment of my own.

Above, left: Portrait of Rev. Tamasaku Watanabe, who was interned along with the artist at the Lordsburg Internment Camp, New Mexico, 1942. By George Hoshida.

Above, right: Wooden cross made by Rev. Tamasaku Watanabe while he was interned at the Santa Fe Internment Camp, New Mexico, ca. 1943.

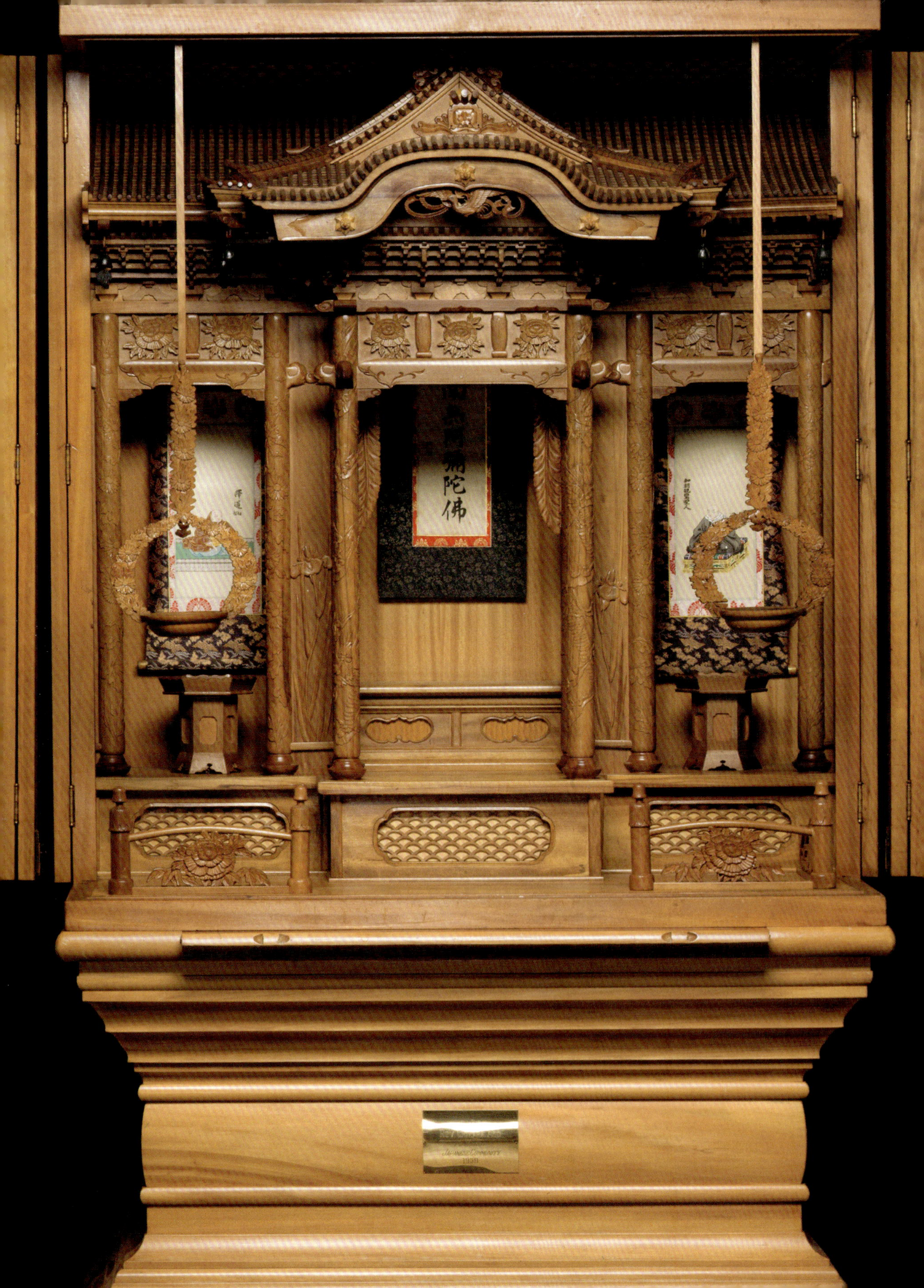

Constructing the Cosmos

Buddhist altars installed in the inner sanctum of temples are crafted to hold a Buddha statue or scrolls representing the Buddha, the Dharma, and depictions of other lineage founders. The altar typically includes stands for offerings of candlelight, water, incense, flowers, and bells. The intricate design of these altars, known formally as *shumidan*, but also referred to colloquially as *butsudan* or *obutsudan*, requires the expertise of highly skilled woodworkers. Constructed according to strict conventions, they are meant to be physical representations of the cosmos itself.

The four Buddhist *shumidan* built at Heart Mountain are the largest such altars to have been built in any of the World War II camps. This was the result of happenstance: a skilled team of master carpenters associated with the Nishiura Construction Company happened to be incarcerated there. Before the war, the Nishiura brothers were perhaps best known for their work on the San Jose Buddhist Temple, which was modeled after the well-known Nishi Hongwanji Temple in Kyoto. The grace and skill with which they crafted these *shumidan* reminded the people of Heart Mountain of all they had left behind, giving them a sense of what was possible even in camp as they contemplated a world beyond.

After the war, the Heart Mountain altars were carefully installed in temples in Stockton (CA), Gilroy (CA), Chicago (IL), and even Japan as beautiful reminders of the Pure Land that exists in the very midst of suffering.

The Aso Obutsudan:
A Heart Mountain Buddhist Altar
Elizabeth and Togo Nishiura

Much of the work done by Shinzaburo and Gentaro Nishiura in the Heart Mountain cabinet shop was the building of large altars for Buddhist churches in the camp. The large altars that were built for the major Buddhist churches were made with fine woods and varnishes and hardware. I saw ads in the Sentinel *placed by the Home Lumber Company of Powell, Wyoming. Probably, the source of the fine wood, paints, varnishes, and hardware was this company. I was told many years after the Center closed that Kiyoshi (Gentaro's son [1923–1999]) brought fine material into the Camp — it is very likely that Kiyoshi accompanied Shinzaburo and Gentaro to Powell to place orders of fine material used in the large altars because the older Nishiura brothers did not speak English and Kiyoshi had worked for the Nishiura Construction Company prior to the war and knew of*

the fine material that the Company used in the building of the many San Jose-area Buddhist temples. Also, Kiyoshi relocated to Denver to work in construction; it is said that he brought building materials and tools on his many visits back to Heart Mountain.

The Aso Obutsudan was commissioned by Reverend Chikara Aso, who lived at 7-10-D, of the San Jose Buddhist Temple, whose Heart Mountain Church was established in Block 8 Building 25.

The material used in the obutsudan is of high quality and was probably bought by the Nishiura brothers through the Home Lumber Company. The two folding doors (amado in Japanese) consist of three panels each, one to cover the side, half of which is open, and the other two covers half of the front. Notice the peony blossoms, the sagari fuji mon (the hanging wisteria crest), the peacock or possibly a crane, and the iris flower; these were probably outlined on the wood or a paper template by my father (Shingo Nishiura [1902–1968],

Opposite: Formal sanctuary altar (*shumidan*) created by Nishiura Construction Company for Buddhist church in Heart Mountain concentration camp, Wyoming.

Shinzaburo's oldest son and an art teacher at Heart Mountain) and carved by the two assistants (in the cabinet shop). The door in the closed position—the panels with the mon (crest) facing inward—will show only undecorated panels.

Let me describe architectural features of the obutsudan. At the top, there is a temple roof with the classical karahafu *(undulating gable), a flattened archery bow, with a peacock or a crane attached to its bottom. In the back above the roof is a lattice* ranma, *a panel. Then one sees the rafters with the classical* kaerumata *(literally, frog legs) supporting the rafters. Below the rafters is a row of* botan *(peony) blossoms. Proceeding downward, between the columns of the* shumidan, *is a panel with two reliefs of* kiri *(paulownia) leaves. Finally, there are three panels of lattice works and two fences with additional peony blossoms. These details are impressive because they were made in a crude shop that would have been considered not typical in Japan.*

—Togo Nishiura

This account of the Aso Obutsudan is an excerpt from an unpublished memoir by my father, Togo Nishiura (1931–2021). The grandson of master carpenter Shinzaburo Nishiura, one of the renowned Nishiura Brothers, my father was a young boy when he and more than twenty members of his family were forced from their California homes and transported to the Heart Mountain concentration camp in Wyoming. After retiring from a long career as a mathematician, my father set forth to learn about and document the family history, including the time spent imprisoned at Heart Mountain.

Reluctant to rely solely on his own memories, he pored through archives and digitized issues of the *Heart Mountain Sentinel*; examined old family letters, photos, and documents, including receipts, pay stubs, and immunization cards; and reached out to historians, his living relatives, childhood acquaintances, and anyone else who might be able to help fill in the details. Tracing the stories of the many Buddhist altars built by the Nishiura Brothers at Heart Mountain soon became a central part of his research, which also expanded to cover *butsudan* built by others at Heart Mountain and in the other concentration camps.

My father was interested in every aspect of these altars: who commissioned them and why, what they cost to build, how construction materials were obtained, and what happened to them after the camps closed. By investigating the history of the *butsudan* that had been painstakingly crafted in camp by his own grandfather and great uncle, he was able to explore the connections between mundane details of daily life such as how the Nishiura Brothers earned their living and spent their days at Heart Mountain and larger questions about the role that faith played in sustaining Japanese Americans during those difficult years. I think my father would encourage you to also reflect on these connections—and the lasting lessons and legacies of incarceration—as you look at the Aso Obutsudan.

Togo Nishiura text reprinted by permission of his estate. Togo Nishiura's research can be found in a forthcoming family history, as well as on the Japanese American National Museum's online project, Discover Nikkei: discovernikkei.org/en/journal/author/nishiura-togo

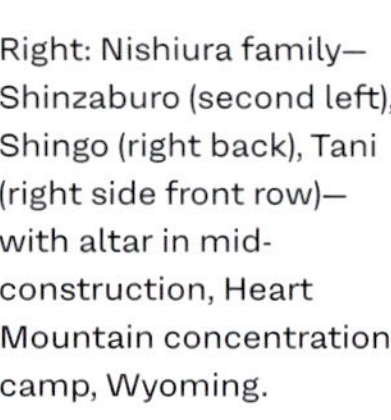

Right: Nishiura family— Shinzaburo (second left), Shingo (right back), Tani (right side front row)— with altar in mid-construction, Heart Mountain concentration camp, Wyoming.

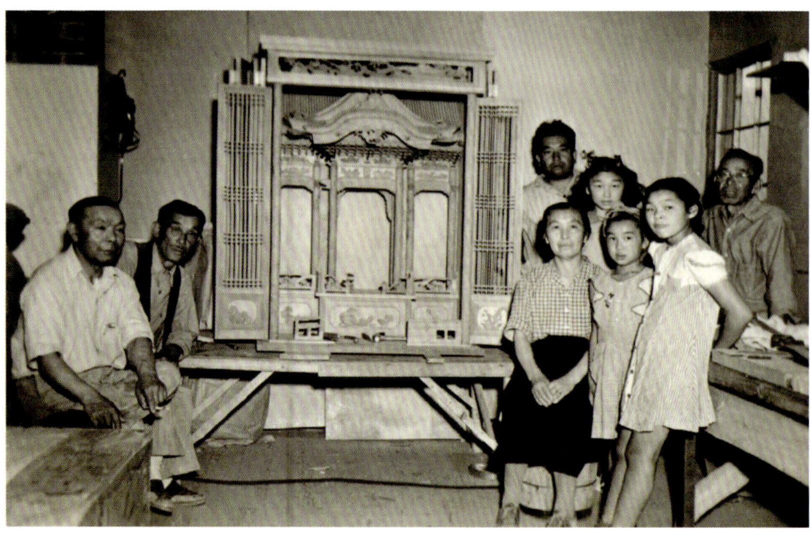

Guard Towers in the Pure Land

According to some Buddhist traditions, enlightenment is to be found in the everyday. One of the Heart Mountain altars made by the Nishiura brothers breaks with convention to show scenes of camp where one might typically expect to see depictions of the Pure Land. The lesson being taught here is that walking the Buddhist path is not to be deferred to a future time, but rather sought in the here and now, regardless of circumstance. This unique altar shows how even everyday moments of incarceration can be considered a rich training ground for Buddhist practice.

Devotion and Resilience through the Shibata Family Obutsudan
Rev. Candice Shibata

Karmic conditions allowed me to finally meet my family in Japan and put my hands together in *gassho* at our family's *obutsudan* like so many others before me at the Heart Mountain concentration camp. Seeing it for the first time, my eyes welled up with tears.

The resiliency of this *obutsudan* is illustrated by its journey—which began at Heart Mountain, where it was crafted by the Nishiura Construction Company, then continued on to Stockton, CA, where it remained at the Buddhist Church of Stockton for approximately thirty years before finding its permanent home in Fukuoka, Japan. For me, this particular *obutsudan* also represents a family legacy: fourteen generations of Shibata ministers have shared the Buddha's teachings, the last four in the United States.

When my grandfather, Reverend Tesshin Shibata, commissioned the *obutsudan*, he had only one special request: he asked the skilled workers to carve images of camp life onto the outer panels of the altar and lotus blossoms on the panels' reverse side. His vision was that the *obutsudan* should capture the reality of the incarcerees' lives in this world of suffering as well as the promise of awakening in the Pure Land.

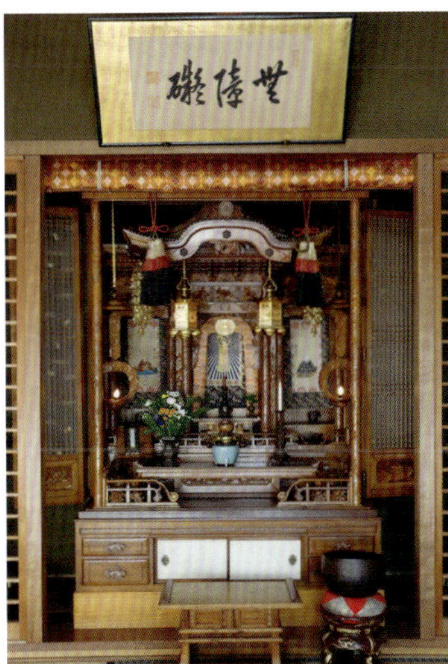

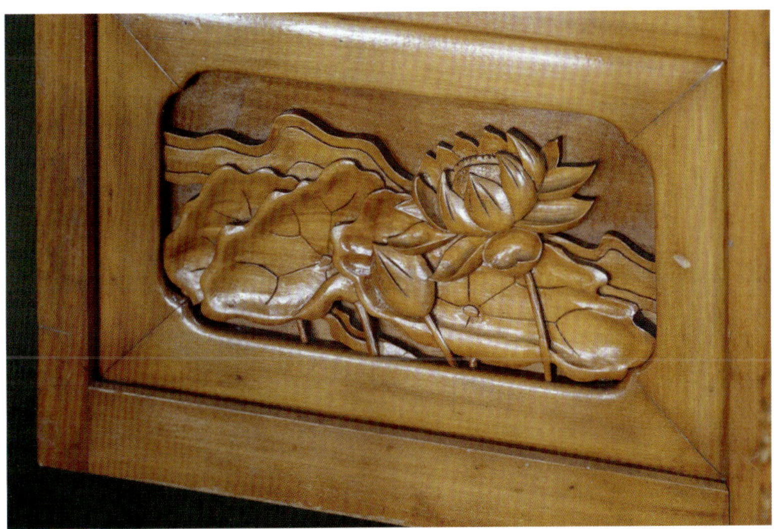

Below, left: Shibata family *shumidan*, made in Heart Mountain concentration camp, now in Joonji Temple in Fukuoka, Japan.

Below: Detail of the Shibata family *shumidan* showing the Pure Land.

Flexibility and Strength:
Shinto and the Martial Arts

In most camps, the authorities prohibited the open practice of Shinto. Yet Shinto ideas and practices, which center around ideas of purification, found their way into camp life nonetheless. In Tule Lake, a small Shinto shrine was located in the martial arts training facility as a reminder that the way of judo was meant to teach physical and mental strength through the purification of one's body and mind.

The Tule Lake Kamidana
Nancy Kyoko Oda

"Dai Ichi Dojo" (First Dojo) were the simple words written on a piece of wood in the *kamidana* (Shinto altar) that would greet you as you arrived for judo practice at the Tule Lake Segregation Center training room in 1944. Judo students would bow upon entry and later, on their way out, they would bow once again as they returned to the world outside the dojo.

The *kamidana*, which was situated in a place of honor, had been made by an expert carpenter who felt that its presence would help bring the essence of the gentle way to this room where judo was being taught under a single light bulb. It was to be the soul of the space. As one judo practitioner reflected: "The *senseis* (teachers) worked together to build the First Dojo to wipe away a gloomy atmosphere of three years of internment life."

My father, Tatsuo Inouye, was devoted to judo up until his death in 1999. Selected to demonstrate the martial art during the 1932 Olympics, he taught judo to Lancaster farm boys before the war, and he taught it to incarcerees and internees at Poston and the Tule Lake Segregation Camp during the war. Afterwards, he resettled in a neighborhood in East Los Angeles, continuing to teach judo at the Senshin Dojo, where the *kamidana* and wooden board were installed, for another fifty-five years.

Wherever my father taught, everyone, young and old alike, learned to bow toward the *kamidana*. The lesson was simple: martial arts and spiritual strength are inseparable.

As an eighth-degree black belt and a highly principled man, my father felt that we all needed to learn to respect one another and to experience physical, mental, and spiritual training in order to set the tone for a successful life.

Right: Judo class held at Rohwer concentration camp, Arkansas, 1942.

Opposite: Kamidana (Shinto altar) dedicated to the deity Hachiman Daimyojin used in the judo dojo of Tule Lake Segregation Center, California, ca. 1944.

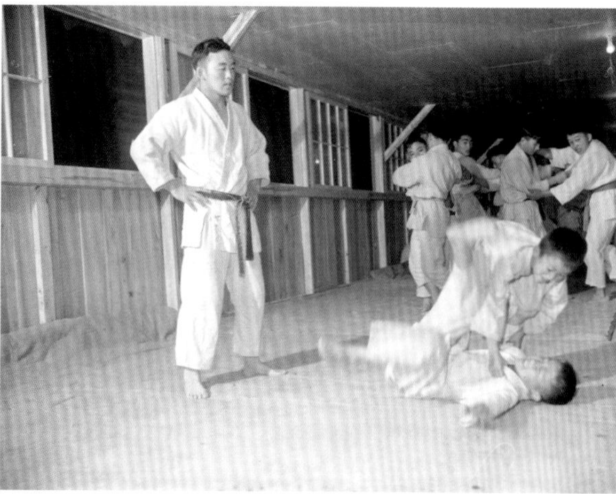

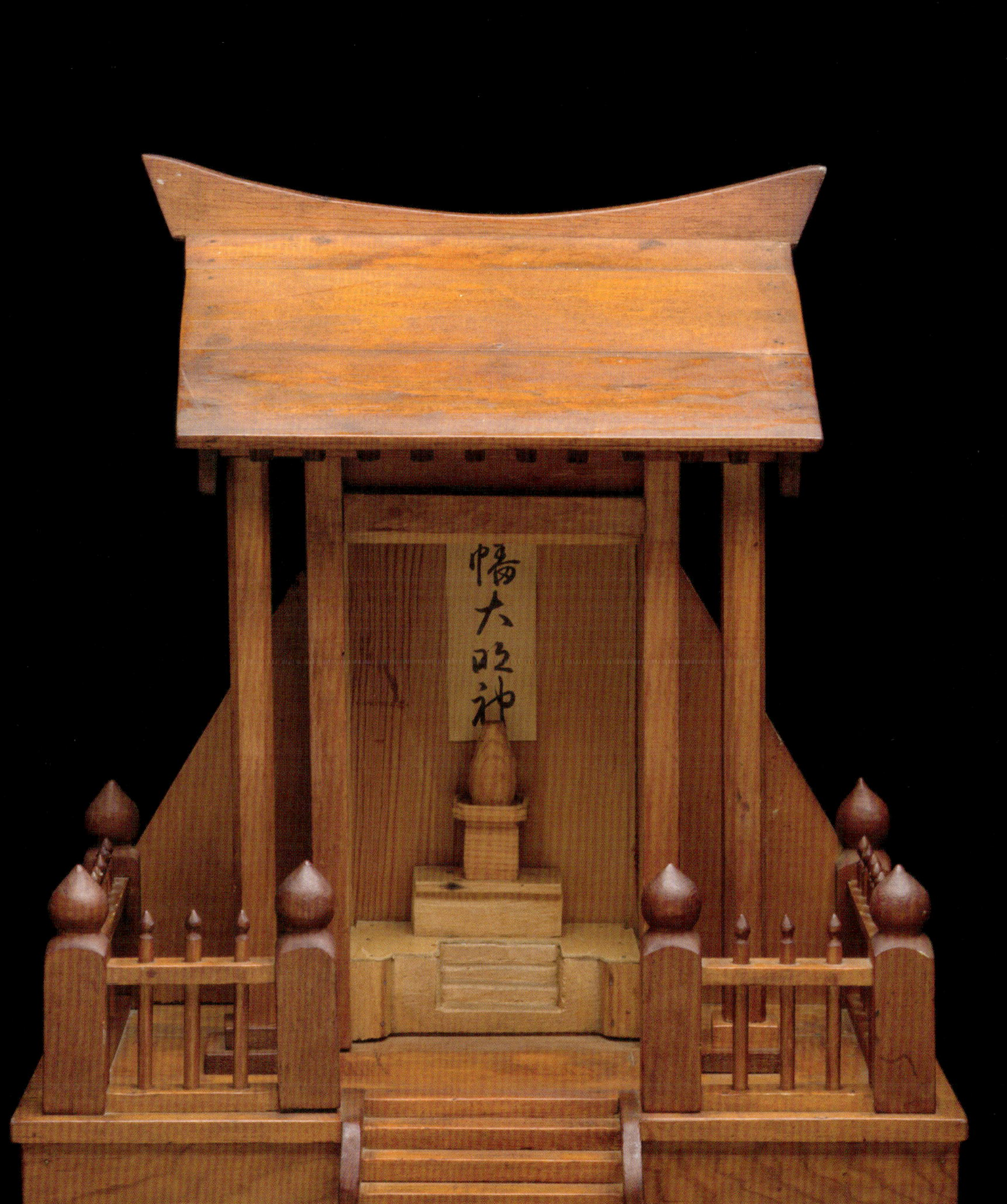

幡大明神

Each Stitch a Prayer

One of the most powerful expressions of religiosity in the camps was meant to impact the world beyond it.

Japanese Americans from the Hawaiian islands and from concentration camps on the mainland served in both the Pacific and European theaters. As these young Nisei soldiers were being sent off to fight, women would band together to create *senninbari* (literally "thousand person stitches"), or belt-sized cloths meant to be worn as a form of protection. Both Buddhist and Christian women participated in stitching their wishes for a soldier's safe return into these waistbands. Each stitched knot was meant as a prayer: the thousand stitches, often gathered by a soldier's mother, sister, or wife, represented the hopes of an entire community.

Minoru Tsubota, a Buddhist, carried a *senninbari* he received from his widowed mother rolled in a plastic covering throughout campaigns in France, Italy, and Germany. Grateful for its protection, he later spoke of how looking at it always reminded him of the tremendous effort his mother must have undertaken to collect the thousand red stitches from the women of the Tule Lake camp.

Christians such as Mickey Makio Akiyama also took great care of his *senninbari*, which was made for him in Manzanar. Trapped by German forces in the October 1944 battle to rescue the "Lost Battalion," he was wounded in the head by a sniper's bullet. Akiyama attributed his survival to his *senninbari* and the photo of his daughter that he kept in his helmet.

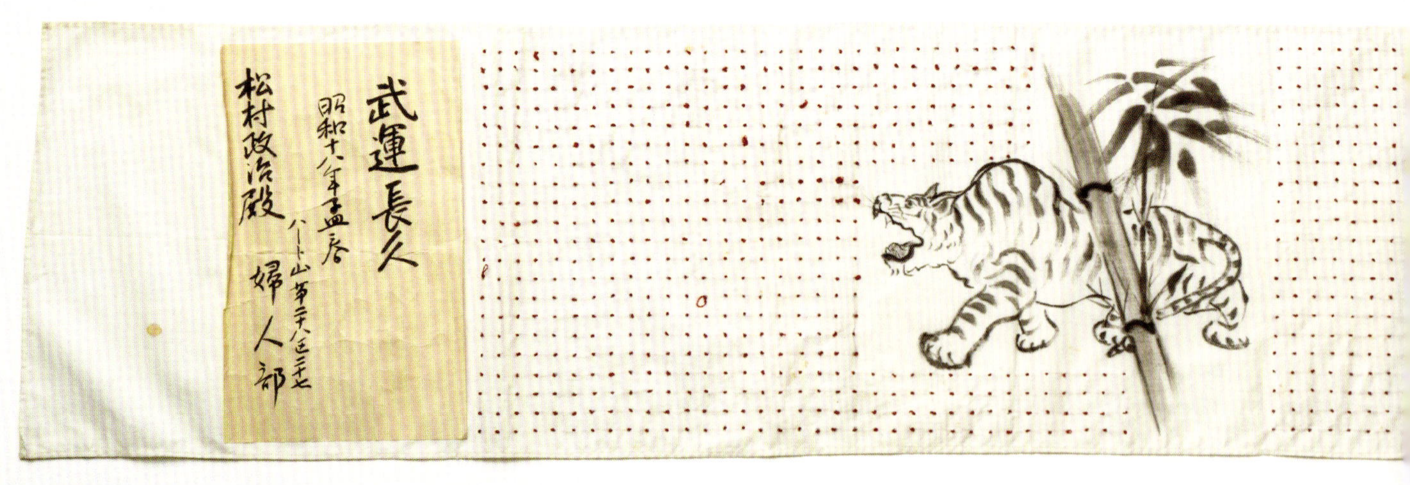

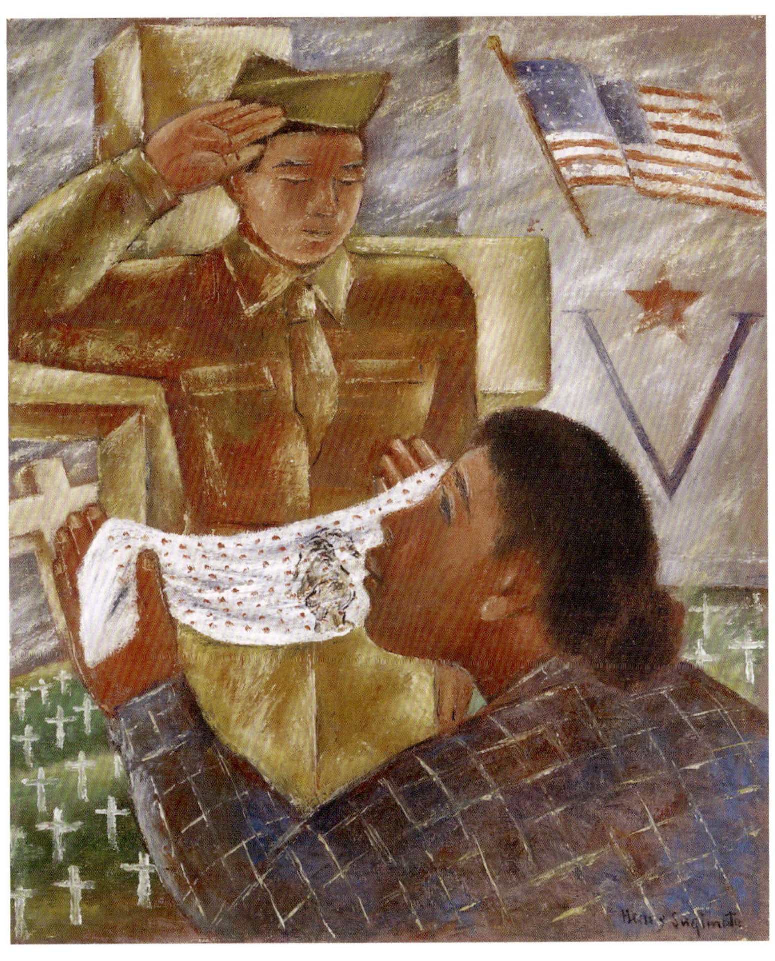

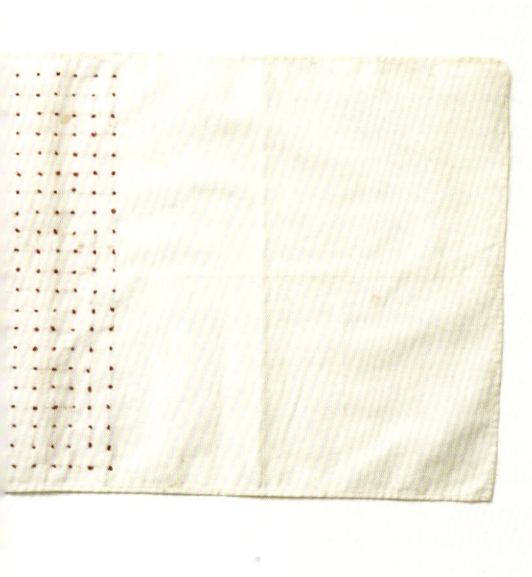

Left: *Senninbari* made
for Jimmie Masaharu
Matsushima by Block 28-27
Women's Club at Heart
Mountain concentration
camp, 1943.

Above: Henry Sugimoto,
"In Camp Jerome," 1943.
Artist Henry Sugimoto,
both a devout Christian and
dedicated artist, devoted
himself to documenting life
in Fresno Assembly Center,
as well as the Jerome and
Rohwer concentration
camps. In this painting that
depicts an Issei mother
offering her Nisei son a
senninbari in the hopes
it will keep him safe,
his service is shown as a
Christ-like sacrifice.

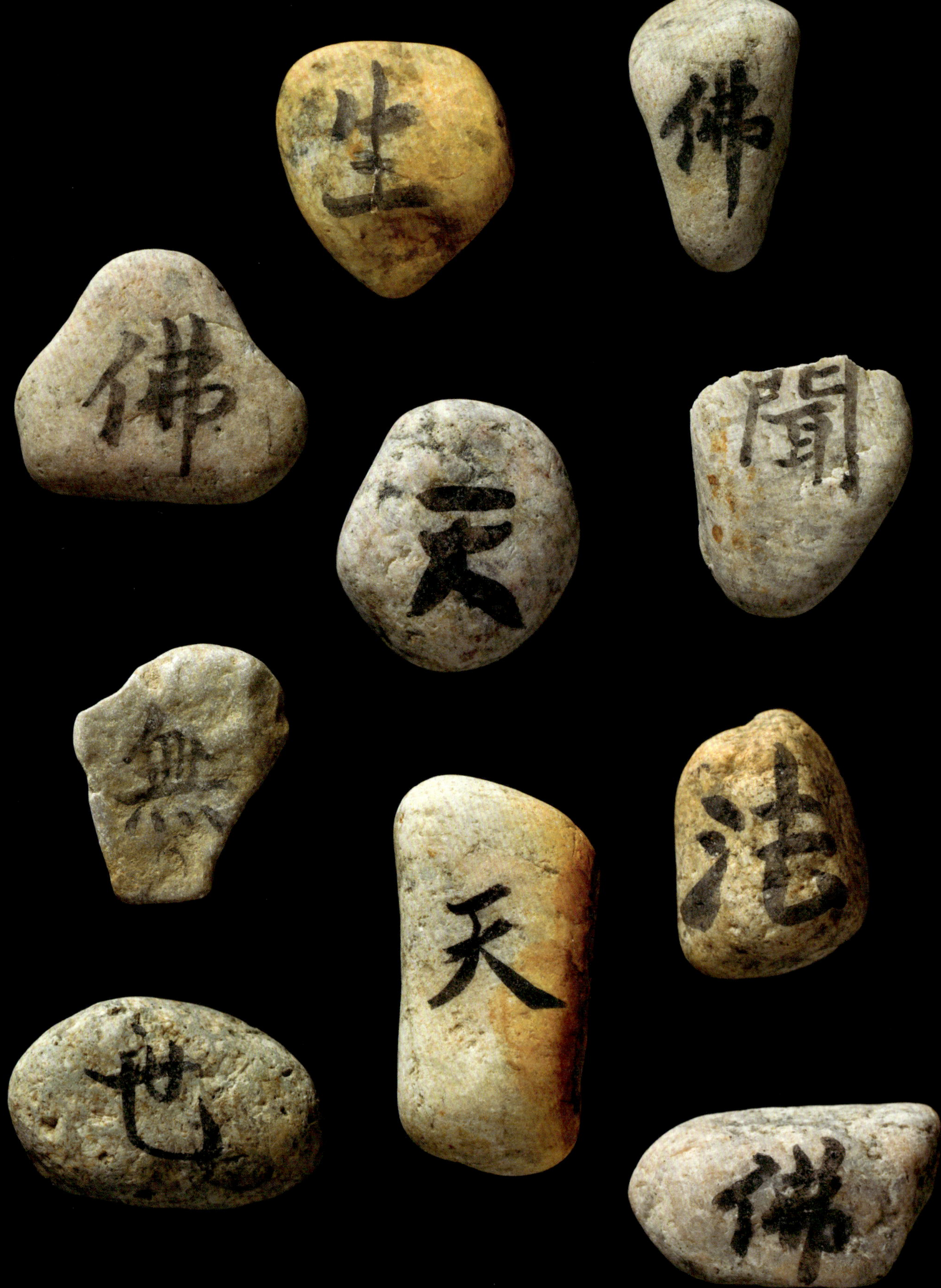

SUTRA
AND BIBLE

When a person who hears the words and phrases of this Sutra is ready for it to happen, a pure faith and clarity can awaken within their minds.

VAJRACCHEDIKA PRAJNAPARAMITA SUTRA
(DIAMOND SUTRA)

Thy word is a lamp unto my feet,

▲ IN 1941. 21ヶ所の Bible Societies より一年に
21,000,000(2千1百万部)の各種版の聖書が 800種
以上の異る国語で印刷された

▲ 米国聖書会社、1816に創始。現在をとに
125年間営業を続けてゐる。其間に
305,555,700(三億五百五十五万五千七百部)を頒布す。

・ 125年間、毎中無休で毎命 四冊宛の割と作る。

・ 現在命会社だけでも毎年 7,000,000(7百万部)印刷する割である

▲ 英国聖書会社 創立美談。 ウェールス住のメリー・Jones、16才。

我は世の光也
我に従ふ者は
暗き中を歩まず
生命の光を得べし。
ヨハネ八十二

これは
汝の行く時汝を導き
汝の寝る時汝を守り
汝の寤る時汝と語らん。
箴言六ノ二二

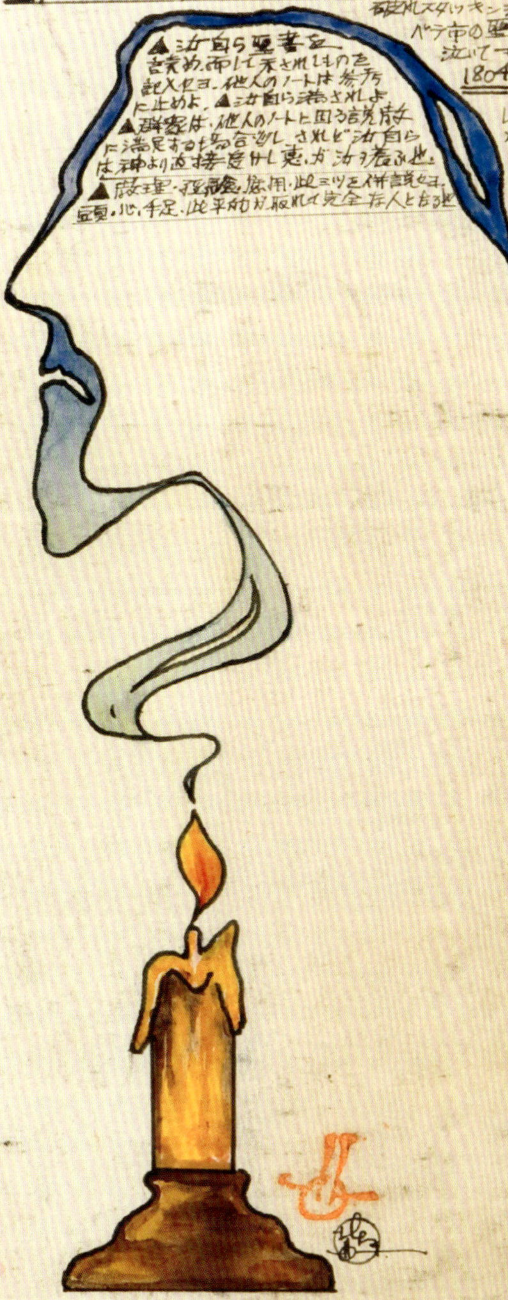

汝の聖言は我が足の燈火
我が路の光也。
詩 一一九・一〇五

All of the religious objects crafted in camp are expressions of faith made manifest, each carved line evidence of the hand that made it. Whether or not we know the specific history of an object, if we attend to it closely, we can see traces of the devotion required to bring it into being. In this way, each has something to teach us.

This is especially true of the most poignant examples of religiosity from the wartime period: ink-inscribed stones that were unearthed in a field in Wyoming, and two heavily annotated bilingual Bibles. These handwritten artifacts, now known as the Heart Mountain Sutra Stones and the Kitaji Bibles, remind us of the potent and transformative power of engaging intimately with religious teachings through scripture.

The fact that both were very nearly lost to time and history is itself a lesson. Confronted by hostility, ignorance, and indifference, the Heart Mountain Sutra Stones and the Kitaji Bibles nevertheless survived, testament to the persistence and resilience of faith in the camps.

Opposite: End pages of the first Kitaji Bible, completed in Poston concentration camp, 1944.

Page 70: A selection of Heart Mountain sutra stones.

The Mystery of the Buried Sutra

Even in the immediate aftermath of Pearl Harbor, it was made clear to the Japanese American community that goods made in Japan or featuring Japanese script could potentially be used to prove their disloyalty. Many families burned or buried such items in the weeks and months leading up to incarceration. When they arrived at the so-called Assembly Centers, they discovered that their fears had not been unfounded; anything written in Japanese, including collections of poetry and Buddhist sutras, were confiscated by the US Army as contraband. The only exceptions to this English-only policy in the earliest days of the incarceration were Japanese-English dictionaries and Japanese translations of the Christian Bible.

Paranoia around being too closely aligned with Japanese culture thus made the idea of possessing Japanese-language sutras a difficult and dangerous one. Unable to own printed versions of sutras, priests and laypeople alike were entirely reliant on their own memories for access to Buddhist scriptures.

How then did a lengthy portion of a Buddhist sutra written on stones in Japanese kanji come to be buried near the cemetery of a Wyoming concentration camp?

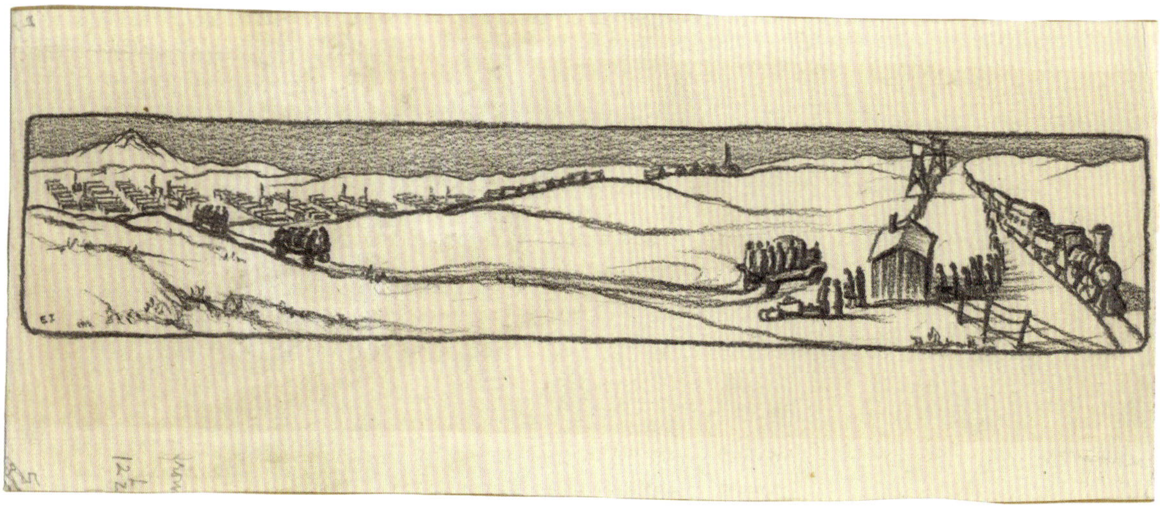

Opposite: Pencil sketch of
Heart Mountain concen-
tration camp landscape by
Estelle Ishigo.

Left: Detail of a section
of a Kamakura-era Lotus
Sutra scroll.

Below: Pencil sketch of
cemetery at Heart Mountain
concentration camp,
Wyoming, by Estelle Ishigo.

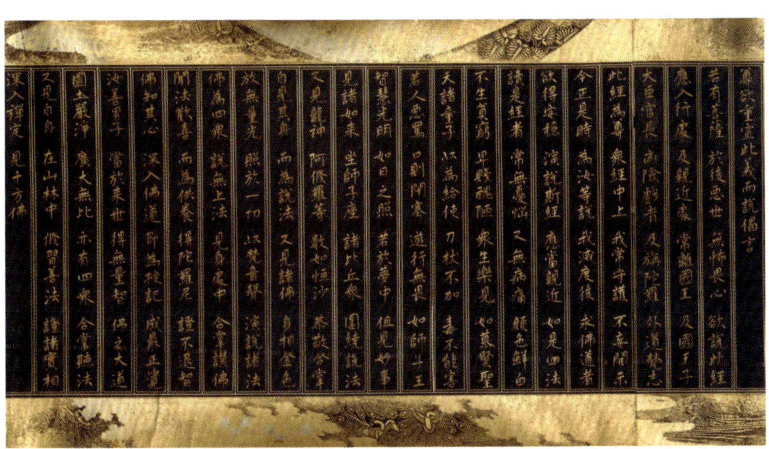

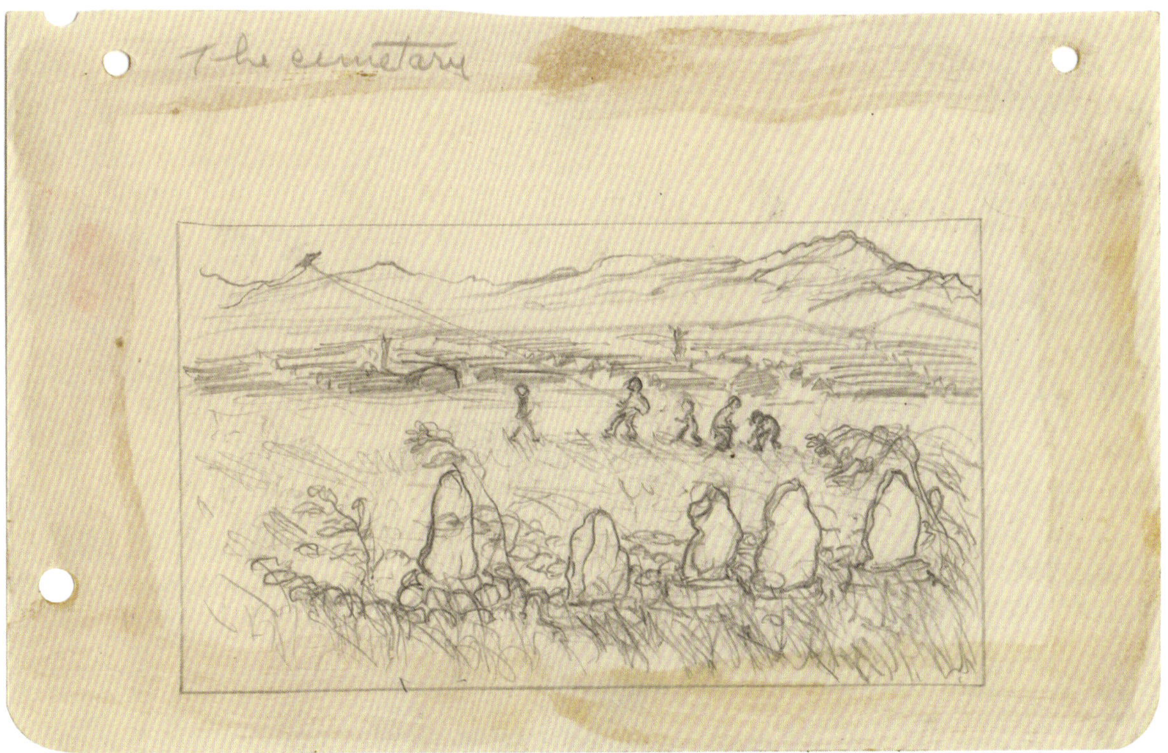

The cemetery

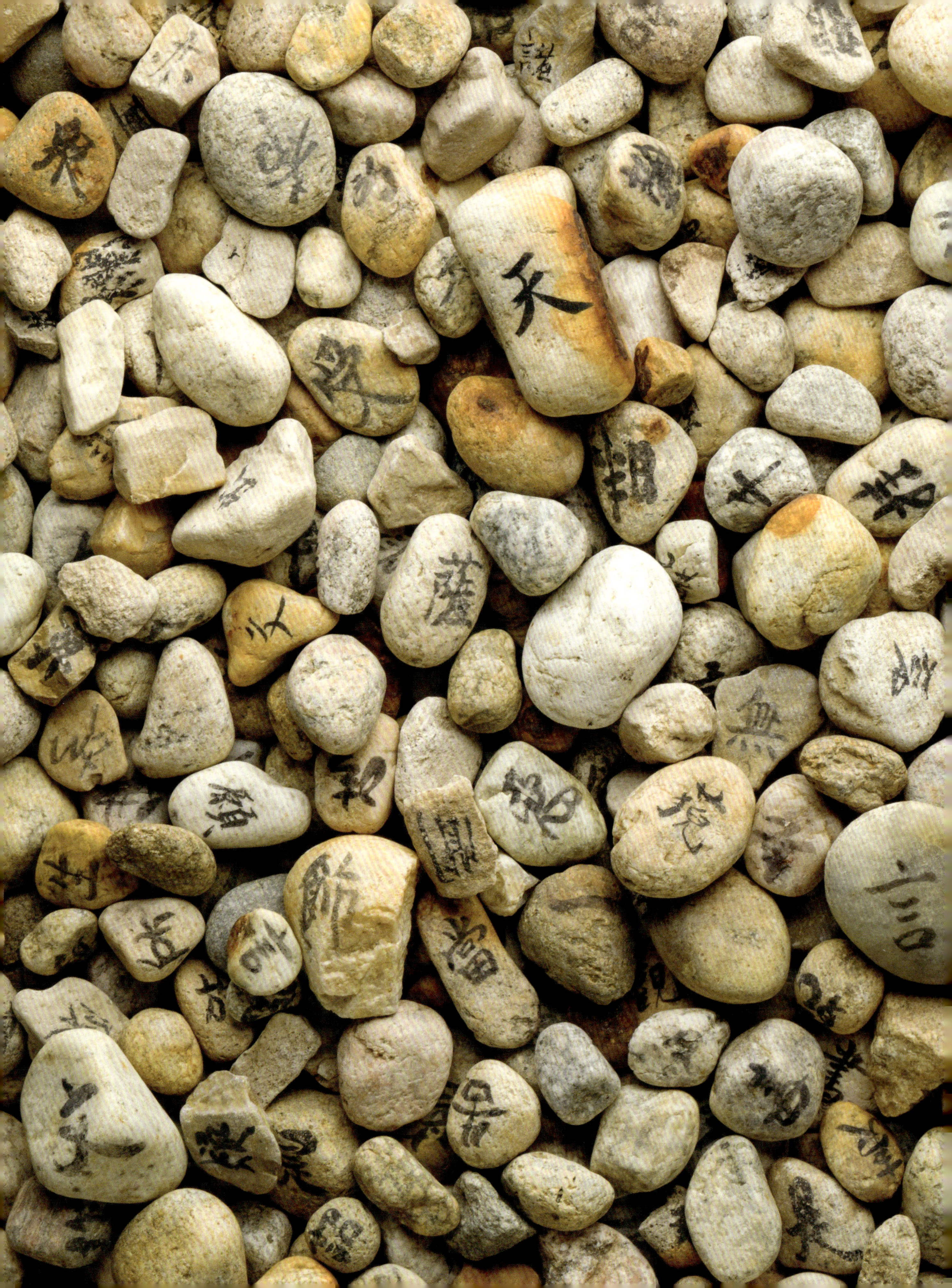

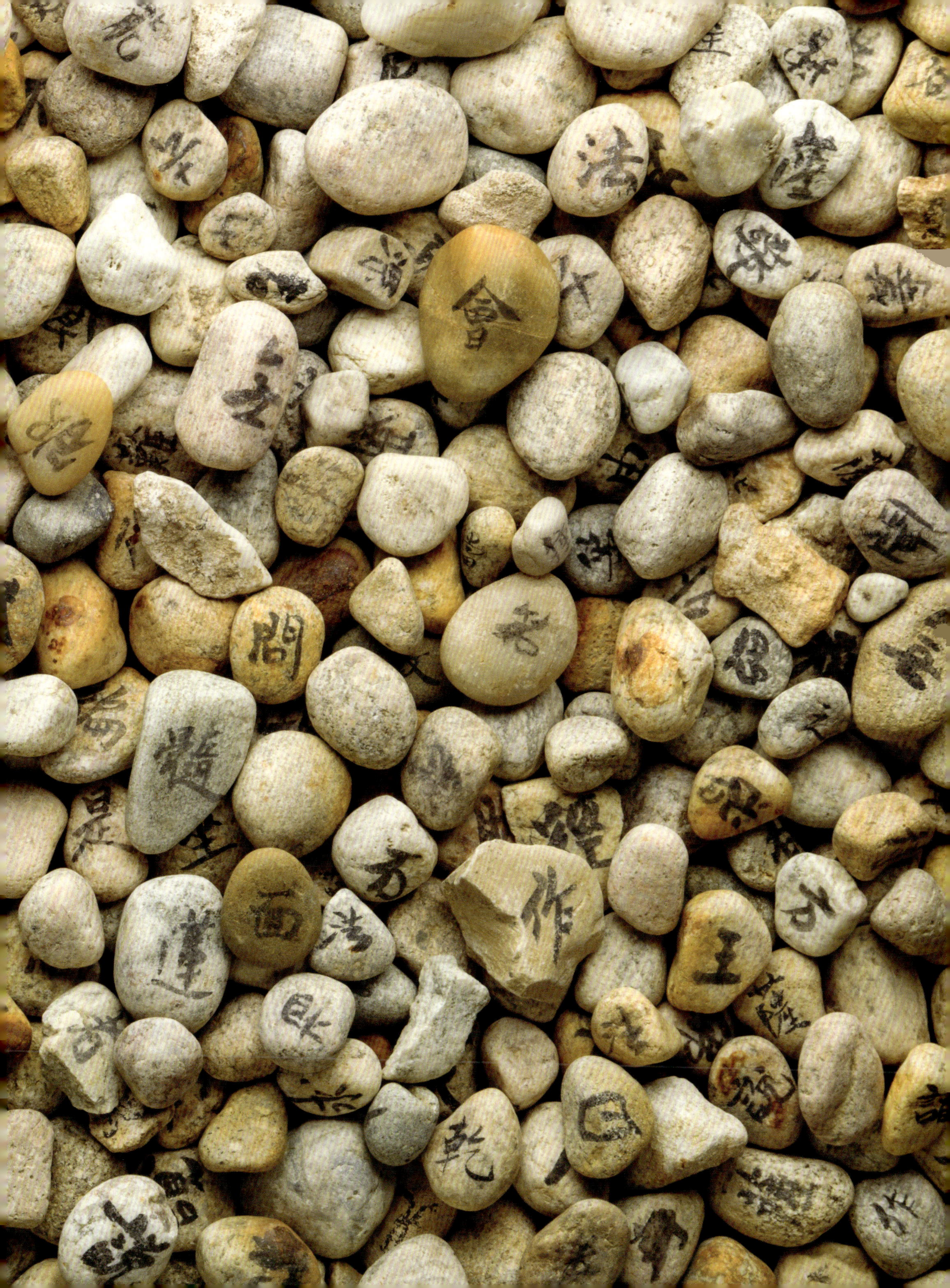

Unearthing the Heart Mountain Sutra Stones

In 1956, near the abandoned camp cemetery at Heart Mountain, a worker employed by the Bureau of Reclamation named Bill Higgins hit something hard just below the surface of the ground with his grader. Concerned at first that he had disturbed a casket, he discovered much to his relief that he had instead unearthed a large metal drum filled with hundreds of small stones. Looking more closely, he saw that each one had been inscribed with a single ideogram. All told, the metal drum contained nearly two thousand stones.

Unable to decipher the Japanese script on the stones, Higgins handed them over to Les and Nora Bovee, owners of the ranch where they had been found. For the next thirty-five years, the Bovees stored them in their barn, occasionally giving one or two away to neighbors or friends or others who came through town to visit the site of the former camp. By the time Bovees donated the remaining stones to the Japanese American National Museum (JANM) in Los Angeles, only 656 were left.

The meaning and purpose of these stones remained a complete mystery for seven more years until 2001, when Sodo Mori, an eminent scholar of Indian Buddhism visiting from Japan, happened to notice them in a JANM exhibit. Examining the stones carefully, he realized that some of the characters written on them could be combined to form Buddhist words. Could they be part of a sutra or sacred Buddhist text?

Mori turned to Professor Kenryo Minowa at the University of Tokyo for help. Minowa, who was working on a project to make one of the largest collections of Buddhist canonical texts available in a digital format, had access to a database capable of making sense of the hundreds of jumbled characters. Using computational analysis, Minowa discovered that the Lotus Sutra—more specifically, the first six volumes of the eight-volume edition of the scripture—perfectly matched what were now known as the "Heart Mountain Mystery Stones."

With this revelation, a possible explanation for how and why the stones came to be written upon has emerged. The practice of copying sutras, which dates back to the late seventh century in Japan, is considered a particularly potent form of meditation: while one's mouth is to be used to chant and give resonance to the Buddha's teachings, one's hands can be used to write and give form to the Buddha. Indeed, the Lotus Sutra itself recommends the pursuit, explaining that by copying out the words of a sacred text, one is placed in deep communion with the Buddha's teachings and thereby transformed.

The Buddhist lineage most associated with the veneration of the Lotus Sutra is the Nichiren tradition. The only ordained Nichiren Buddhist priest at Heart Mountain, Nichikan Murakita, was a master calligrapher who was also known to have taught calligraphy in the camp. Minowa and Mori concluded that Reverend Murakita was in all likelihood the only person at Heart Mountain

Opposite: Heart Mountain sutra stone with the character for *kokoro* (heart-mind-spirit).

Pages 76 & 77: Heart Mountain sutra stones.

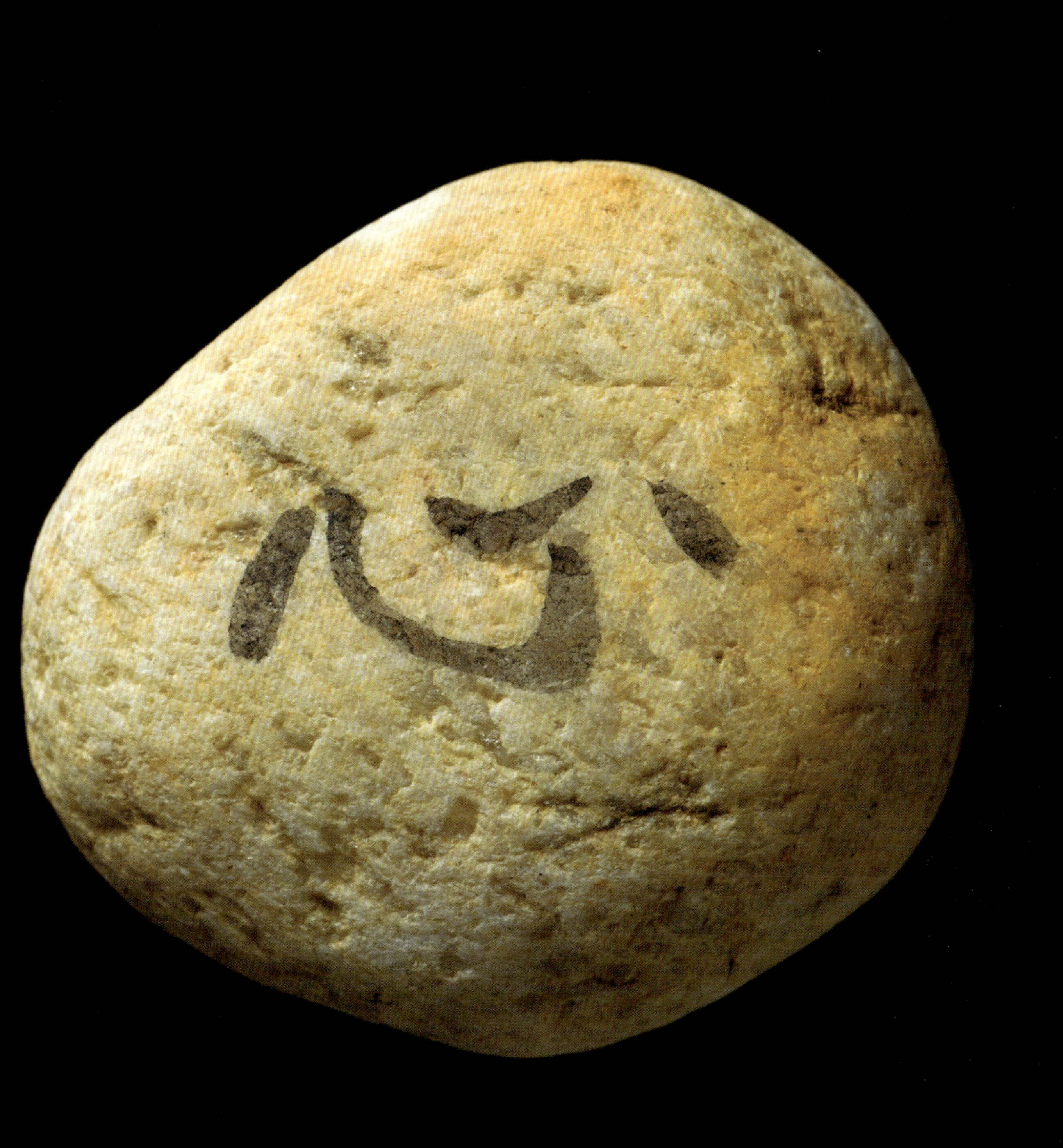

familiar enough with the Lotus Sutra to have conceived of the idea of writing the scripture out, character by character, on stones from the Shoshone River.

While we still do not know with absolute certainty — and may never know — if Murakita was indeed the person responsible for writing on and then burying the Sutra Stones, what has become clear is that they were not buried near the Heart Mountain cemetery by accident. The chain of coincidences, circumstances, and karmic conditions that make it possible for us to appreciate them today is both mundane and mysterious. If they hadn't been placed in a container and buried in the ground, they might never have been discovered. If Bill Higgins hadn't thought to look more closely at the contents of the metal drum he hit while grading, they might have been thrown away. If the Bovees hadn't talked about them to visitors to Heart Mountain, or if Minowa and Mori hadn't discovered the secret of the scripture they spelled out, they might still be considered little more than a curiosity. Instead, the stones continue to speak to us about the innumerable and often private ways that those in camp sought to find meaning in their faith.

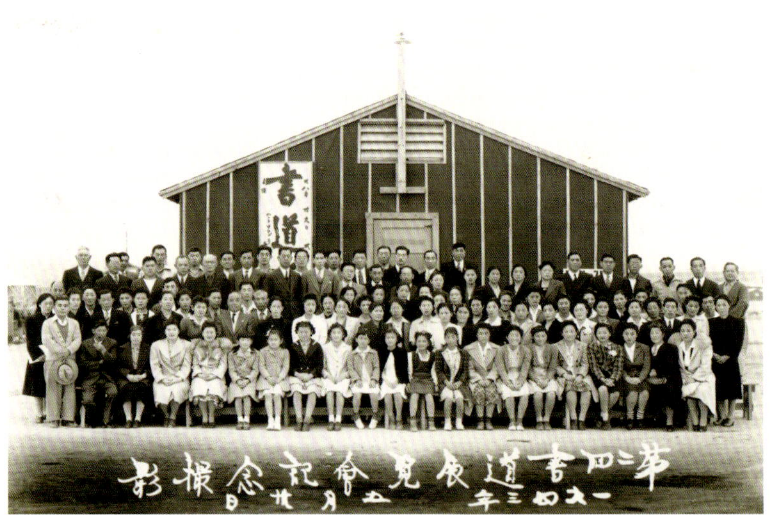

Above: Rev. Nichikan Murakita (back row center, in front of door) and members of the Calligraphy Association that he led at an exhibition at Heart Mountain concentration camp, Wyoming, 1943.

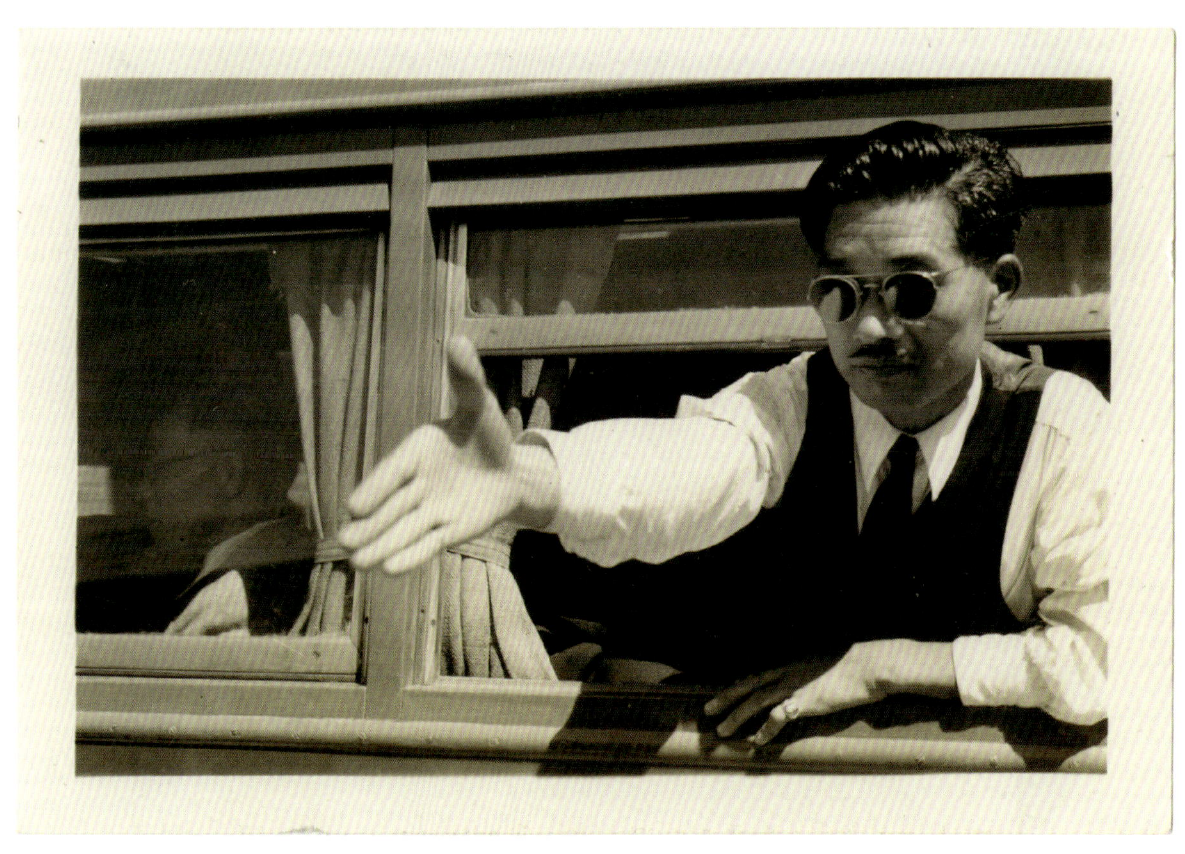

Above: Rev. Nichikan Murakita waving from train as he is leaving Heart Mountain concentration camp for the prisoner exchange ship that will take him to Japan, 1943.

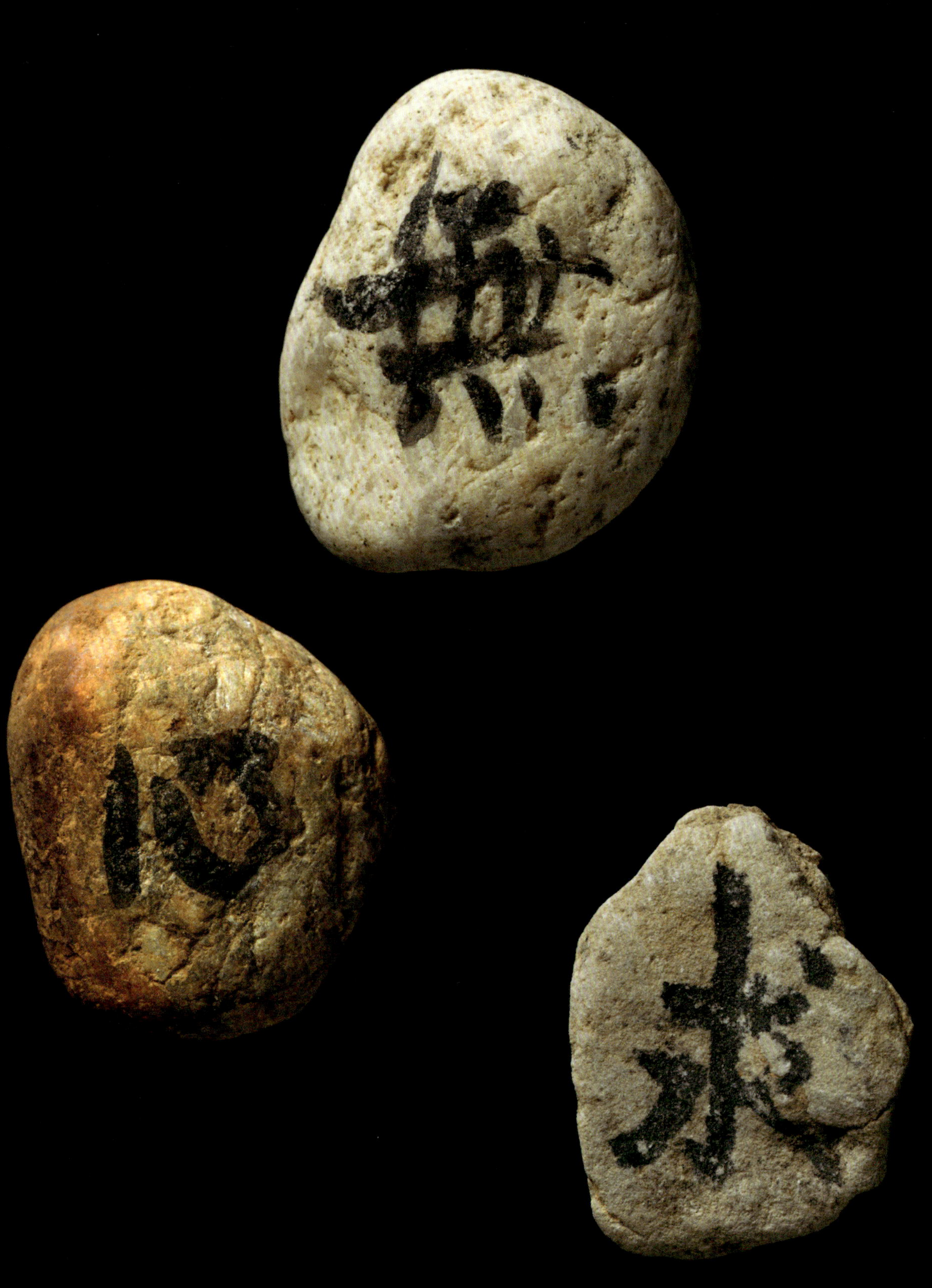

無
心
本

Recollecting the Scattered Stones

Hundreds of Heart Mountain Sutra Stones were distributed or lost in the decades after their discovery. The largest cache of stones outside the Japanese American National Museum now resides in Wyoming at the Heart Mountain Interpretive Center.

Wyoming Regards a Sutra
Dakota Russell

When I first encountered the "Mystery Stones" in Heart Mountain's collections, I was filled with questions—questions that I began asking the locals. A neighbor remembered Nora Bovee once displayed them in her ceramics shop in the hopes that a visitor might explain them to her. Another told me his family had a bowl of stones sitting on the mantle in the old homeplace, but ho couldn't recall how they came to be there.

None of the people I spoke to knew what the stones were, but they held them in reverence just the same. I could understand that. My grandfather owned an arrowhead collection he felt similarly about. He saw himself as a steward of the farm he worked, and he understood that there had been many other stewards before him. He knew next to nothing about the people who used those arrowheads, but he knew that they shared one thing in common—a home. That was enough, in his view, to make them sacred objects.

Eventually, I learned of Dr. Mori's work to uncover the story of the Sutra Stones. I was also able to fill in some details about their probable creator, Nichikan Murakita. I began giving talks about the stones. One day, a farmer arrived at Heart Mountain Interpretive Center, hefting a three-gallon bucket of sutra stones he had found in an old shed. He kept them for years, suspecting they were something special. Now, after reading about one of my talks in the local paper, he wanted to return them back to where they belonged.

And so, here in Wyoming, the "Mystery Stones" hold a bit less mystery than they used to. I do feel a bit guilty. It's good to preserve some wonder in the world. But mystery should never get in the way of our efforts to learn more about each other, to try and *understand* each other. I would like to think Nichikan Murakita would agree.

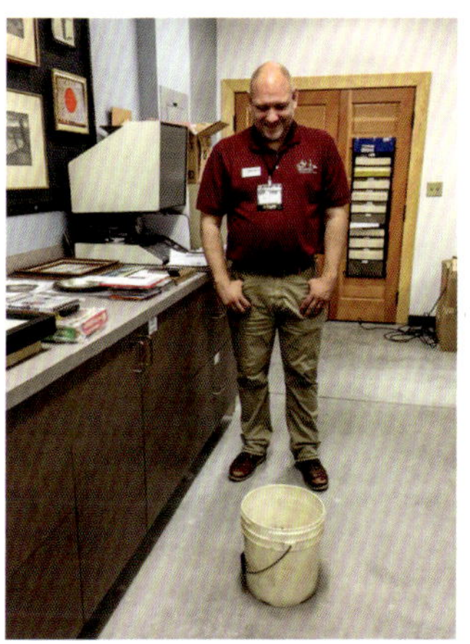

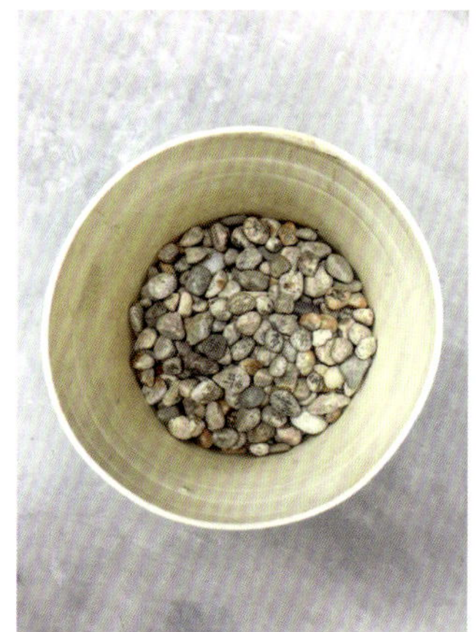

Opposite: Heart Mountain sutra stones with characters for "nothing," "heart and soul," and "desire."

Above, left: Dakota Russell stands with bucket filled with Heart Mountain sutra stones.

Above, right: Sutra stones donated by a local farmer to the Heart Mountain Interpretive Center, Wyoming.

The Word Carries On:
Bibles in Camp

Christians might have been allowed free access to their most important religious texts in camp, but they were not immune from the indignities of camp life. Included in this collection of Bibles and other religious texts are volumes that bear the marks of incarceration, including a censor's stamp showing that it had been checked for subversive material. Mitsuji Furuta's worn copy of the New Testament & Psalms, one of the few items he managed to grab while being arrested in February 1942 by the FBI, traveled with him to the Tuna Canyon Detention Station, the Santa Fe Internment Camp, and ultimately the Poston concentration camp where he was finally reunited with his family. Reverend Wada used his *Ritual: Japanese Methodist Church* to record the temporary camp addresses of his congregation.

Well-thumbed and creased with use, these sacred books give mute testimony to the unique and personal meaning they had for their owners in difficult times. They were also meant to teach and inspire: Seiji Iwanaga's copy of *The Words of Jesus* bears a Christmas 1944 dedication by Salvation Army Captain Masuo Kitaji that reads, "Thy word is a lamp unto my feet, and a light unto my path. Psalms 119:105."

Opposite, top row: Bible given to Marian Koyama in Santa Anita Assembly Center, California; Bible examined by censors and taken into Fort Lincoln (Bismarck) Internment Camp by Genzo Nakahiro, North Dakota.

Opposite, middle row: Tetsuo Taguchi's Japanese translation of the New Testament; Rev. Masahiko Wada's Methodist Church Ritual Book with former congregants' temporary addresses written onto the end pages; Roman Catholic version of the New Testament issued to a US Army soldier.

Opposite, bottom row: Military New Testament issued to MIS officer Don Okubo; New Testament given to Kyle Iwanaga by Captain Masuo Kitaji; Mitsuji Furuta's Bible taken into Tuna Canyon Detention Station, Santa Fe Internment Camp, and Poston concentration camp.

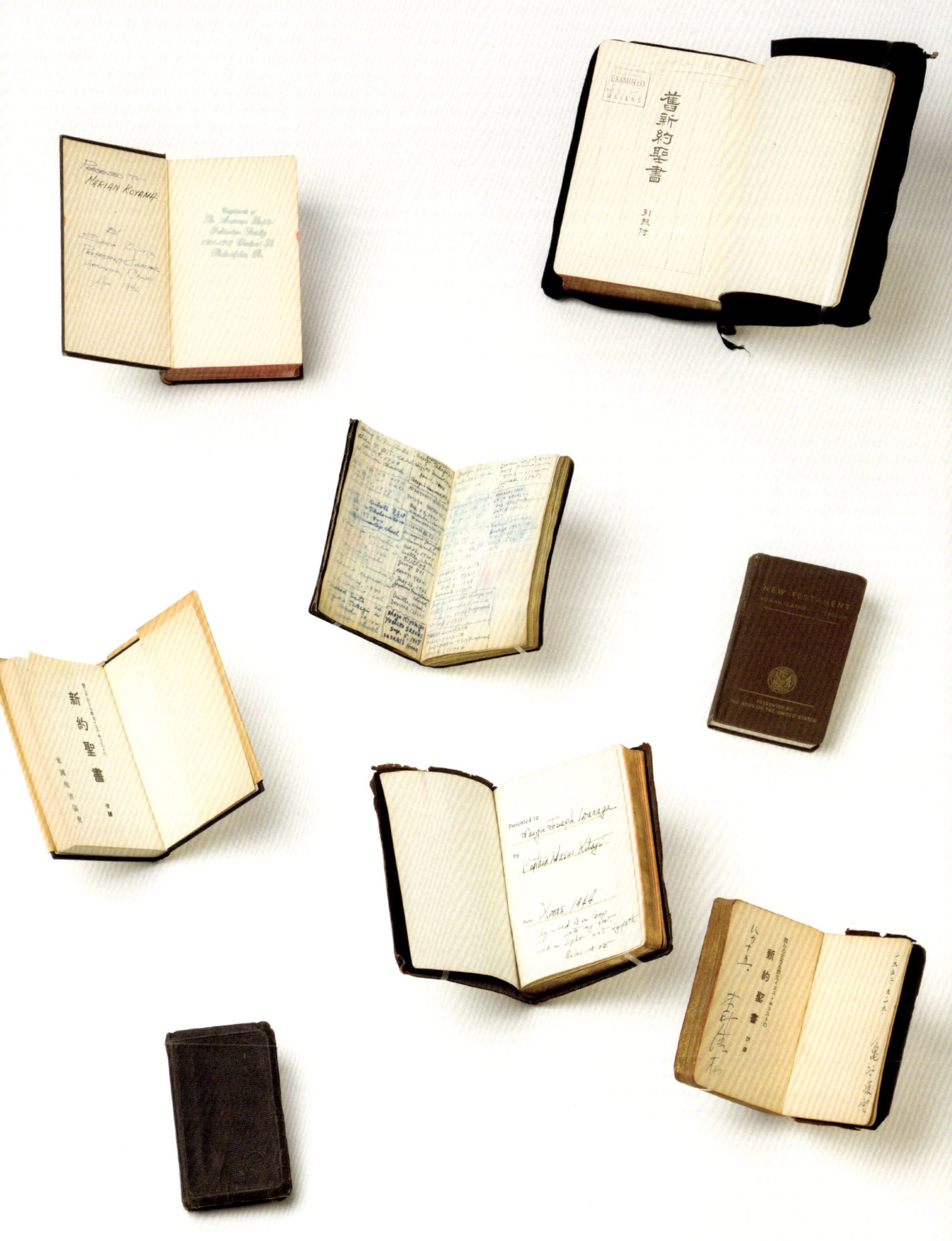

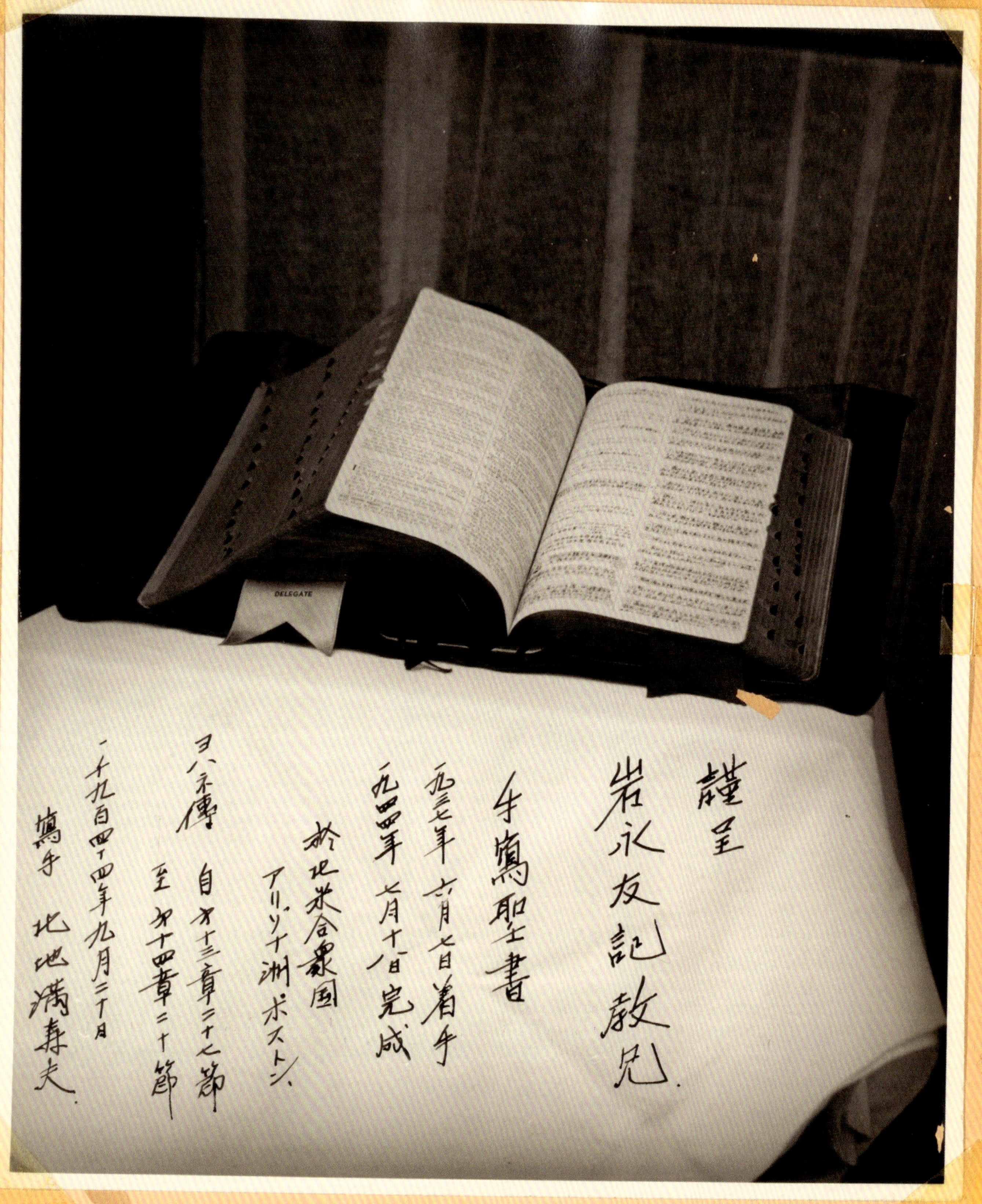

Captain Kitaji's work
from 6-7-1937 to 7-18-1944. 7 year's work

The Kitaji Bibles:
The Gospel in Two Languages

Unlike the Heart Mountain sutra stones, there is no mystery surrounding the provenance of the two Bibles into which former Salvation Army Captain Masuo Kitaji meticulously handwrote commentary and full Japanese translations. Now known as the Kitaji Bibles, these monumental volumes, the product of close to two decades of persistent, painstaking work, are perhaps the most spectacular demonstrations of Christian devotion to have emerged from the wartime camp experience.

Even before the war and incarceration, Captain Kitaji saw his mission in life as sharing the Gospel with members of the Japanese American community. He quickly realized that to do this effectively, he needed to be able to communicate in both Japanese and English. A newspaper article from February 3, 1945 that was found tucked inside the front cover of one of the Kitaji Bibles explains: "When he took charge of the Salvation Army Corps in 1933, he had difficulty conducting the meetings because travel difficulties made it necessary that he conduct joint meetings in the English and Japanese language. All songs, Bible readings, and messages had to be duplicated in both languages. Captain Kitaji conceived the plan of [hand]writing [a word-for-word Japanese-language translation into] the Bible, page by page, interleaving the pages in his own language with the standard leaves."

Captain Kitaji's unique solution to the problem of how to teach the Gospel in both languages at once required an almost unthinkable level of dedication. While in camp, Kitaji would devote the period from 5 a.m. to noon working on the first of these Bibles, writing in such minuscule text that he sometimes needed the aid of a magnifying glass.

Like the practice of sutra copying, transcribing Biblical texts has centuries of precedent. Most commonly associated with the labor of cloistered monks in the Middle Ages seeking to preserve the word of God, this kind of work is also referred to in Deuteronomy 17:18–20, which commands the kings of Israel to copy God's law by hand. In Japan, a similar set of beliefs often associated with Buddhist and Shinto traditions teaches that the act of writing out characters in a sacred text is a way of transmitting or channeling spiritual power.

Kitaji's thoughts on how to unite these two traditions can be extrapolated from a lecture that he gave to a fellowship group of the Poston II Christian Church on November 23, 1943 entitled, "Gospel Found in Japanese Ideograph." It appears that for him, the act of transcribing, translating, and commenting on the Bible using Japanese ideographs was not only a way of delivering the Gospel to new converts; it was itself a means of enhancing the glory of God.

Opposite: Photo of Bible when Captain Masuo Kitaji completed the Japanese-language portion, with notations by his friend and colleague Major Tomoki Iwanaga, in Poston concentration camp, Arizona, 1944.

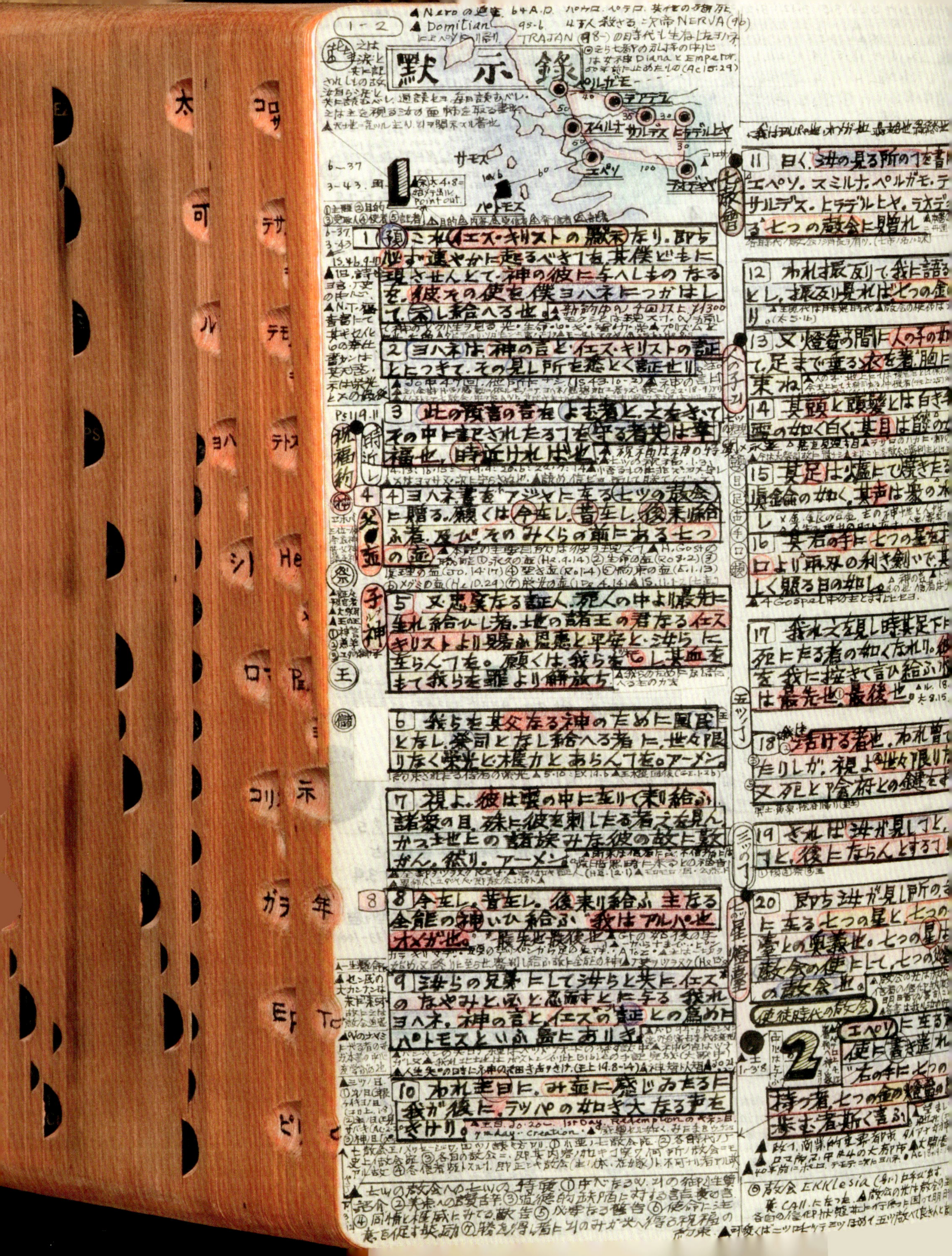

CHAPTER 1.

*revelation to the seven churches of Asia.
of Christ. 14 His glorious power and*

ation of Jḗ'-ṡŭs Chrĭst, which
unto him, to shew unto his
s which must shortly come to
sent and signified *it* by his
servant John:
Jo. 3.32; 12.49.

e record [witness] of the word
of the testimony of Jḗ'-ṡŭs
all things that he saw.
.6; 1 Jo. 1.1.

s he that readeth, and they
words of this prophecy, and
ngs which are written therein:
s at hand.
1.28; Jam. 5.8; 1 Pe. 4.7.

o the seven churches which
Ā'-ṡĭă: Grace *be* unto you, and
im which is, and which was,
to come; and from the seven
are before his throne;
; Jo. 1.1.

n Jḗ'-ṡŭs Chrĭst, *who is* the
ss, *and* the first begotten of
the prince of the kings of the
im that loved us, and washed
m our sins in his own blood,
20; 1 Ti. 6.13; He. 9.14; 1 Jo. 1.7.

made us kings [to be a king-
sts [to be priests] unto God
his Father; to him *be* glory,
for ever and ever. Ä'-mĕn.
.16; He. 13.21; 1 Pe. 2.5,9.

e cometh with clouds; and
l see him, and they *also* which
nd all kindreds of the earth
ause of [mourn over] him.
ĕn.
9.37; Ac. 1.11.

phă and Ō-mĕg'-ă, the begin-
nding, saith the Lord, which
was, and which is to come,

4.8; 11.17; 21.6; 22.13.

ho also am your brother, and
tribulation, and in the king-
ience of Jḗ'-ṡŭs Chrĭst [omit
in the isle that is called
the word of God, and for the
Jḗ'-ṡŭs Chrĭst [omit Christ].
; 2 Ti. 1.8; 2.12.

the Spirit on the Lord's day,
nd me a great voice, as of a
0.26; Ch. 17.3; 21.10
0.26; Ac. 10.10; 2 Co. 12.2.

I am Ăl'-phă and Ō-mĕg'-ă,

the first and the last: and [R. V. omits this
first sentence], What thou seest, write in
a book, and send *it* unto the seven churches
which are in Ā'-ṡĭă [R. V. omits which are
in Asia]; unto Ĕph'-ĕ-ṡŭs, and unto Smȳr'-
nă, and unto Pĕr'-gă-mŏs, and unto Thȳ-ă-
tī'-ră, and unto Sär'-dĭs, and unto Phĭl-ă-
dĕl'-phĭ-ă, and unto Lā-ŏd-ĭ-çē'-ă.

12 And I turned to see the voice that
spake with me. And being turned, I saw
seven golden candlesticks;
Ver. 20; Ex. 25.37; Ze. 4.2.

13 And in the midst of the seven candlesticks *one* like unto the Son [a son] of man,
clothed with a garment down to the foot,
and girt about the paps with a golden girdle.
Ch. 15.6; Eze. 1.26; Da. 7.13; 10.5.

14 His head and *his* hairs *were* white like
wool, as white as snow; and his eyes *were*
as a flame of fire;
Ch. 19.12; Da. 7.9; 10.6.

15 And his feet like unto fine [burnished]
brass, as if they burned [as if it had been
refined] in a furnace; and his voice as the
sound of many waters.
Ch. 14.2; Eze. 43.2; Da. 10.6.

16 And he had in his right hand seven
stars: and out of his mouth went a sharp
twoedged sword: and his countenance *was*
as the sun shineth in his strength.
Ch. 2.1,12,16; 3.1; Ep. 6.17; He. 4.12.

17 And when I saw him, I fell at his feet
as dead. And he laid his right hand upon
me, saying unto me, Fear not; I am the
first and the last:
Ver. 11; Is. 41.4; Eze. 1.28; Da. 8.18; 10.10.

18 *I am* he that liveth [And the living
one], and was [and I was] dead; and, behold,
I am alive for evermore, A'-mĕn; and have
the keys of hell and of death [death and
Hades].
Ch. 4.9; 5.14; Ps. 68.20; Ro. 6.9.

19 Write the things which thou hast seen,
and the things which are, and the things
which shall be hereafter;
Ver. 12; Ch. 2.1; 4.1.

20 The mystery of the seven stars which
thou sawest in my right hand, and the
seven golden candlesticks. The seven stars
are the angels of the seven churches: and
the seven candlesticks which thou sawest
are the seven churches.
Ze. 4.2; Mal. 2.7; Ph. 2.15.

CHAPTER 2.

*What is commanded to be written to the angels, that is, the
ministers of the churches.*

UNTO the angel of the church of Ĕph'-ĕ-
ṡŭs write; These things saith he that

The Man Behind the Bibles

Laura (Kitaji) Dominguez-Yon

Masuo Kitaji was born in Wakayama Prefecture and raised in a Buddhist monastery where he received an education in literature, poetry, math, science, music, art, martial arts, and shiatsu massage.

From his arrival in the US in 1915 until 1925, his main job was helping the family business, a dry goods store in Watsonville, CA called Kitaji Sokai (Mercantile), where the goods were not so dry. As he would later recall, he often took the liberty of "sampling the goods" while making deliveries on his motorcycle.

The death of Kitaji's favorite sister from tuberculosis in 1925 was a turning point for the 28-year-old. Distraught at the senseless loss, he got drunk enough that he crashed his motorcycle, sustaining serious injuries. The Salvation Army officer who found him at the wreck stayed at his bedside every day while he recuperated in the hospital. What better convert than a drunken bartender?

By 1933, Kitaji was leading the Salvation Army's Oakland Corps, a job that entailed conducting meetings in both English and Japanese, as well as translating songs, Bible readings, and messages so they could be more accessible to his flock. In 1935, he began working on a dual-language Bible.

Seven years later, in a move that was designed to protect the new Salvation Army Captain from the forced removal of all Japanese from the West Coast, Kitaji's superiors planned to transfer him to Boston. When he asked who would take his place, he was told his replacement would be a Caucasian officer who did not know Japanese. This was unacceptable to Kitaji, who believed that people still young in their faith needed a leader who could communicate with them in their own language. He refused the transfer, saying he would instead stay with his people. When told he was disobeying a direct order, he quit the Corps. Upon being told, "You can quit, but you can no longer use the title 'Captain' because it indicates an official organizational rank," he responded: "Every ship has a captain. Every sports team has a captain. I am the Captain of my people!"

It is for this reason that he's remembered by his followers as "Captain Kitaji," a name and title that remains clearly visible on the Bibles into which he meticulously inscribed full Japanese translations as well as his own commentaries and illustrations.

After the war, Captain Kitaji returned to California to resettle as the new manager of the Gilroy Hot Springs, a Japanese-owned mineral water resort. Having visited the site before the war, he knew and respected the owner, H. K. Sakata, also of Watsonville. Some sixty families—about 150 people all told—settled temporarily at the hot springs after coming out of the concentration camps.

Impressed with the healing properties of the water there, Kitaji dreamed of running a rest home for the aging Japanese immigrants he had served throughout so much of his life. Two years later, he got permission from Sakata to expand his single-room cabin in order to build the Church of the New Born where he could hold services. Kitaji soon became the spiritual heart of the hot springs, playing the role of confidant and healer for its residents and visitors.

In 1953 he acquired a new, larger Bible and once again began copying out its Japanese translation by hand, this time adding his own interpretive artwork to the pages. This second Bible, which included copious cross-referenced materials and personal notes on sermon topics, was meant as a practical tool for ministers dealing with dual-language followers. Together, these two Bibles that Kitaji worked so hard on reflect the fullness of his life experience, modeling leadership and creativity for the Japanese American community.

Right: Back of the cover for the first Kitaji Bible.

Opposite: Photo of Captain Kitaji taken to commemorate his completion of the first Bible while he was incarcerated at Poston concentration camp, Arizona, 1944. The photo is glued onto an end page of the Bible.

Pages 88 & 89: Handwritten Japanese and printed English of the first page of Revelations in the first Kitaji Bible.

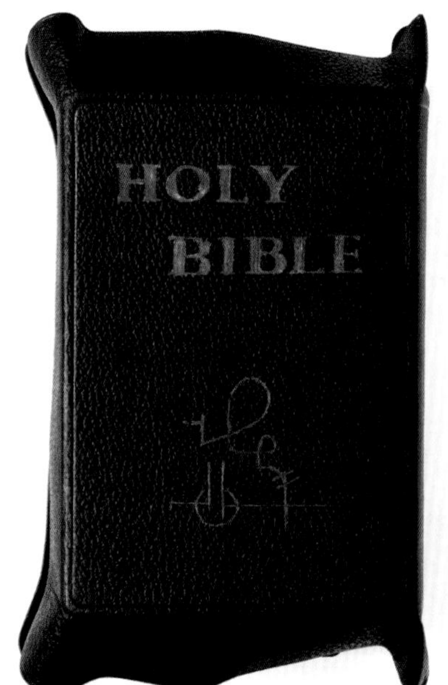

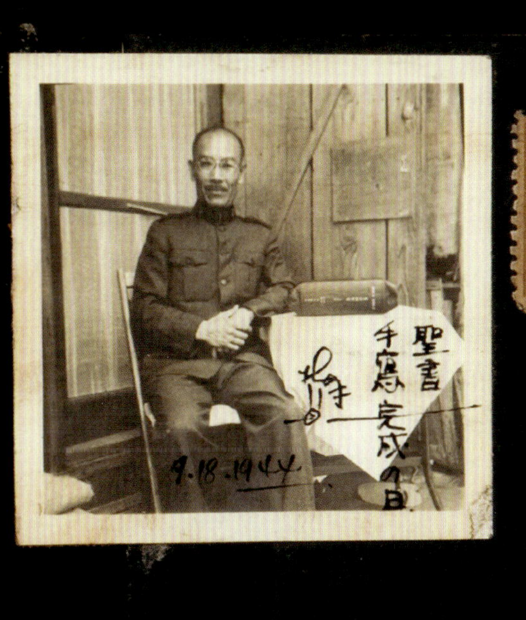

聖書
手寫完成の日
9.18.1944.

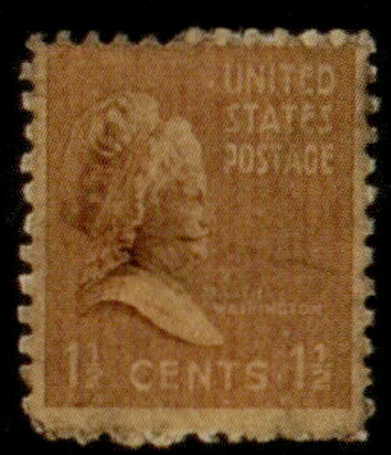

UNITED
STATES
POSTAGE
1½ CENTS 1½

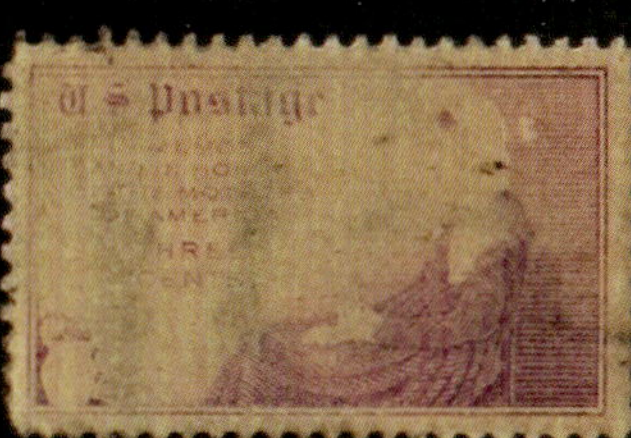

of Postage

Opposite left, top:
Illustration accompanying
the story of Jonah and the
whale that appears in
the Book of Jonah in the
second Kitaji Bible.

Opposite left, bottom:
Illustration of Matthew
14:30–31 when Jesus
pulls Simon Peter out of a
stormy Sea of Galilee from
the second Kitaji Bible.

Opposite right, top:
Illustration and commen-
tary accompanying the
introduction to the gospels
in the second Kitaji Bible.

Opposite right, bottom:
Drawing that illustrates
1 Corinthians 3:4–8 from
the second Kitaji Bible.

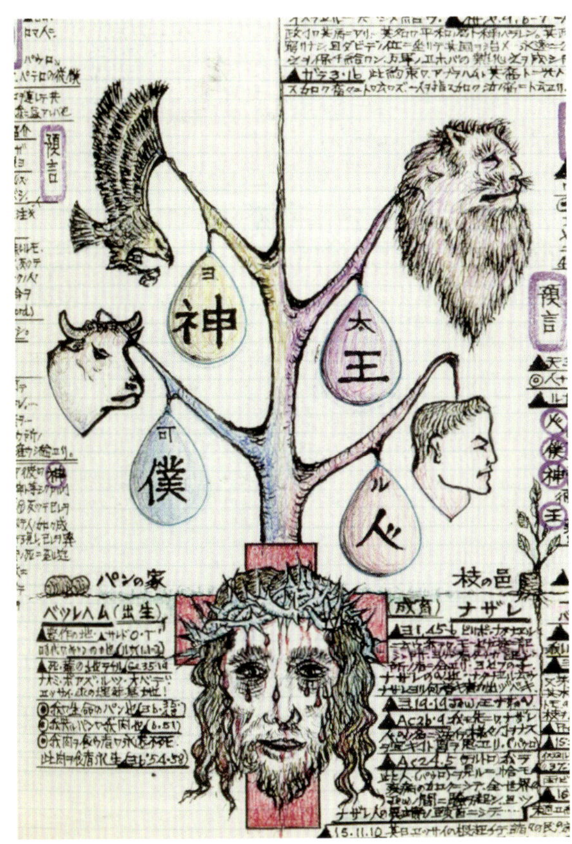

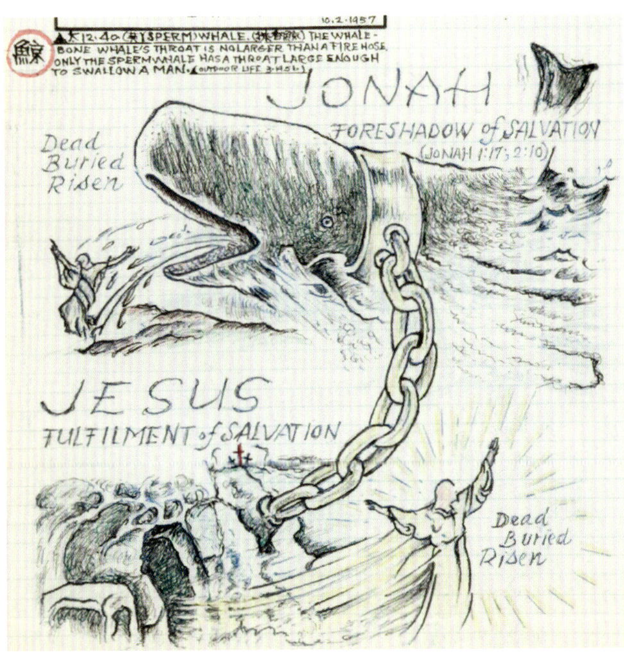
LK. 12.40 (A) SPERM) WHALE. THE WHALE-
BONE WHALE'S THROAT IS NO LARGER THAN A FIRE HOSE,
ONLY THE SPERM WHALE HAS A THROAT LARGE ENOUGH
TO SWALLOW A MAN. (OUTDOOR LIFE 3-1957)
JONAH
FORESHADOW of SALVATION
(JONAH 1:17; 2:10)
Dead
Buried
Risen
JESUS
FULFILMENT of SALVATION
Dead
Buried
Risen

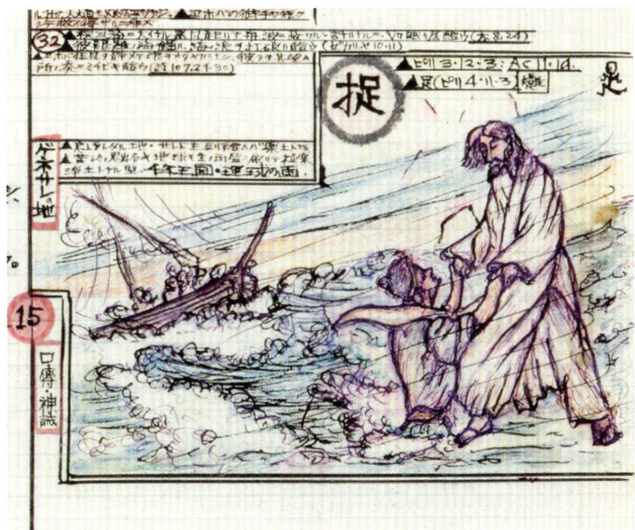

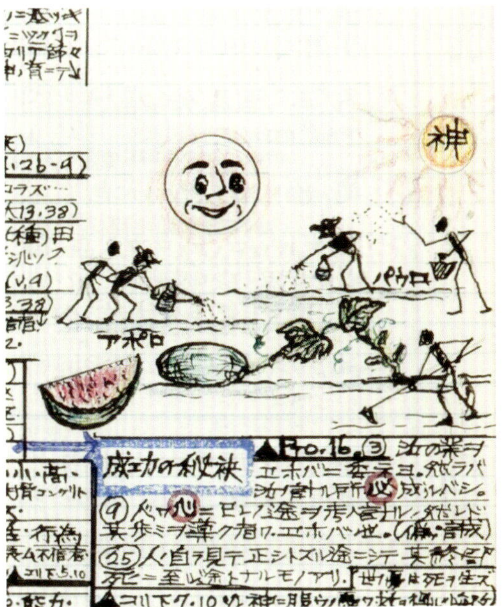

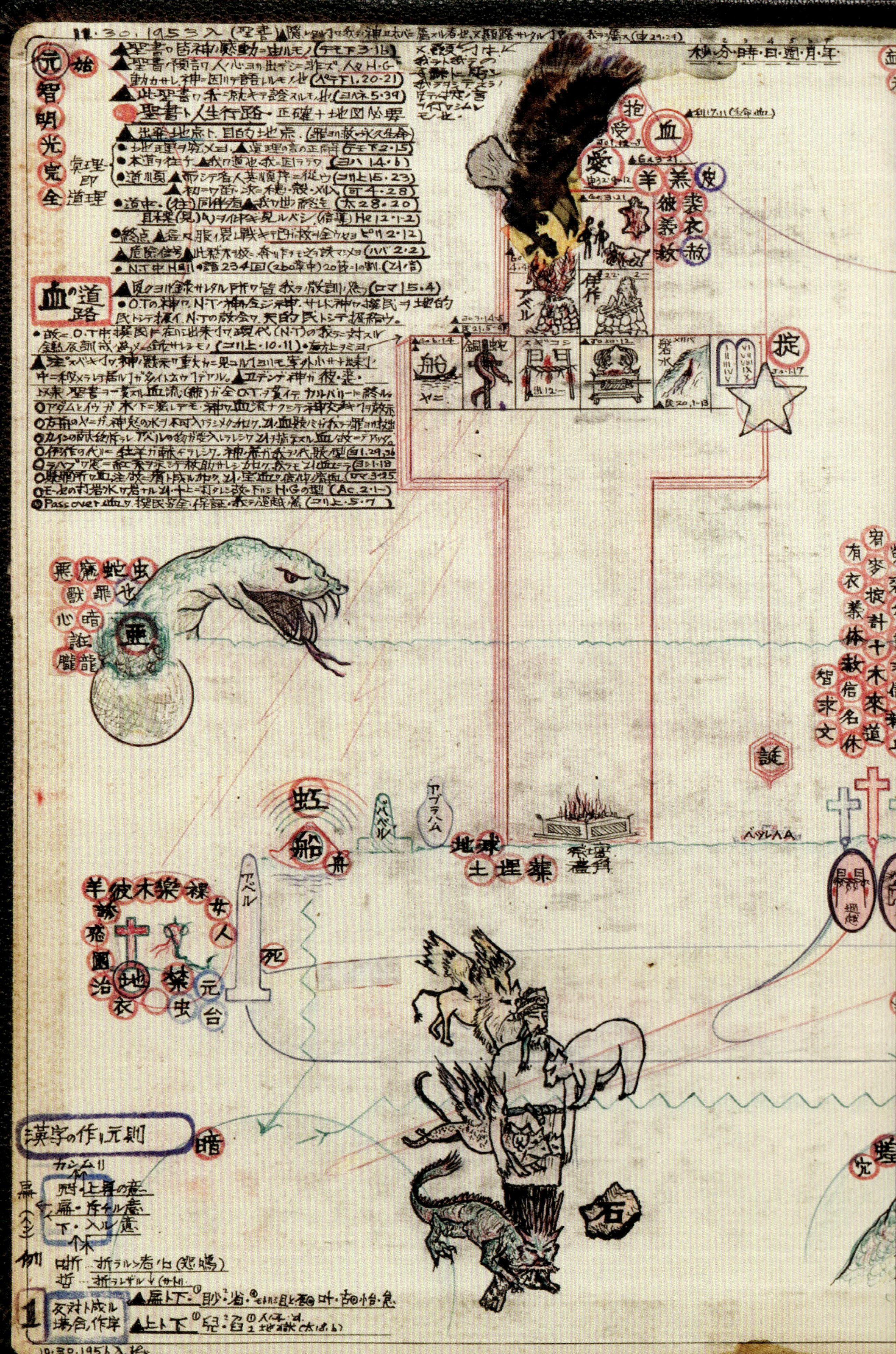

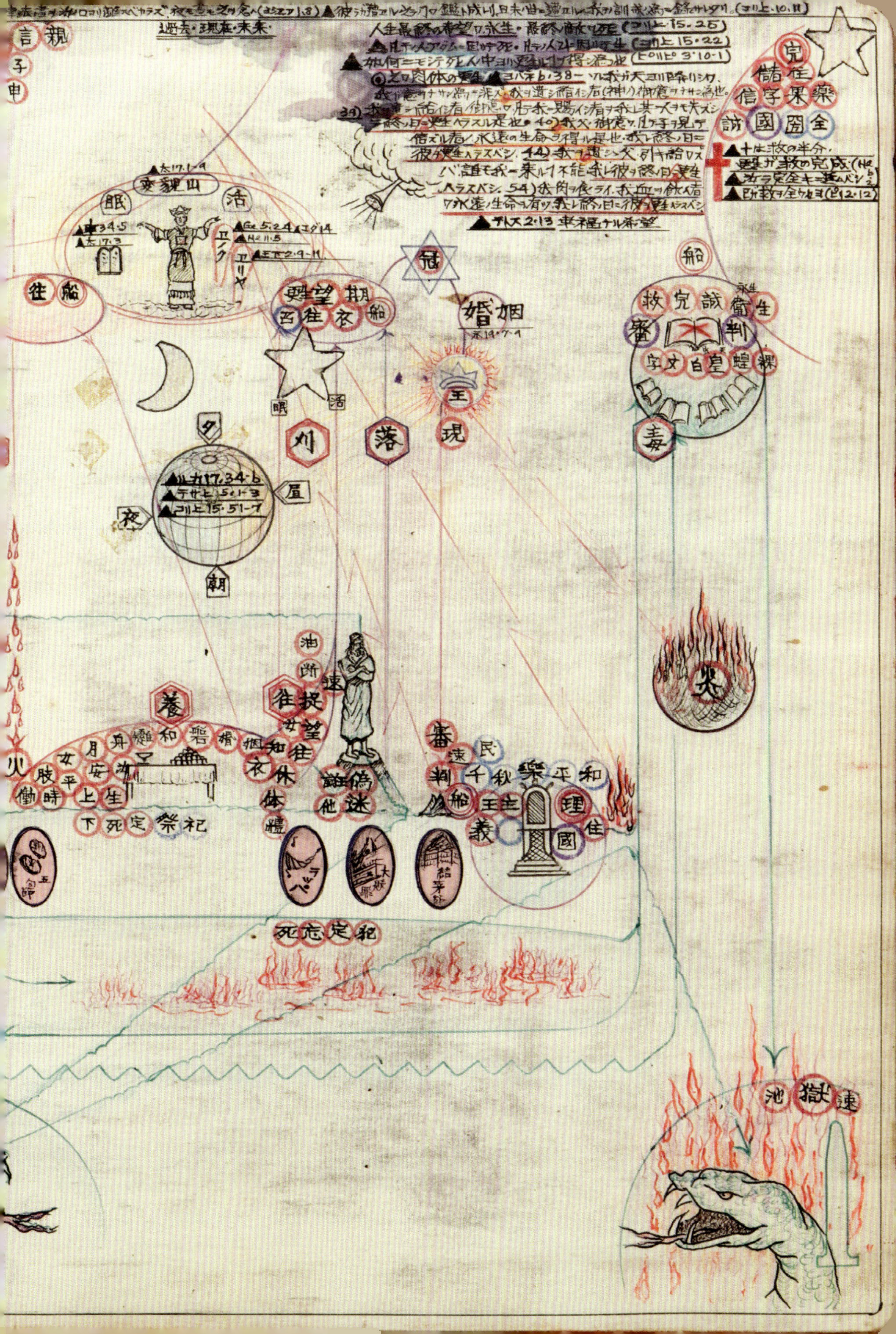

Saving the Kitaji Bibles

As articles in camp newsletters and postwar newspapers attest, Kitaji's dedication to his unique Bibles was known and celebrated amongst family and friends. Yet in the years following his death in 1973, their whereabouts remained a mystery. Kitaji's extended family assumed they remained with his widow, at least until her death in 1985. Then, sometime in 2016, they turned up in a recycling bin in the San Francisco Bay Area. From there, they were offered up for private sale by a New York auction house and would have been auctioned off if members of the Japanese American community had not intervened. Already concerned that pieces of Japanese American history were being offered for sale by companies running auctions and online, they rallied around Kitaji's descendants to help bring the Bibles to Stanford University's Hoover Institute, where they could be preserved for posterity.

Not for Sale
Nancy Ukai

Thirty-four Kitaji family members, two of whom had themselves been born in the Poston concentration camp, were stunned in early 2017 to learn that a 1944 photo of their uncle was being used to advertise the auction of their uncle's Bibles. In a letter to the New York-based Swann Auction Galleries protesting the impending sale, they wrote that the Bibles were "family heirlooms" that were "used to teach us when we were children" and that selling them would be an "inappropriate attempt to exploit the unconstitutional World War II incarceration of 120,000 Japanese Americans for profit." If Swann had been serious about doing due diligence, they pointed out, all the auction house had to do was look at the baptismal records written in the Bibles themselves.

The firm immediately withdrew the Bibles—which had been priced at $85,000— from availability. After private discussions, they were instead transferred to the family.

This rescue of the Kitaji Bibles came in the wake of a previous protest that had successfully prevented the sale of camp crafts and artifacts collected by folk-art expert Allen Eaton. In 2015, the New Jersey-based Rago auction house had been scheduled to sell the Eaton collection, but community outrage and legal action had forced the sale to be suspended.

In the case of the Kitaji Bibles, Swann had privately solicited a public institution for a bid, but that institution had instead alerted a community member. Informal networks built through activism enabled a quick response.

Similar battles against profiteering from the material culture of Japanese American incarceration continue to this day. Each act of resistance helps to heighten consciousness that Japanese American history should not be bought and sold, but rather preserved and studied.

Opposite: Handwritten Japanese translation of Malachi 3:11–17 in the first Kitaji Bible.

Pages 94 & 95: End papers of the second Kitaji Bible.

Printed Bible text (left column, Malachi 3):

LORD of hosts. But ye... all we return?

1.3; Ac. 7.51.

a man rob God? Yet ye... But ye say, Wherein have... In tithes and offerings.

cursed with a curse: for ye... even this whole nation.

ye all the [the whole]... the storehouse, that there... ine house, and prove me... aith the LORD of hosts, if... ou the windows of heaven... t a blessing, that there... ugh *to receive it.*

Ch. 26.20; 2 Ch. 31.10; Ne. 10...

I will rebuke the devou... and he shall not destr... r ground; neither shall... uit before the time in the... ORD of hosts.

25; Am. 4.9.

all nations shall call you... be a delightsome land... sts.

4; Da. 8.9.

ur words have been stout... e LORD. Yet ye say, Wh... so much against thee?

3; 2.17.

ve said, It is vain to serv... profit *is it* that we have... and that we have walked... the LORD of hosts?

p. 1.12.

how we call the proud happy... work wickedness are set u... mpt God are even deliver...

s. 73.12; 95.9; Je. 7.10.

en they that feared... h one to another: and th... and heard *it,* and a boo... was written before him for... the LORD, and that thou...

6; He. 3.13; Re. 20.12.

hey shall be mine, saith th... that day when I make... I will spare them, as a ma... son that serveth him.

103.13; Is. 62.3; Tit. 2.14; 1 Pe...

shall ye return, and disce... righteous and the wicked... that serveth God and h... not.

Am. 5.15.

CHAPTER 4.

...ent on the wicked, 2 and his blessing... exhorteth to the study of the law... jah's coming and office.

hold, the day cometh, that... an oven; and all the prou... t do wickedly, shall b...

Handwritten Japanese text (文語訳 マラキ書 第三章):

…汝らに歸らん、萬軍のエホバ之を言ふ。然るに汝らは、我ら何に於て歸るべきやと言へり。

（什）なんぢ獻物に於てなり。

⑧ 人、神の物を盗むことをせんや、然れど汝らは我物を盗めり。汝らは又、何に於て汝の物を盗みしやと言へり。十分の一...

⑨ 汝らは呪詛をもて詛はる、又汝ら凡ての國人は我物を盗めり。

⑩ 我が宮殿に食物あらしめん爲に汝ら什一を盡て我倉に携へ來れ、而して之をもて我を試み、吾が天の窓を開きて容るべき所なき迄に恩澤を汝らに注ぐや否やを見るべし。萬軍のエホバ之を言ふ。

⑪ 我れ又噬食ふものを汝らの爲に抑へて汝らの地の産物を壊らざらしめん、又汝らのブドーの木をして時の至らざる前に其實を畑に落さざらしめん。萬軍のエホバ之を言ふ。

⑫ 又萬國の人、汝らを幸福なる者と稱へん、そは汝ら樂き地となるべければなり。萬軍のエホバ之を言ふ。（楽）

⑬ エホバ言ひ給ふ、汝らは言をはげしくして我に逆へり。然るも汝らは我ら何を汝に逆ひて何を言ひしやと言へり。

⑭ 汝らは云へらく、神に服仕ることは徒然なり。我ら其命令を守り、且萬軍のエホバの前に悲みて歩みたりとて何の益あらんや。

⑮ 今我らは高ぶる者を幸福なりと稱ふ。又惡を行ふ者も盛になれり、神を試むる者すらも救はると。

⑯ 其時エホバを畏るる者互に相語れり。エホバ耳を傾けて之をきゝ給へり。又エホバを畏るる者および其名を記憶ゆる者の爲にエホバの前に記念の書をかき記せり。

⑰ 萬軍のエホバ言ひ給ふ、我れ吾が設くる日に彼らをもて我寶となすべし。又人の己に仕ふる子を憐むがごとく、我れ彼らを憐まん。

⑱ 其時、汝らは更に又義者と惡き者と、神に仕ふる者と、仕へざる者との区別を知らん。

（欄外記号：心・審判・不信以上・来らん者・再初・火・理・日・時・名・楽）

DEDICATED IN MEMORY OF THE BUDDHIST SOLDIERS
WHO GAVE THEIR LIVES FOR THEIR COUNTRY
DURING WORLD WAR II ··· MAY 30, 1948
HONOLULU, HAWAII, U.S.A. ··· HONPA HONGWANJI MISSION OF HAWAII
HAWAII FEDERATION OF YOUNG BUDDHIST ASSOCIATIONS

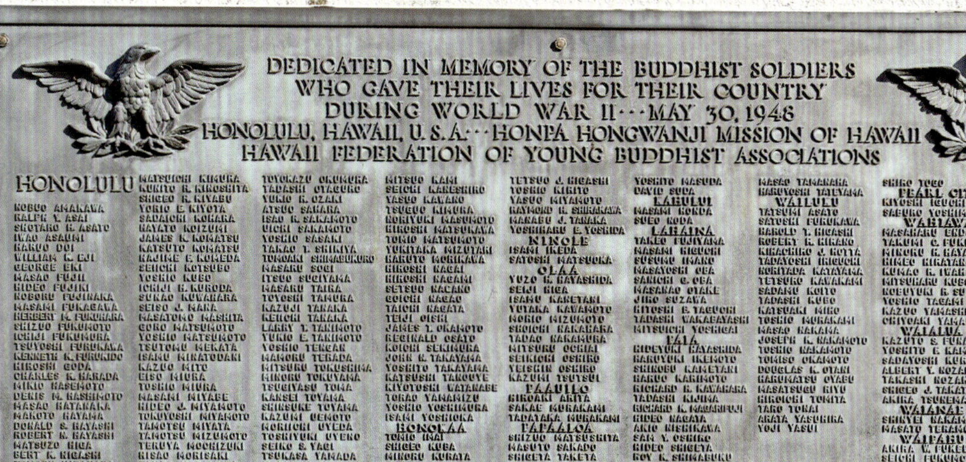

HONOLULU
NOBUO AMAKAWA
RALPH Y. ASAI
SHOTARO H. ASATO
IWAO ASAUMI
HARUO DOI
WILLIAM K. EJI
GEORGE EKI
MASAO FUJII
HIDEO FUJIKI
NOBORU FUJIHARA
MASAMI FUKAGAWA
HERBERT M. FUKUHARA
SHIZUO FUKUMOTO
ICHIJI FUKUMURA
TSUYOSHI FURUKAWA
KENNETH K. FURUMIDO
HIROSHI GODA
CHARLES K. HARADA
MIKIO HASEMOTO
DENIS M. HASHIMOTO
MASAO HATAKA
MAKOTO HAYAMA
DONALD S. HAYASHI
ROBERT K. HAYASHI
MATSUZO HIGA
BERT K. HIGASHI
TOMOSU HIRAHARA
KAZUO L. HIRAMATSU
HIROYUKI HIRAMOTO
GEROME M. HIRATA
MASAO HISANO
JAMES G. HORINOUCHI
KENICHI ICHIMURA
WILLIAM Y. IKEDA
MASAMI IKARAZU
MINORU INOUYE
MASAYUKI ISHII
SHICHIRO ISHII
SHINICHI M. ISHIKI
HACHIRO ITO
TETSUO ITO
MUNEMASA JICHAKU
JUNICHI J. KAGIHARA
ETSUTOSHI M. KAMAYA
TETSUO KATAKO
GORO A. KAWATA
SATOSHI KAYA

MATSUICHI KIMURA
KUNITO R. KINOSHITA
SHIGEO R. KIYABU
YORIO E. KIYOTA
SADAICHI KOHARA
HAYATO KOIZUMI
JAMES K. KOMATSU
KATSUTO KOMATSU
HAJIME E. KOMEDA
SEICHI KOTSUBO
YOSHIO KUBO
ICHIJI H. KURODA
SUNAO KUWAHARA
SEISO J. MANA
MASATOMO MASHITA
GORO MATSUMOTO
YOSHIO MATSUMOTO
TSUTOMU MEKATA
ISAMU MINATODAKI
KAZUO MITO
EISO MIURA
TOSHIO MIURA
MASAMI MIYABE
HIDEO J. MIYAMOTO
TOKUYOSHI MIYAMOTO
TAMOTSU MIYATA
TAMOTSU MIZUMOTO
TERUYA MOCHIZUKI
HISAO MORISAKI
TAKEO MORISHITA
MASAO MOTOKANE
SUSUMU MOTONAGA
ISAMU MURAKAMI
KANO MURASHIGE
SHIGERU MURATA
YOSHIO NAKAMURA
TAKASHI NAKAUYE
CHIKAO NISHI
KATSUYUKI NISHIMURA
SHIGERU NISHIMURA
JYUN NISHISHITA
CHIETO NISHITANI
TARO NISHITANI
SHIZUO A. NOZAWA
TOSHIO NUNA
TSUGIO OGATA
YOSHIO OGOMORI
MITSUMI OKAMOTO
SUEO OKAMOTO
MASAO OKIMOTO

TOYOKAZU OKUMURA
TADASHI OTAGURO
YUKIO H. OZAKI
ATSUO SAHARA
ISAO K. SAKAMOTO
UICHI SAKAMOTO
YOSHIO SASAKI
TAKAO T. SHIKIYA
TOMOAKI SHIMABUKURO
MASARU SOGI
ITSUO SUGIYAMA
MASARU TAIRA
TOYOSHI TAMURA
KAZUJI TANAKA
KENICHI TANAKA
LARRY T. TANIMOTO
YUKIO E. TANIMOTO
YOSHIO TENGAN
MAMORU TERADA
MITSURU TOKUSHIMA
MINORU TOKUYAMA
TSUGIYASU TOMA
KANSEI TOYAMA
SHINSUKE TOYAMA
KAZUMI UEMOTO
NORIICHI UYEDA
TOSHIYUKI UYENO
SEIKO S. YAGI
TSUKASA YAMADA
MORIO YAMAGUCHI
MASARU YAMAMOTO
ISAMU YAMANAGA
SHIZUO YAMASAKI
MINORU YOSHIMURA
KAORU MORIWAKI
YUKIO IDE
TORAO MIGITA

MITSUO KAMI
SEICHI KAMESHIRO
YASUO KAWANO
TSUGUO KIMURA
NORIYUKI MASUMOTO
HIROSHI MATSUKAWA
TOMIO MATSUMOTO
YUKITAKA MIZUTARI
MAKOTO MORIKAWA
HIROSHI NAGAI
HIROSHI NAGAMI
SETSUO NAKANO
GOICHI NAGAO
TAICHI NAGATA
TEIJI OISHI
JAMES T. OKAMOTO
REGINALD OSATO
KOICHI SEKIMURA
JOHN K. TAKAYAMA
YOSHITO TAKAYAMA
KATSUSHI TAKOUYE
KIYOTOSHI WATANABE
TORAO YAMAMIZU
YOSHIO YOSHIMURA
ISAMI YOSHIOKA
HONOKAA
TOMIO IMAI
SHIGEO KUBA
MINORU KURATA
HITOSHI NAJITA
HONOMU
SHIGETO NIIDE
SHOJI OKIDO
SHIZUO TERAMOTO
KONA
TOSHIO R. FUJII
SHIRO IKENO
TSUYOSHI L. IWAMOTO
HITOSHI W. KADOOKA
GORO G. MATSUDA
KUSUO MATSUMOTO
KYUICHI MATSUMOTO
TOMIICHI MATSUMOTO
KIYOSHI MATSUNAGA
AKIRA MORIHARA
IWAO NAKAMURA
HISAYUKI A. YANO
NAALEHU
SHISUKE W. FUJIOKA
MITSUO L. FURUICHI
KIYOSHI MASUNAGA
KAMEO TSUTANI
YONEYO YONEMURA

HAWAII
HILO
JITSURO FUJIKAWA
YOSHIMI FUJINO
KAZUO GOYA
YASUO HIRAYAMA
KAZUO IHARA
TETSUO J. HIGASHI
TOSHIO KIRITO
YASUO MIYAMOTO
RAYMOND H. SHIRAKAWA
MANABU J. TANAKA
YOSHIHARU E. YOSHIDA
KINOOLE
ISAMI IKEDA
SATOSHI MATSUOKA
OLAA
YUZO H. HAYASHIDA
SEIJI HIGA
ISAMU KANETANI
YUTAKA KAWAMOTO
NOBIO MIZUMOTO
SHOICHI NAKAHARA
TADAO NAKAMURA
MITSURU OCHIAI
SEIKICHI OSHIRO
YEISHIN OSHIRO
KAZUMI TSUTSUI
PAAUILO
HIROAKI ARITA
SAKAE MURAKAMI
TADATAKA MURAKAMI
PAPAALOA
SHIZUO MATSUSHITA
MASUTO SAKADO
SHIGETA TAKETA
YASUJI K. UCHIMA
PAPAIKOU
KANEICHI E. HIGA
KIKUMATSU KAWANISHI
MITSUGI MUROOKA
HITOSHI NAKAI
YOSHITO NII
AKIRA OJIRI
BUSHICHI TAKI
TSUTOMU YAMAOKA
SHINTARO HANAUMI
MASAYOSHI OGATA
RIAKI MORIMOTO
SABURO NAKASATO

MAUI
HAIKU
KATSUSHIRO KANEMITSU
YOSHITO MASUDA
DAVID SUDA
KAHULUI
MASAMI HONDA
SUEO KODA
LAHAINA
TAKEO FUJIYAMA
MASAMI HIGUCHI
SUSUMU IMANO
MASAYOSHI OBA
SAMICHI G. OBA
MASARAO OTAKE
JIRO SUZAWA
HITOSHI E. TAGUCHI
TADASHI WAKABAYASHI
MITSUICHI YOSHIKAI
PAIA
HIDEYUKI HAYASHIDA
HARUYUKI IKEMOTO
SHINOBU KANETANI
HARUO KARIMOTO
RICHARD H. KAWAHARA
TADASHI KIJIMA
RICHARD K. MASARIFUJI
HIDEO NAGATA
AKIO NISHIKAWA
SAM Y. OSHIRO
HIDEO SHIGETA
ROY K. SHIMABUKU
TERUTO TANIMOTO
MINORU TOSAKA
SHIGEO WASANO
HIDEO YAMADA
PUUNENE
HAROLD J. ARAKAWA
HIDEO ARAKAKI
YEIKO GOYA
TETSUO HAMADA
HENRY S. IKEHARA
SHOMATSU KIRA
SABURO MAEHARA
MASAO MATSUI
ISAMI MIYASATO
HIROMU MORIKAWA
EDWARD E. NAKAMURA
KAZUO NISHIHARA
MASAMI SAIKI
TAKESHI SHIGIHARA
TAKEO SHIMIZU
YOSHINOBU TAKEI

OAHU
AIEA
EWA
WAHIAWA
WAIALUA
WAIANAE
WAIPAHU
PEARL CITY
KAUAI
ELEELE
LANAI

REMEMBRANCE

If someone born into a warrior house who loses
his life on the battlefield, if he dies having said the
nenbutsu, then, in accordance with the original vow,
Amitābha [Buddha] will come to welcome him
and he will achieve birth in the Pure Land.

念仏 – TO RECALL THE BUDDHA
SHINRAN SHONIN (1173–1263)

And that these days should be remembered
and kept throughout every generation,
every family, every province, and every city;…
nor the memorial of them perish from their seed.

ESTHER 9:28

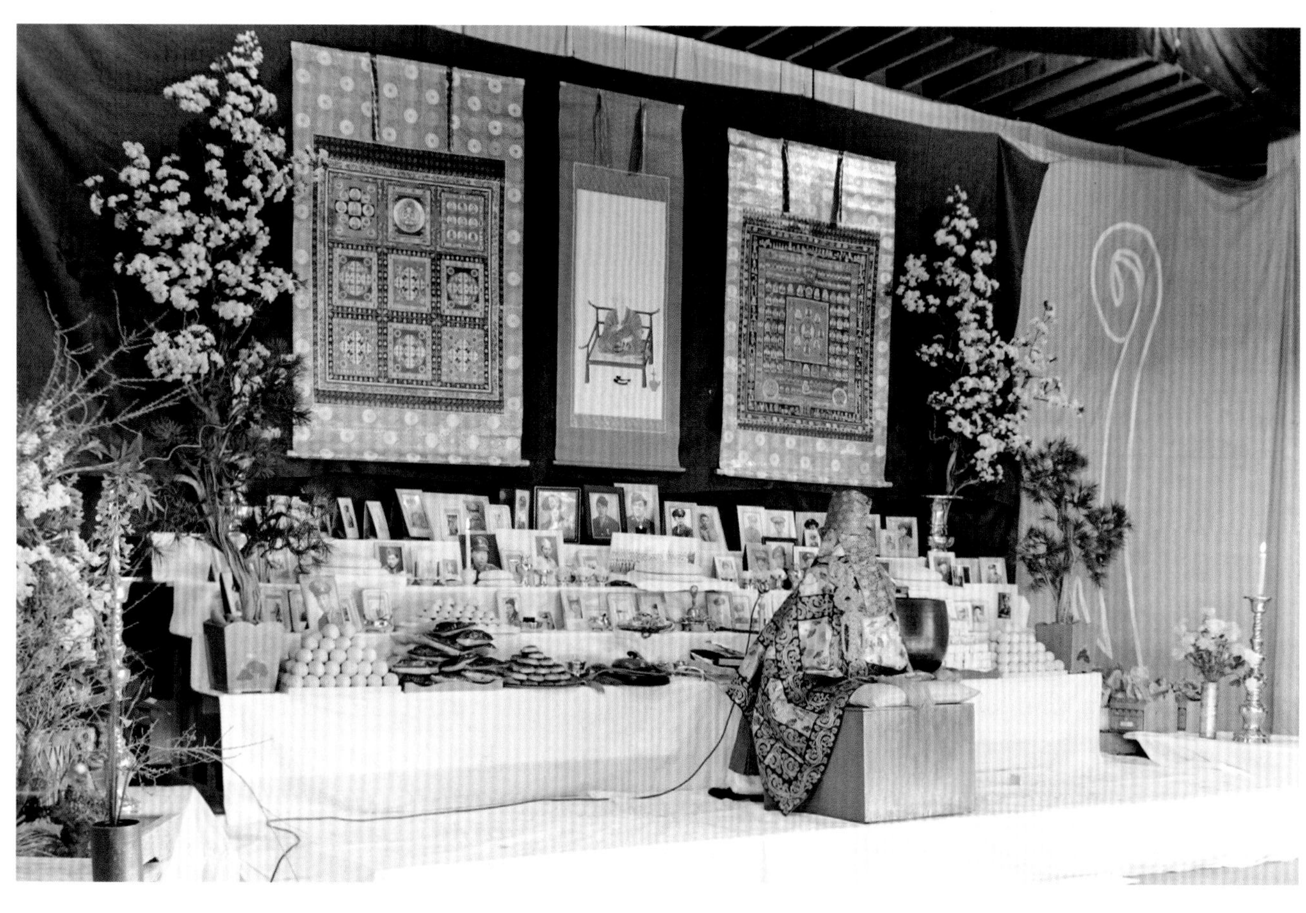

As loved ones and community members started dying in the camps—whether due to natural causes or from inadequate food, shelter, or healthcare—Japanese Americans turned to their faith traditions to help mourn their loss.

Such remembrances often involved public acts of memorialization. Buddhists and Christians have distinct theological views of death and the afterlife, and their rituals for funerals and memorial services likewise differ, but during World War II, they would often come together to grieve. Both Buddhist and Christian clergy led families in funerals and remembrances that took place in cemeteries, barrack churches, and auditoriums. They also spearheaded collaborative efforts to build large-scale monuments to honor the dead.

For Nisei soldiers, the question of religious affiliation was particularly significant; it represented how their passing would be marked on the battlefields. The US Army did not permit "Buddhist" as a designation on dog tags, and the only chaplains made available to the Japanese American soldiers were Christian. The question of how to administer religiously appropriate last rites to the Nisei who died in combat, the vast majority of whom were Buddhists, remained a concern for the duration of the war.

Opposite: Shingon Buddhist memorial service with altar photos of fallen Nisei soldiers at Minidoka concentration camp, Idaho, ca. 1944.

Page 98: Bronze plaque at the main headquarter temple of the Honpa Hongwanji Mission in Honolulu, created and installed after the war, continues to serve as a reminder of the sacrifice of the majority-Buddhist volunteers and draftees who served in the Military Intelligence Service in the Pacific and in the segregated 100th/442nd Regimental Combat Team in the European theater.

Dedication ceremony of Manzanar Ireito, officiated by Rev. Shinjo Nagatomi of the Nishi Hongwanji Buddhist tradition and Rev. Junro Kashitani of the Holiness Church, 1943, California.

Rev. Nagatomi's daughter recalled that her father practiced for hours every day on "large rolls of paper with a huge brush, about 3⅛ inches in diameter, and black paint…. Sometimes he was unable to sleep, thinking about his task, and would rise early and tackle the words, i-rei-to, until the words seemed to dance off the paper." After several weeks, the Buddhist priest was satisfied that he had produced a version that could be engraved on the monument in perpetuity.

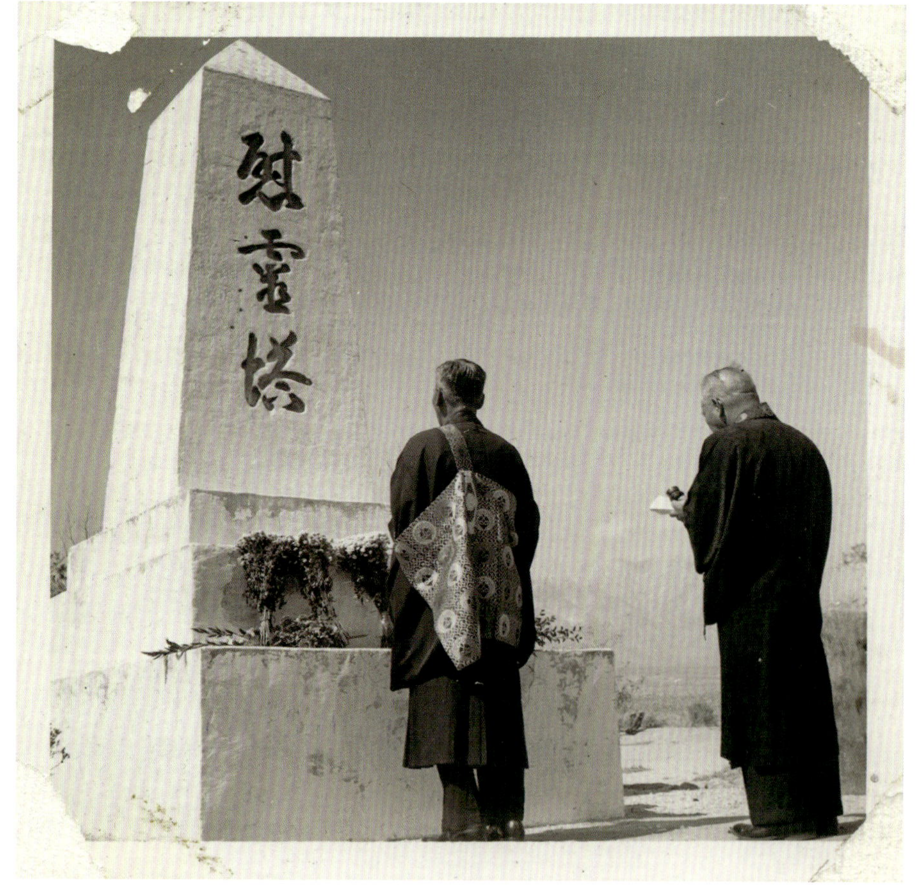

Irei: Remembering the Spirits of the Dead

The Manzanar Ireito, a monument built in 1943 to honor those who would never return home from camp, is one of the most striking examples of interfaith cooperation to take place during the World War II incarceration. The initial idea for a structure that could memorialize the dead was proposed by the senior Buddhist priest at Manzanar, Reverend Shinjo Nagatomi, who also contributed the calligraphy for the characters "I-rei-to," or "consoling spirits tower," that give the monument its name. Ryozo Kado, a Catholic landscape architect, gardener, and stonemason, helped with the design of the monument, which is based on the five-tiered structure of a Buddhist stupa (*gorinto*).

Various Buddhist and Christian clergy worked together with the camp's Town Hall Committee to decide where the Ireito would be placed. Each family in camp was asked to donate ten to fifteen cents to pay for the concrete required to build the monument, and residents of Block 9 and sixty Young Buddhist Association members provided the labor to build it.

On the afternoon of August 14, 1943—a date chosen to coincide with the Buddhist Obon festival honoring ancestors—Reverend Nagatomi and the Holiness Church's Reverend Junro Kashitani officiated over the dedication of the Ireito in a ceremony that was attended by other clergy as well as most of the general population in camp.

In the postwar years, the Manzanar Ireito has become one of the most widely recognized symbols of incarceration. But it is just one of many monuments that were erected in the camps to commemorate the dead. The Japanese word "Irei"—literally "to console the spirit"—is used in a slightly different formulation—"Ireihi" or "consoling spirits monument"—on the stupa built in the Rohwer camp in Arkansas. Made from found rebar and bits of barbed wire, and engraved with calligraphy by Buddhist priest Reverend Daitetsu Hayashima, the Rohwer Ireihi is yet another reminder that the living as well as the dead require consolation.

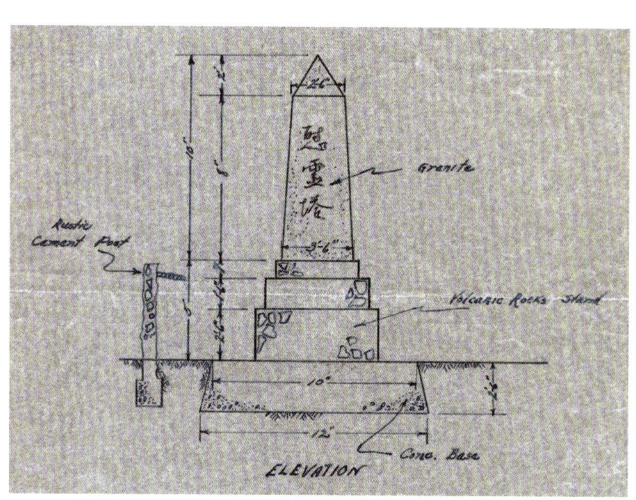

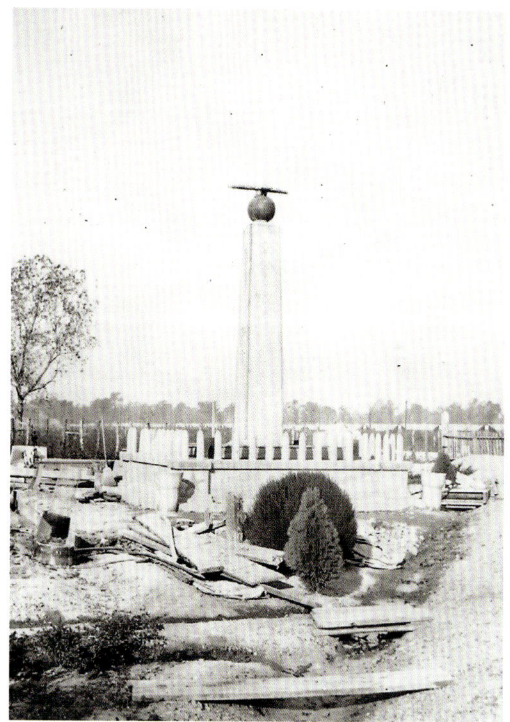

Above, left: Manzanar Ireito construction sketch, 1943.

Above, right: Ireihi monument under construction at Rohwer concentration camp, Arkansas, 1944.

Right: Ireito were also made for more personal and intimate forms of memorial, such as these carved memorials made in concentration and internment camps that are now in the Japanese American National Museum collection. Some were made to memorialize the experience of incarceration itself, while others were made to honor a loved one who had died. The small rectangular one was made to honor the memory of a twelve-year-old who died while incarcerated.

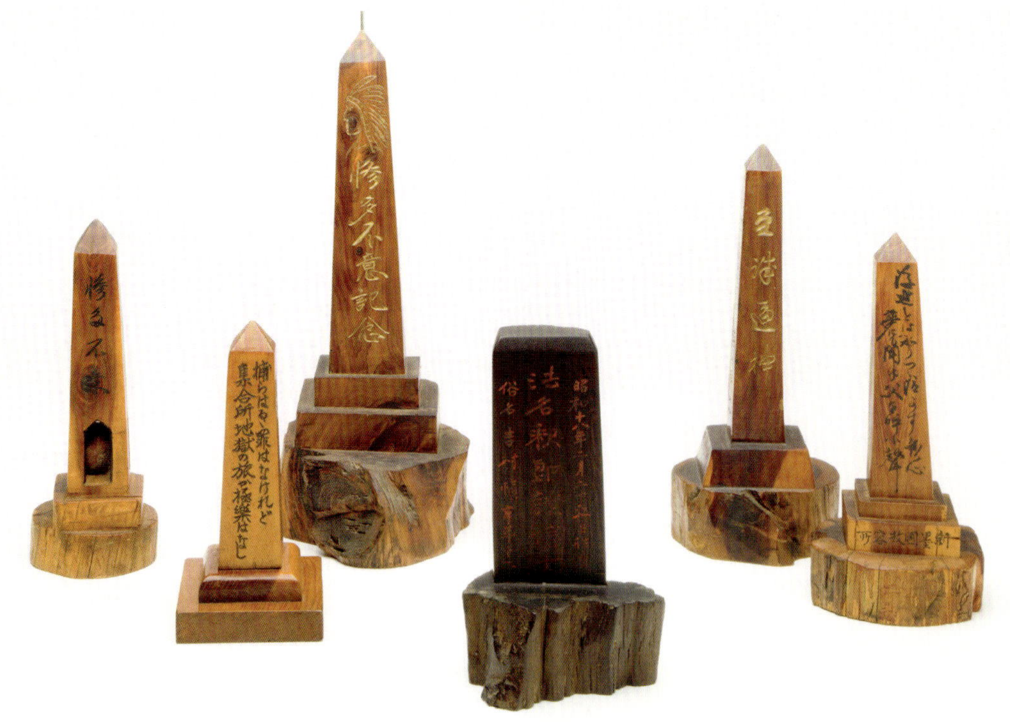

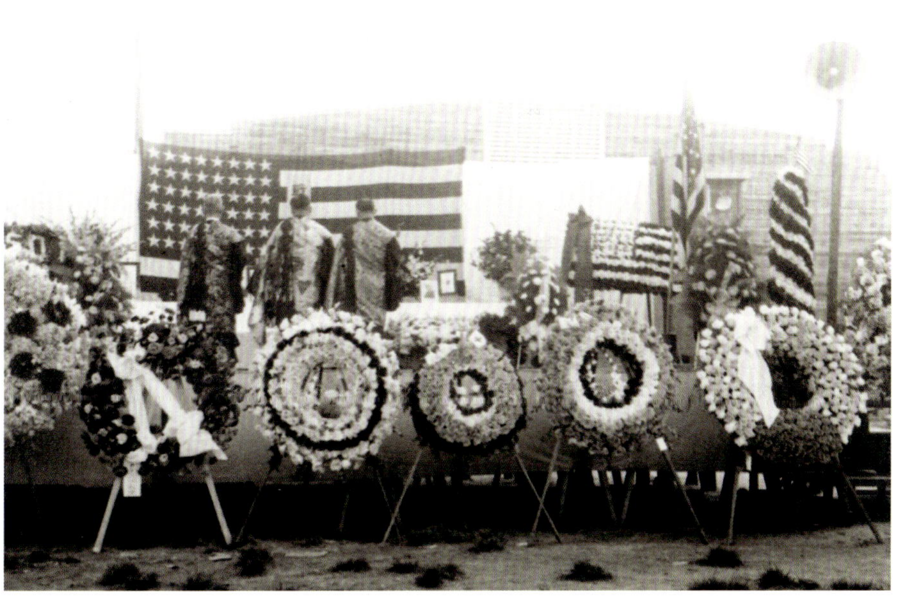

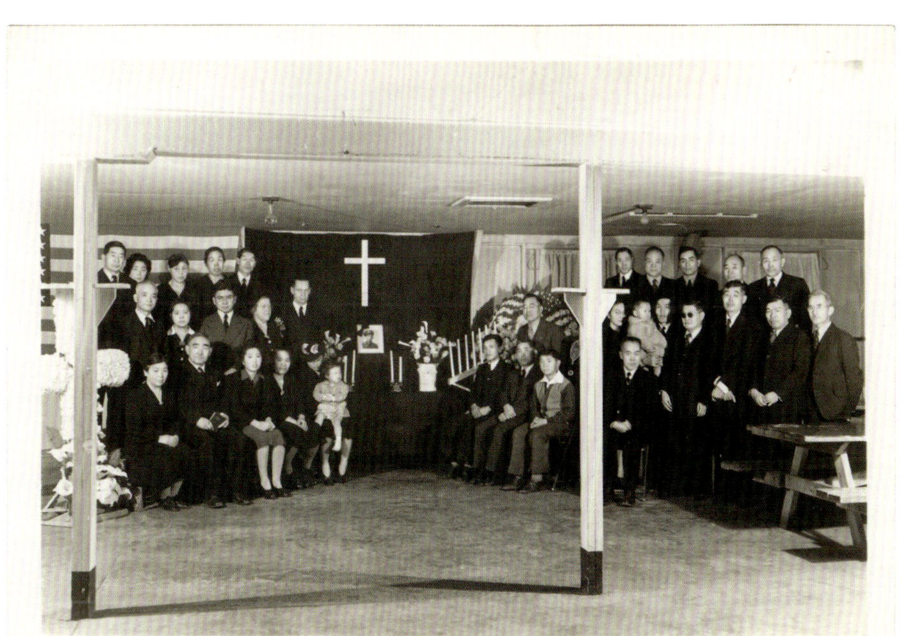

Above: Buddhist funeral for Nisei soldiers with three priests officiating, Rohwer concentration camp, Arkansas.

Left: Christian funeral for Sgt. Ned T. Nakamura of the 442nd RCT's G Company who was killed in action during the rescue of the "Lost Battalion" in the Vosges Mountains, Minidoka concentration camp, 1944.

Honoring the War Dead

As news trickled in about the high rate of casualties among Japanese American soldiers on the front lines of the Pacific and European theaters, special efforts were made to remember the war dead.

A unique war memorial, consisting of eighty-eight artillery-shell-shaped structures inside each of which are statues of the Buddha, was built on the grounds of Waimea's Shingon Mission in the final months of the war. This memorial, the design and construction of which was coordinated by Gold Star mothers on Kaua'i, was meant to reference the eighty-eight stations that comprise the famous pilgrimage route on Japan's Shikoku Island. By creating a memorial that could simultaneously also function as a pilgrimage destination, they hoped to ensure that the sacrifice made by their sons who had given their lives for the US would be remembered, visited, and honored into perpetuity, long after they themselves had passed.

Opposite: Waimea Shingon Mission War Memorial.

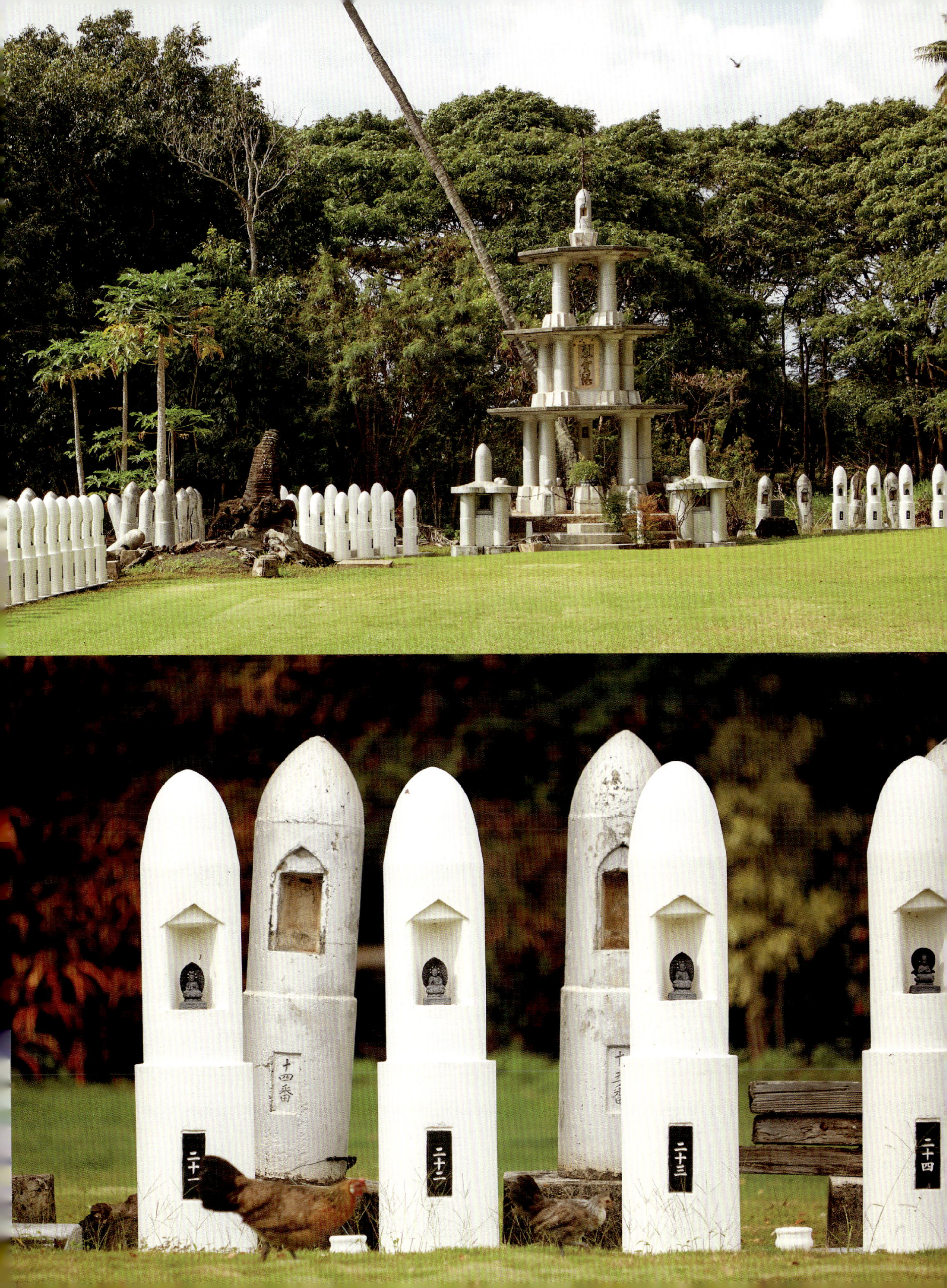

十四番
十三番
二十二
二十二
二十三
二十四

The Amache Memorial

Baptist pastor Reverend Masahiko Wada took the lead in mobilizing the community in Colorado's Amache concentration camp to build an Ireito monument that would also include a special honor roll plaque for Nisei soldiers who had lost their lives in combat.

Remembering Strength and Resilience
Mitch Homma

Whenever I think or talk about the wartime Amache Memorial, I'm overtaken by mixed emotions. The three-piece memorial, designed by my great-grandfather Reverend Masahiko Wada, is one of many that he helped create in Japan and the US. As such, the physical structure itself is a piece of his lasting legacy.

I grew up hearing so many stories about my great grandparents' service to the Christian church and people that I can't help but see the Amache Memorial and feel pride and honor.

But when I reflect upon it, I can see how its three parts represent three aspects of the wartime experience. The granite stone at its base evokes the strength and resilience of the people of Japanese descent who were forced to live behind barbed wire. Engraved in both Japanese and English, it commemorates their time at Amache and shows Japanese and American cultures coming together.

The wood monument that makes up the middle of the monument features the handwritten names of 148 people, including thirty-one Nisei soldiers who died in the service of their country. Written in Japanese, the monument wall honors those who would never have a chance to leave Amache, as well as those who gave their lives overseas while their families were imprisoned there. Among the names on that wall is that of my grandfather, Kyushiro Homma. A dentist interned at Amache, he was only 44 years old when he passed. My father was seven at the time. So looking at this part of the memorial, I can't help but be reminded of the life-changing impact our time at Amache had on my family.

The third piece of the Amache Memorial is an honor roll plaque accompanied by a gold-colored star on top that commemorates those who died while serving their country. On the plaque, written in English, are the names of Nisei soldiers. The gold star serves to remind us of those service members who fell fighting for freedom and democracy while their families remained unfree behind barbed wire. Written in English, the names of these Nisei soldiers are a reminder of their loyalty and sacrifice.

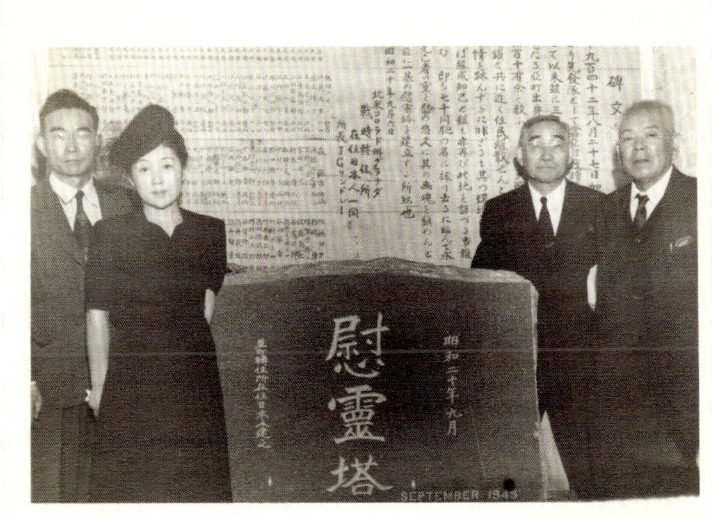

Opposite: Amache Memorial Wall for those who died in camp and during military service.

Left: Dedication of Amache Ireito and Memorial Wall, 1945.

Memorial Tablets for Nisei Soldiers

On the Hawaiian islands, Reverend Mitsumyo Tottori of the Hale‘iwa Shingon Mission, the only Issei Buddhist priest not arrested and interned on the mainland, handwrote roughly 420 *toba* (wooden memorial tablets) for those Nisei soldiers from the islands who were killed in action. Placed in the inner alcove of his temple, these tablets were not made for display, but rather were meant to ensure that every soldier who died in battle would be prayed for. The first tablet Reverend Tottori wrote was for Sergeant Shigeo "Joe" Takata of Waialua, who died on September 29, 1943. The posthumous name that he gave to Sergeant Takata in keeping with Buddhist custom—"Yu-mon-in Chu-sei Ho-koku Ko-ji"—translates to "For the sake of America, he gave his life." Reverend Tottori continued this practice of creating memorial tablets for soldiers' death as he learned of them—regardless of whether they were Buddhist or Christian—until the end of the war.

The Heartbeat of a Soldier-Ancestor
Wendy Egyoku Nakao

My Zen Buddhist teacher instructed me as follows: "Please treat a memorial tablet as though it is the body of the deceased person, as the body of a Buddha."

Seeing these tablets, I become aware of my breath slowing and my heart beating; I feel drawn to sit and feel my body upon the earth. Death has a way of pulling me down into the ground of being, into the deep roots and the bloodvein of all that connects with the lifestream flowing throughout space and time.

These humble wooden tablets, upon which each soldier's name has been so carefully written, are a reminder that freedom is neither easily gained nor maintained. Here are hundreds of memorial tablets for beloved sons, brothers, husbands, and friends—Buddhists and Christians—who took their place among the myriad ancestors by selflessly serving a cause greater than themselves.

All of our efforts together are needed to turn the wheels of peace and justice. Constant vigilance is required to address the cruelty of racism and white supremacy. An undeniable thread of love and compassion unspools from each life that is given up for others. True freedom comes from serving. I ask, "How am I serving? How am I honoring the debt? In what ways must I evolve in order to live in a truly life-giving way?"

As the ancestral vein interweaves with our breaths and heartbeats, let us raise a great vow to serve each other, all beings, and the Earth. I bow in gratitude with my forehead touching the ground. May it be so.

Below: Funeral of Sgt. Shigeo "Joe" Takata, first soldier of the 100th Infantry Battalion to be killed in action, Hawai‘i, 1943.

Opposite: Memorial tablets for Hawai‘i soldiers killed in action during World War II.

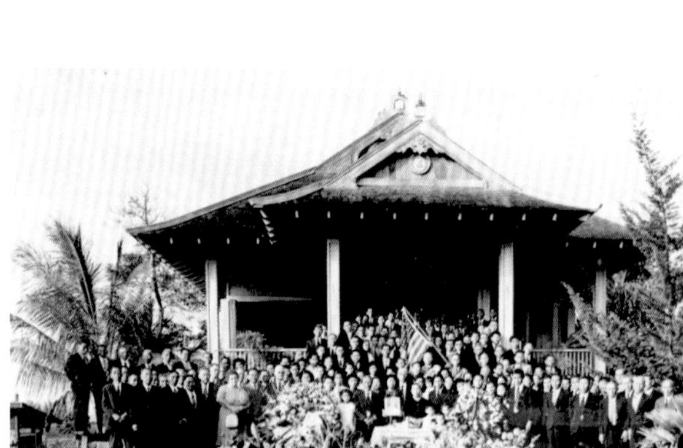

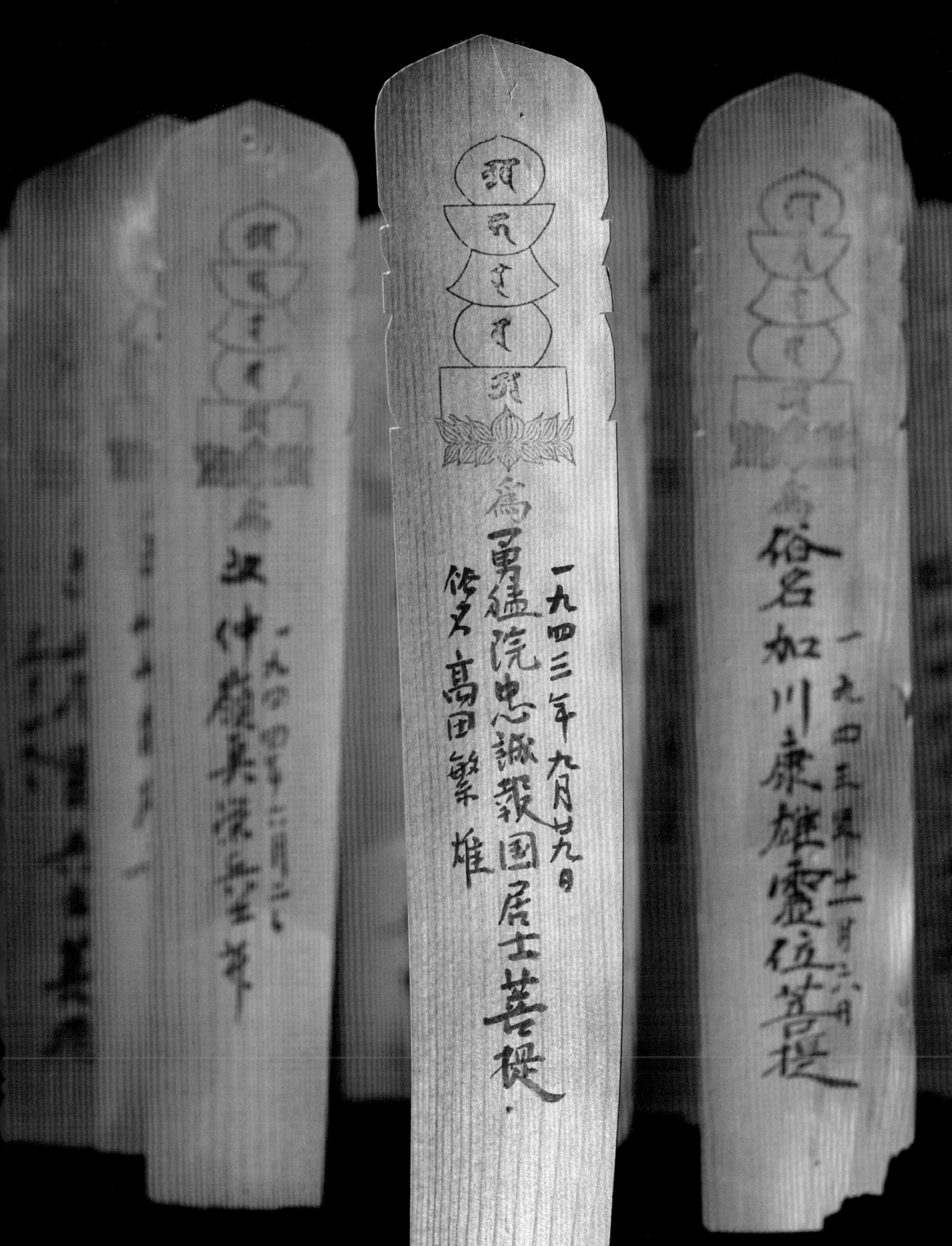

為
勇邁院忠誠報国居士菩提
一九四三年九月廿九日
修文　高田繁雄
為
俗名加川康雄霊位菩提
一九四五年十二月

Chaplains and the 100th/442nd Regimental Combat Team

Properly memorializing those who died in combat was a priority not just on the home front, but on the front lines as well. Although the majority of the segregated 100th/442nd Regimental Combat Team were Buddhist soldiers, all five chaplains associated with the unit were Christian. The longest serving chaplain in the unit, Israel Yost, noted that while he never attempted to conduct a Buddhist religious rite, he would pray "with any soldier who wanted a prayer."

Nisei soldiers who lost their lives invariably ended up in Christian graves, regardless of whether they were Christian or Buddhist. One such burial site was described by a medic in a letter to his wife as "a bare new plot of ground where many of our boys lie … and white crosses will dot that acre." Congregationalist Hiro Higuchi, a Nisei from Hawai'i who was assigned to the Second Battalion as chaplain, wrote in a letter to his wife: "We don't get to perform the funeral service as we are at the front all the time and the bodies are interred in the rear echelon. However, some chaplain takes care of the funeral services. We go back when we can to say a prayer for them."

Despite many appeals that a Buddhist chaplain be assigned to the Japanese American unit, Assistant Secretary of War John McCloy ultimately ruled against doing so. According to the Japanese American Citizens League's Mike Masaoka, McCloy believed that "since there was widespread suspicion of, as well as ignorance about Asian religions, it would be better public relations to approve only Christian chaplains for the 442nd."

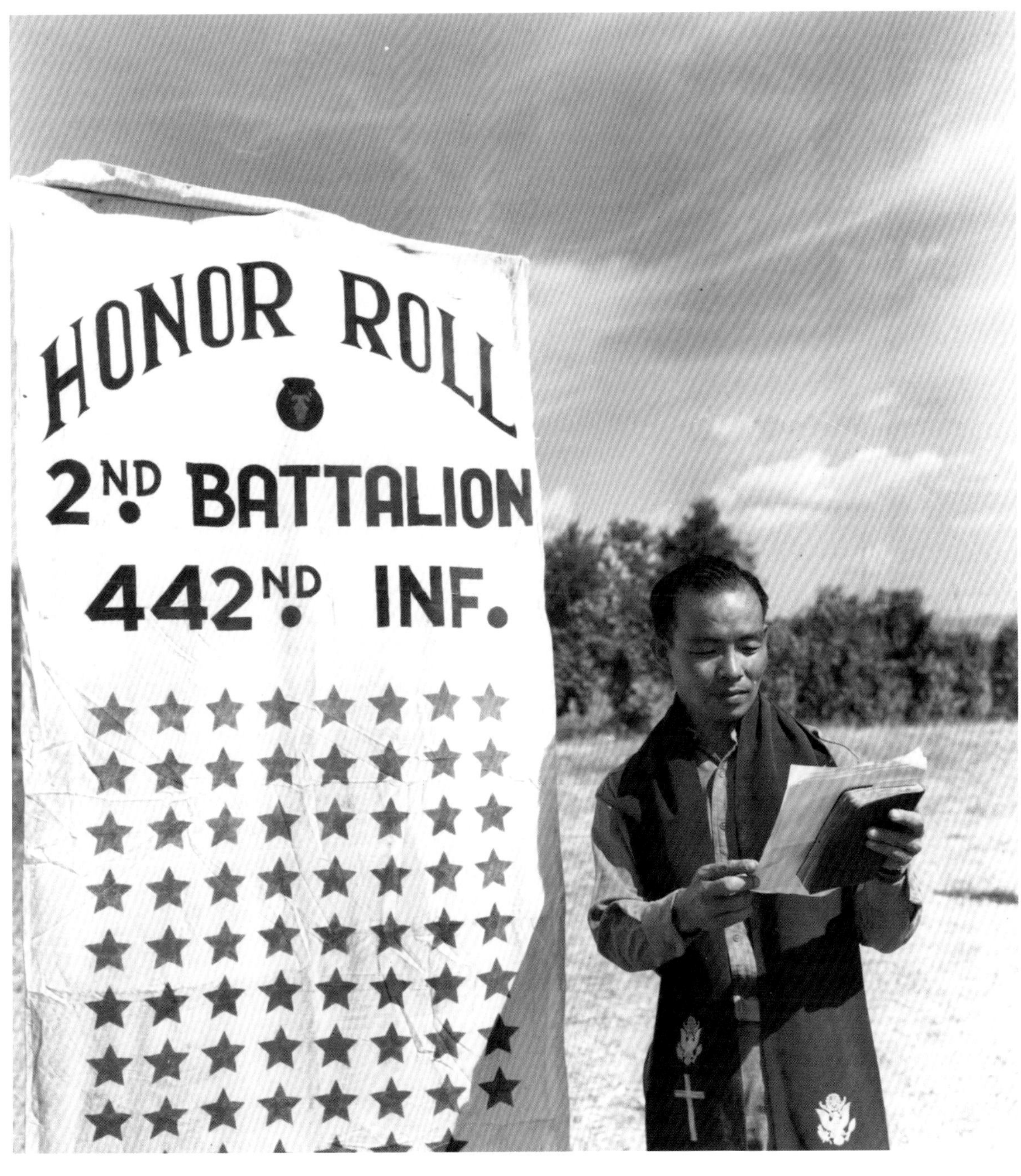

442nd RCT Chaplain
Hiro Higuchi reads a list
of casualties from
his regiment, European
Theater, 1944.

Dog Tags and Religious Affiliation

The Army's practice during World War II was to stamp the dog tags of soldiers with their religious affiliation so that appropriate last rites could be administered if they were to die in combat. As the war in Europe progressed, soldiers and their families began calling for the US Army to officially recognize Buddhism as a religious affiliation; at the time, the only available options were "P" for Protestant, "C" for Catholic, "H" for Hebrew (or Jewish), and "blank" for no religious affiliation. Buddhist soldiers were generally assigned "P" for "Protestant" as a matter of expediency.

One Hawai'i-based volunteer recollected being asked about his background while reporting to the draft board. When he replied "Japanese," the person filling out the intake form corrected him: "the army's classification for us was 'Mongolian.'" When asked about his religion, the newly inducted soldier answered, "Buddhist," but was informed the army would be classifying him as "Protestant." Throughout his time in the army, this Japanese American Buddhist was thus formally deemed a "Mongolian-Protestant."

Another Nisei veteran recalled that when he asked that his dog tag be marked "Buddhist," a "scornful Caucasian officer [said]: 'Let me tell you that we don't have the Buddhist religion in the American army. Pick another one.' [I] then chose Protestant, and when the officer asked why I selected Protestant, [I] said, 'Because I protest!'" The angry officer then assigned the young Buddhist soldier to latrine duty.

Sutra Lost in Dog Tags
Gene Oishi

In 1953, I enlisted in the Army to lose myself like a masked, anonymous anybody and nobody in a Mardi Gras parade. I was twenty, eight years after our release from an American concentration camp, and still unsure of who or what I was. My family was Buddhist, but when asked for my religion, I would always say Protestant. It seemed simpler that way. No explanation or apology needed. After basic training, I was assigned to an Army band in France, where I had ample time for desultory reading, mostly fiction. But mixed in were works on religion and philosophy—books I stumbled on in the post library and the PX. Among these was a book called *The Wisdom of the Buddha*. I wasn't sure why I bought it. It stood in my wall locker unread for months.

We had monthly inspections in the band. We would clean the windows, mop the floors, make the bunks wrinkle free and airtight, polish our boots and instruments, and stand at attention next to our open footlockers with all our toiletries placed with military precision in their assigned places. Most important was the Bible, placed straight and tall at the center. I don't know what got into me. On an impulse one day, just before the commanding officer entered the barrack, I replaced the Bible with *The Wisdom of the Buddha*.

The C.O. looked at the Buddhist text, then quietly asked to see my dog tags. After glancing at it, he continued his inspection without a word. I got the message. For the next inspection, the Holy Bible was in its rightful place. As I look back at what I now see as a milestone on my road to self-discovery and acceptance, I see that moment as one small baby step toward being at peace with who and what I am. Years later, after my retirement, I began an intensive and fulfilling study of Buddhism, and have continued my search for my identity and "The Wisdom of the Buddha" ever since.

Opposite, top: Dog tags belonging to brothers Calvin and Joji "George" Saito, both showing "P" for Protestant.

Opposite, bottom: George Saito's YMCA membership card and Methodist Church membership card.

The Saito family were longtime members of the Los Angeles Japanese Methodist church before and after World War II. The brothers were killed in action months apart in the European theater.

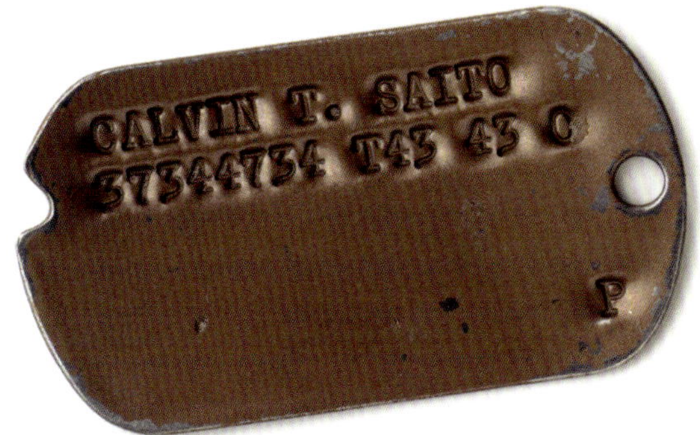

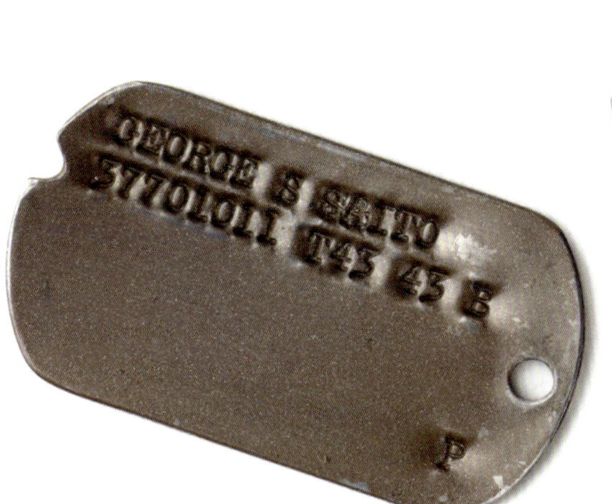

MEMBERSHIP CARD

JAPANESE BRANCH

Young Men's Christian Association

OF LOS ANGELES

certify that GEORGE SAITO

is a member of the Association

for the year of 19 42

2 YEARS CONTINUOUS MEMBERSHIP

_______________ Chairman   _______________ Secretary

Certificate of Christian Church Membership

This is to certify that George S. Saito

whose signature appears below is a member in good standing of the

Japanese Methodist Church.

Rev. Y. Yamaka PASTOR

ADDRESS 1517 W. 36 St.   ADDRESS 3600 S. Normandie

Los Angeles, Calif.   L. A.

DATE March 8, 1942   PHONE Pa. 6655

153   COUNTER SIGNED

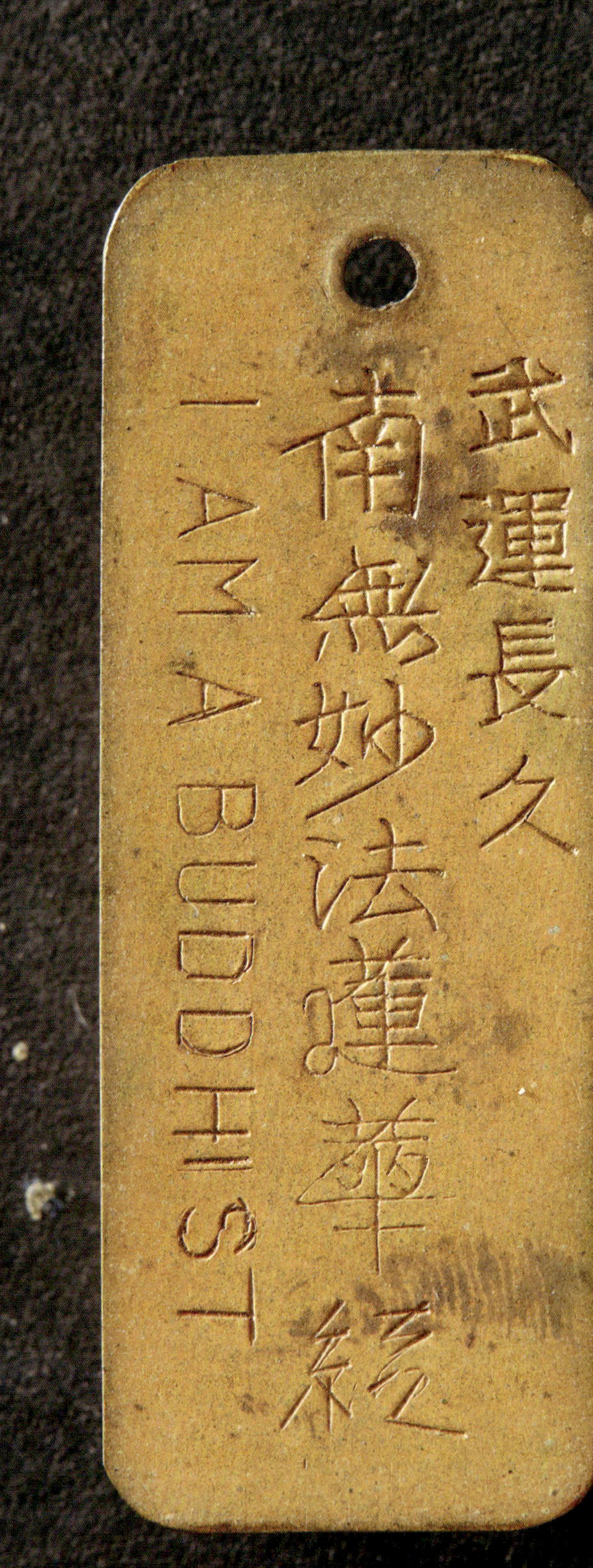
武運長久
南無妙法蓮華経
I AM A BUDDHIST

Faith Etched in Steel
Mikoto Yoshida

Name, serial number, blood type, religion: these would be used to identify me should something happen during my three combat deployments to Afghanistan. I had two dog tags with this information threaded around my belt loop and tucked into my back pocket. I attached a third to the laces of my left boot as a precautionary measure, should the rest of my body be unidentifiable. I barely noticed these pieces of metal that I carried with me as if they were part of my own body. They weren't meant for me; they were meant for someone who would be trying to identify me.

During my stint in the Marine Corps, and before that, in the Naval Academy, I had read numerous books about the history and tactics of war, trying to ingest the lived experiences of those who had gone through combat before me and what it means to be a Marine. I had pored over accounts of the Greek infantry in the Battle of Thermopylae, German trench warfare in World War I, the island-hopping campaigns of World War II, and the killing fields of Vietnam. I never learned about American servicemen, who, like me, were Japanese Americans. It wasn't until 2019 that I discovered that the Fort Sill Army Base where I had trained for seven months had been used as a detention site for people of Japanese ancestry following the attacks on Pearl Harbor. Nor did I learn during my time as a Marine about the 442nd Regimental Combat Team of the US Army, a unit composed entirely of Japanese American soldiers, many of whom had gone off to fight while their family members remained behind barbed wire. This unit of Japanese American soldiers fought so fiercely overseas for the freedoms they had been denied back home that they remain to this day the highest decorated unit of its size in American military history.

A Nisei veteran myself, I, too, had gone to war for my country, but without even knowing who I really was or who had come before me. I had been so conditioned by the absence of people like me in my textbooks that it had not even occurred to me to entertain the possibility of heroes such as these.

While monuments have been built to generals who fought to maintain the enslavement of an entire people on American soil, this history of Japanese American heroism, along with the contributions of other men and women of color, have been largely erased from the lexicon of military heroes taught about in the military.

We need to shout to be heard in order to survive. Despite the rust and wear and tear on this dog tag, the simple yet bold statement "I am a Buddhist" reminds us to hold on to who we are, to etch it in steel if we must, and to fight.

Opposite: Handmade US Army dog tag made by Buddhist soldier during World War II.

Church Women Ask:

How Can WE help Japanese American Evacuees?

By Gracia D. Booth

5

SOLIDARITY

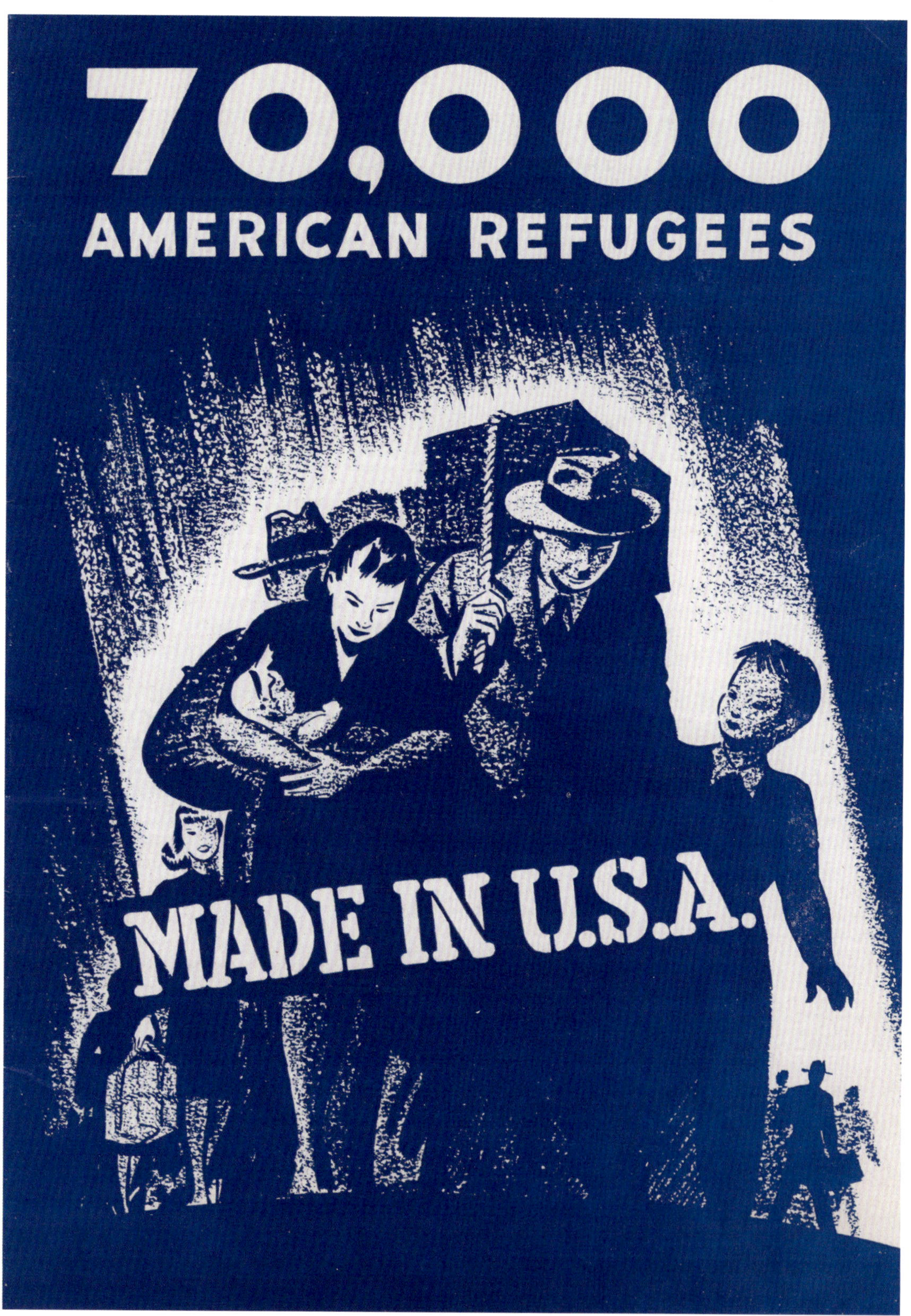

70,000
AMERICAN REFUGEES
MADE IN U.S.A.

When Japanese Americans were forcibly removed from their homes, they were shocked to realize how few people stood up in their defense. The handful of individuals and organizations who did actively pursue solidarity with Japanese Americans were often deeply religious.

For them, solidarity as a spiritual practice took many forms: protecting churches and temples against vandalism; transporting household and religious items from storage sites to the camps where they were needed; and helping procure educational and employment opportunities for those allowed to take advantage of them. After the war, when Japanese Americans returning to the Pacific Coast faced hostility and racial prejudice, they helped create church- and temple-based hostels and assisted with the purchase of food and supplies.

The few non-Japanese Americans who chose to stand up for justice during and in the immediate aftermath of the war often did so at considerable personal cost. Not only did they use their own savings to travel to the often remote camps at a time when gas was being rationed, they were also often harassed and accused of giving aid and comfort to the enemy.

Nevertheless, these religious leaders and laypeople held firm in their belief that doing the right thing over the popular thing was always the correct choice. Their acts of compassion reminded the incarcerees that they were not alone.

Opposite and page118: Booklets published by Christian organizations advocating on behalf of incarcerated Japanese Americans.

Pre-Incarceration Support for Japanese Americans

The vast majority of people who testified at the Tolan Commission hearings that took place prior to the forced removal were hostile towards Japanese Americans. Those who stood up to defend them were, almost without exception, deeply religious. Quakers, former missionaries to Japan, and a lone convert Buddhist priest defended the Japanese Americans they had known. But despite their best efforts to frame the argument against incarceration as a moral one, they were ultimately unable to stop the incarceration from happening.

Reverend Ronald Lane Latimer

Ordained in July 1940 as a Shingon Buddhist priest, Reverend Ronald Lane Latimer was serving the Koyasan Beikoku Betsuin in Los Angeles when the war broke out. When the Tolan Commission came through Los Angeles, he volunteered to testify. In his remarks, he argued emphatically for the loyalty of the Japanese Americans with whom he had worked.

After the forced removal, he continued his support of Japanese Americans by making frequent trips to Santa Anita Assembly Center and later to the Heart Mountain and Poston concentration camps, encouraging Buddhists to maintain their faith from behind barbed wire.

Azalia Emma Peet

The only non-Japanese American to support the community during the Tolan Commission hearings in Portland was Azalia Emma Peet, a Methodist missionary in Japan from 1916 to 1941. In her testimony, she appealed to a sense of ethics and practicality. When her fellow Oregonians were sent to the camp in Nyssa, Oregon, she relocated there as well, choosing to live alongside them.

Below, left: News coverage of Rev. Ronald Latimer's ordination ceremony at Los Angeles Koyasan Beikoku Betsuin that appeared in the *Rafu shimpo*, one of the Japanese American newspapers in Los Angeles, on August 25, 1940.

Below, right: Azalia Emma Peet spent twenty-five years in Japan as a Christian missionary and left only when she had to because of the outbreak of war. Pictured here in Orange, California, July 1945.

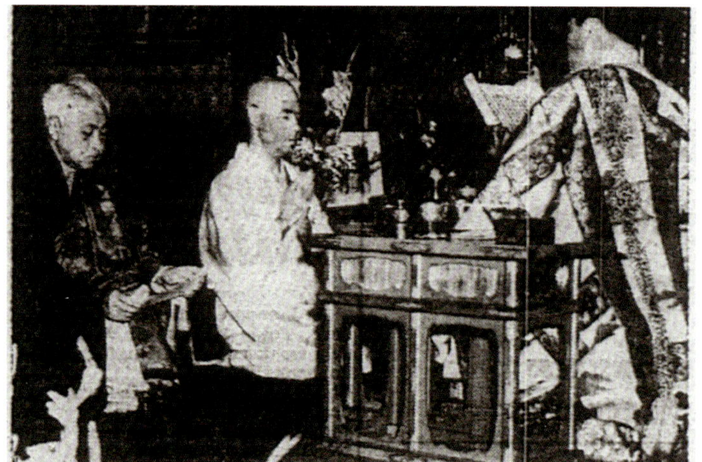

AMERICAN PRIEST — R e v. Latimer Ren-jyo is pictured as he was ordained Shingon priest by Bishop Setsu S. Takahashi of the Koyasan Shingon temple in a special ceremony on July 20. At the left is Rev. Nyogen Senzaki, who assisted in the rites.

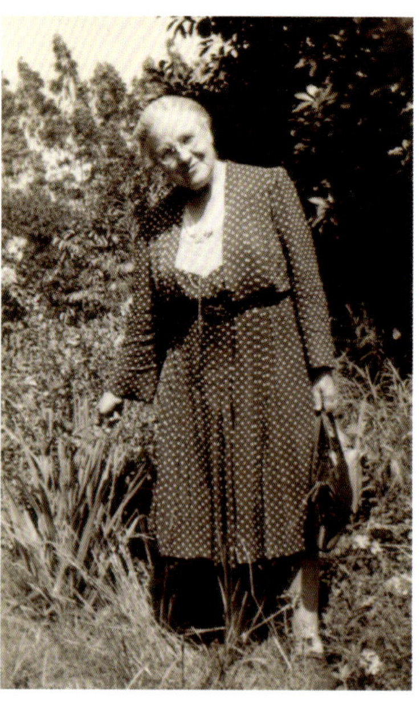

There was a charge, which I have read many times in the press, that the Buddhist temples encourage the worship of the Japanese Emperor, and many other statements equally fantastic, and as an American citizen, and a very loyal one, I wanted to correct some of these errors in your records.... I have not only been in my own temple, which happens to be the second largest in the Japanese section, but I have spoken and taken part in activities both with the older Japanese and with the Japanese-Americans in other temples. I would certainly emphatically deny that those temples encourage any disloyalty; quite the contrary.... However, I want to say that Buddhism and Shintoism are completely unconnected; that Buddhism in India is an Indian religion; in China it is a Chinese religion; in Japan it is a Japanese religion; and in America it is an American religion.

— Reverend Ronald Lane Latimer, convert Buddhist Priest
  at Los Angeles Tolan Commission hearings

To put 126,000 Japanese on the Pacific coast into concentration camps, 85,000 of whom are American citizens, educated in the democratic schools of America, would deprive Caucasians in this area of much-needed food for the defense program. It will put the burden of their support on the already overtaxed and overburdened taxpayers. It will cause a serious social problem, to say nothing of taking from 85,000 American citizens their civil liberties. All this, besides causing untold suffering among our Japanese neighbors.

— Azalia Emma Peet, former Christian missionary to Japan
  at Portland (OR) Tolan Commission hearings

The Work of Solidarity: Convert Buddhist Priests

Despite the fact that the majority of Japanese Americans were Buddhist, only a small handful of Buddhists in the world outside of camp—all recent converts—worked actively to assist them. A number of individuals who had been ordained as priests before the war—including Sunya Pratt, Ernest Hunt, Julius Goldwater, Bhikunni Dhammadena, Frank Boden Udale, and Ronald Lane Latimer—worked hard to protect the now-shuttered temples and helped transport items that were stored there to the camps where they were needed. These non-Japanese clergy were also instrumental in delivering English-language service books and other materials helpful to Buddhist study and practice. In their dharma talks, they encouraged Young Buddhist Association members to be confident of their right to be American citizens as Buddhists.

```
[I]t is the sum total of the thoughts of
the individuals that comprise the nation,
their inmost feelings, their lack
of understanding, or their knowledge,
that direct their nation's destiny.
```

— Sunya Pratt at a convention of
  Northern California Young Buddhists in 1941

Sunya Pratt
Michihiro Ama

Gladys Pratt (1898–1986), better known as Sunya Pratt, is an extraordinary figure in the history of American Buddhism. Ordained in 1936, she was the first ever fully recognized female Buddhist priest of European descent in the world, and thus the only woman amongst the small handful of convert Buddhist priests who provided invaluable help to Japanese Americans throughout their World War II incarceration. In addition to obtaining permission from the US Army to run the Dharma School for Nisei Buddhists at Camp Harmony (Puyallup Assembly Center) in Washington State, she protected the household belongings of hundreds of Japanese American families that were being stored at the Tacoma Buddhist Church, which she served until her death.

Pratt's message—that individual karma leads to a collective karma, which in turn shapes the karma of a country—still resonates with us today. Herself an immigrant, she was sympathetic to Japanese Americans not just because of their shared faith, but also perhaps because she understood what it was like to be considered an outsider. At a time when the United States continues to be challenged by racial discrimination, ethnic exclusion, gender inequality, and religious intolerance, Sunya Pratt's example still resonates.

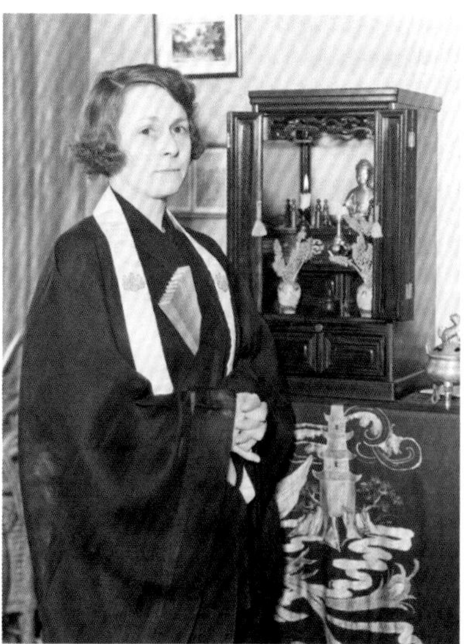

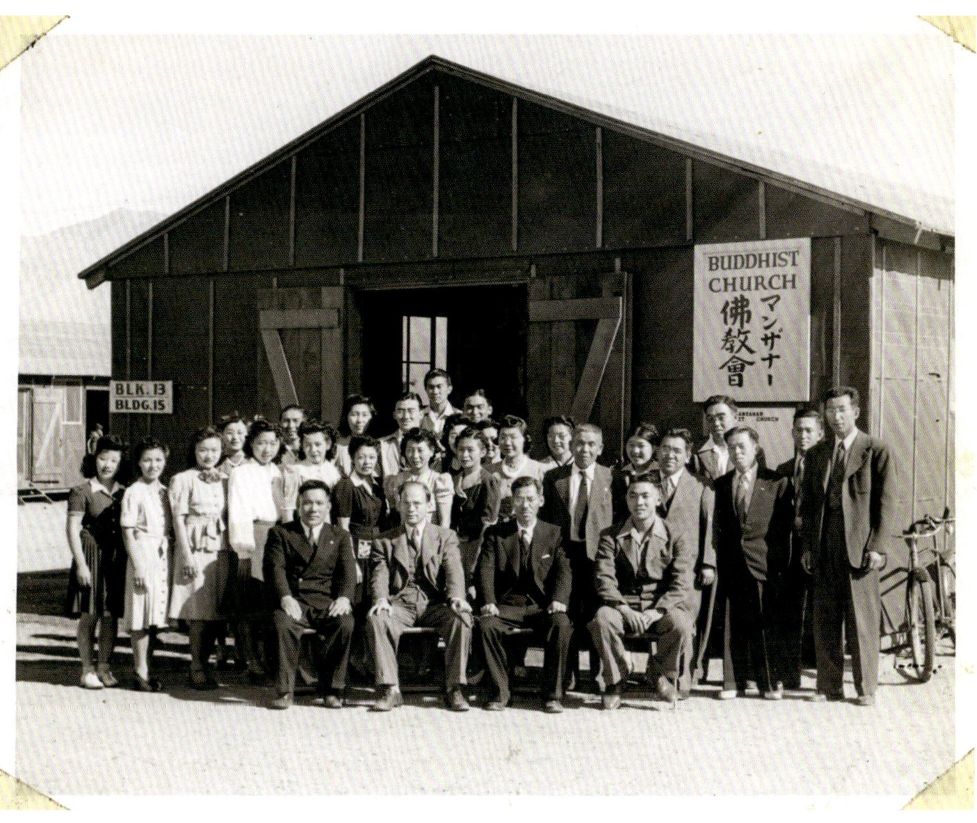

Julius Goldwater
Michihiro Ama

Julius A. Goldwater (1908–2001) ordained as a Buddhist priest in the Nishi Hongwanji tradition in 1934. One of the earliest non-Asian Buddhist clergy in America, Goldwater is perhaps the most well-known of the convert Buddhist priests who assisted incarcerated Japanese Americans during World War II. According to his obituary in the *Los Angeles Times*, Goldwater "traveled to [concentration camps] in California, Arizona, Wyoming, Colorado, and Arkansas, bearing gifts, Buddhist study materials, and news of the outside world. He watched over internees' homes, preventing the illegal sale of one by alerting the FBI. He wrangled with suspicious officials, trying to make them understand that Buddhism was autonomous and not connected with the Japanese government."

For the duration of the war, Goldwater took care of three temples in Los Angeles, ensuring that Senshin Buddhist Temple, Gardena Buddhist Church, and the Los Angeles Hompa Hongwanji Buddhist Temple were protected from looting and vandalism. In the postwar period, he helped set up the hostel at Senshin Buddhist Temple that provided Japanese Americans with much-needed housing at a time when lingering anti-Japanese racism made finding a place to live difficult. When grocery stores refused to sell to returning internees, he would buy and distribute food for them.

These efforts on behalf of the Japanese community got him called "Jap lover" and led to attacks on his own home. But he continued to remain a steadfast advocate for a multi-ethnic American Buddhist future, stating that in Buddhism "there can be no thought of discrimination in sect, race, or color." For Goldwater, American Buddhism needed to reflect the full diversity of the United States if it was to live up to its ideal of equality.

Opposite: Sunya Pratt, shown here when she was ordained as the first female Buddhist priest of European descent in 1936, was born in England as Gladys Pratt. Serving the Tacoma Buddhist Church, she had a particularly close relationship with English-speaking Nisei Buddhists.

Above: Rev. Julius Goldwater and Rev. Nagatomi in front of Buddhist church in the Manzanar concentration camp, California, ca. 1943. Photo by Toyo Miyatake.

The Work of Solidarity:
Catholic and Mainline Protestant Clergy

For Japanese American Catholics, pastoral care was provided by priests who even before the war had been assigned to serve them. Though small in number, they provided critical religious and practical assistance. Father Leo Tibesar followed his Japanese American parishioners to the Minidoka concentration camp, taking up residence nearby so he could continue to minister to them, while Father Hugh Lavery traveled to all ten concentration camps to conduct masses and otherwise offer support. Brother Theophane Walsh worked to help Japanese Americans resettle in Chicago, while Father Edward J. Flanagan, the renowned founder of Boys Town, sponsored Nisei to come to the home for abandoned youth in Nebraska.

Father Hugh Lavery
Jonathan van Harmelen

The story of the incarceration cannot be told without mentioning Father Hugh Lavery (1895–1970). As the head of Los Angeles' Maryknoll Mission and the school it ran at St. Francis Xavier from 1927 to 1956, Father Lavery oversaw the expansion of the school and the transformation of the Maryknoll Mission from a religious center into a cultural hub for the Japanese American community of Los Angeles.

Lavery's support for Japanese Americans during the incarceration embodied his devotion to principles of spiritual justice. Immediately following the outbreak of war on December 7, 1941, Father Lavery spent months working with the Japanese American community. He hosted meetings of Japanese American leaders at the Maryknoll center and, in February 1942, testified on behalf of Issei interned by the FBI at Fort Missoula, Montana. When he challenged Wartime Civil Control Administration (WCCA) director Karl Bendetsen on the need to send orphans of partial Japanese descent to camp, Bendetsen replied that anyone with even "one drop of Japanese blood in them must all go to camp."

Father Lavery spent the next four years traveling to the ten WRA concentration camps that held Japanese Americans, providing spiritual guidance, negotiating for the release of Japanese American families, and helping Nisei students enroll in Catholic schools. When WRA leaders announced that the camps were closing, Lavery shepherded Japanese American families back to Los Angeles and helped them find housing amid widespread prejudice.

In 1949, remembering the bitter experience of his exchange with Bendetsen, Lavery wrote an open letter to President Harry Truman to protest Bendetsen's appointment as Assistant Secretary of the Army. Shortly before his death, Lavery received the Order of the Sacred Treasure from the Emperor of Japan. Although he was not the only Maryknoller to support the Japanese American community, Lavery's many actions during the war and after give proof of his strong moral compass.

Below: Father Hugh Lavery visits the Maryknoll congregation in the Manzanar concentration camp, ca. 1943.

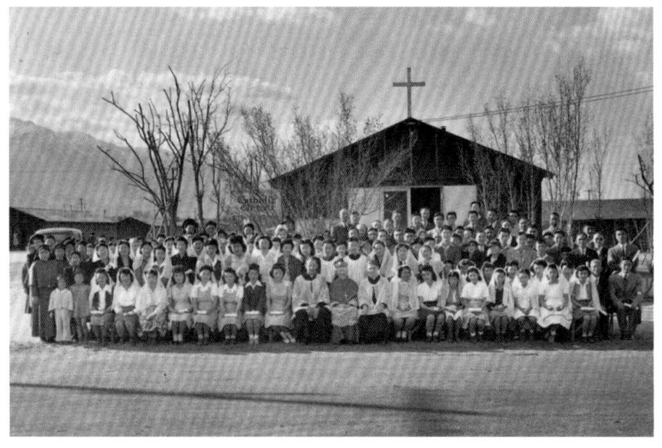

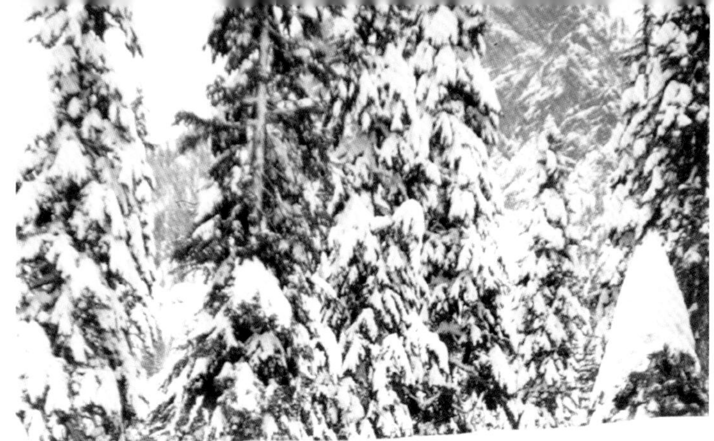

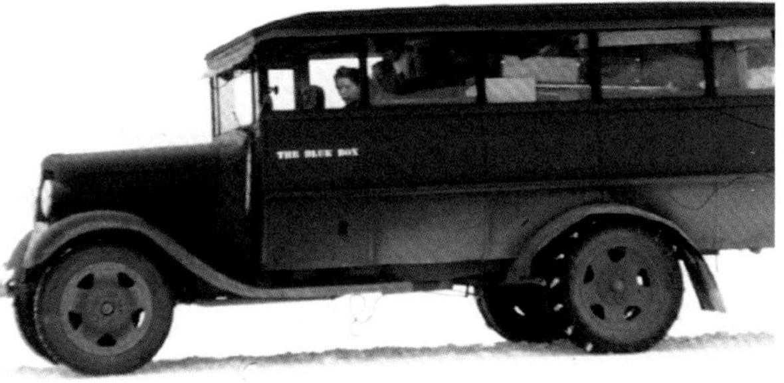

The decision made by Reverend Emery Andrews, a Baptist pastor who served the Seattle Japanese Baptist Church, to move his entire family to Idaho so he could continue to minister to his congregants while they were incarcerated at Minidoka is one of the more remarkable acts of wartime solidarity with Japanese Americans. Despite the more than 600 miles between Seattle and Minidoka, he made over fifty round trips with a church bus, incurring enormous cost to himself at a time when gas was being rationed.

The Blue Box
Brooks Andrews

Writing about the Blue Box, the old jalopy used by my father to bring goods to Minidoka throughout the war, is like reminiscing about an old friend. Conversations regarding camp life always included the Blue Box. Smiles and laughter brought life to a very important character that played a significant part in bringing hope in a practical way to those languishing behind barbed wire.

The Blue Box made an average of a trip and a half each month between Minidoka and Seattle to aid and cheer the displaced residents. By the end of 1945, my father had completed fifty-six round trips. It was a rare occasion when Reverend Andrews left Minidoka without a request for a sewing machine, a pair of boots, a baby crib, or other comforts of home that had been stored in the gymnasium of the Japanese Baptist Church in Seattle. Sagebrush, heat, dust, and ticks were no accoutrements for a home away from home, and the incarcerated longed for some semblance of the lives they had left behind in Seattle. These recipients of Christian love were not just

Above: Rev. Emery Andrews drove "the Blue Box" bus between Seattle and the Minidoka concentration camp over fifty times during the war, transporting items that had been stored by Japanese Americans at the Seattle Japanese Baptist Church.

members of the Baptist faith: my father aided the entire Japanese American community, no matter their religious background.

The Blue Box was a symbol of love and hope for those in Minidoka during the war. But for those prejudiced against the "Japs," as they were called, it represented a kind of treason. Epithets such as "turncoat" and "Jap lover" were frequently bandied about. This persecution extended beyond words. It was not unusual for Reverend Andrews to be refused service at gas stations. Visits from the FBI were the norm, and he was once thrown out of a café in Twin Falls. A local of Twin Falls who bought the house our family had been renting forced us to vacate it and move on.

I often reflect upon the origin of the Blue Box: the truck chassis of a Chinese Baptist Church bus that was no longer in use had been joined together with the passenger compartment of an old Japanese Baptist Church bus to birth the Blue Box. The result was the physical representation of Christian ministry in action: one was of no use without the other.

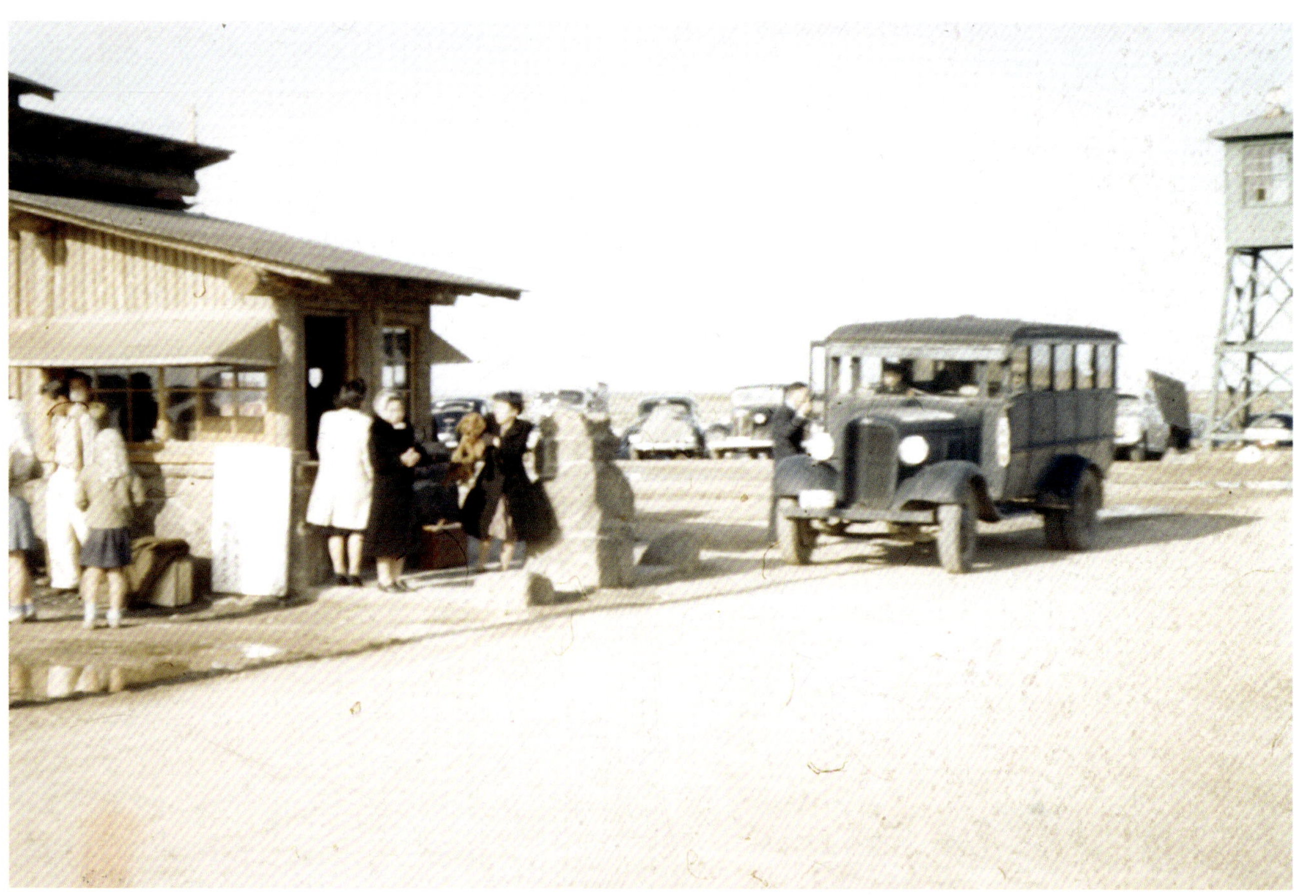

Above: The Blue Box pulls up to the front gate of the Minidoka concentration camp, ca. 1943.

128

Quaker Support for Japanese Americans

Quakers were by far the most outspoken and engaged advocates for Japanese Americans during World War II. Despite their relatively small numbers throughout the US, and their relative lack of membership amongst Japanese Americans, they played an outsized role in assisting the community, regardless of religious affiliation, both in camp and in resettlement. They were instrumental in opening a dozen hostels for those who were able to find their way to the Midwest and the East Coast during the war, including the very first resettler-era hostel in Chicago in February of 1943.

Some of the first Japanese Americans allowed to leave camp were college-aged students who found institutions of higher education outside the Western Defense Command zone willing to accept them as transfer students. After vetting by camp authorities, the resettled students were assisted by numerous Christian organizations and colleges sympathetic to their situation. Most notably, the Quaker-affiliated American Friends Service Committee created the National Japanese American Student Relocation Council (NJASRC) in May 1942, which ultimately placed more than 4,000 students in over 600 colleges and universities.

In addition to students, Japanese Americans who could find sponsors willing to provide employment in the so-called "free zones" were also allowed to leave camp. The majority of those who managed to do so were Christian, in part because those who listed their religious affiliation as Christian in loyalty questionnaires administered in camp were given preference. By contrast, Buddhists were penalized, and those who identified as Shinto were denied leave clearance entirely.

American Friends Service Committee: Solidarity in Action
Anne M. Blankenship

No organization did more to exemplify the spirit of conscientious solidarity with Japanese Americans during World War II than the Society of Friends, more commonly known as Quakers. Their social aid organization, the American Friends Service Committee (AFSC), challenged the injustice of the forced relocation of Japanese Americans in courts, transferred students to inland universities, arranged jobs, and opened hostels for those who couldn't find housing upon leaving the camps. These efforts made by the Quakers on behalf of Japanese Americans during World War II and the immediate postwar period—and their choice to immediately and consistently stand for justice while also performing innumerable smaller and more humble tasks, such as preparing baby clothing for incarcerated mothers—made a deep impression on the Japanese American community.

When the AFSC and its leaders failed in their efforts to persuade the US government against the incarceration of Japanese Americans, they professed an obligation to do what they could to mitigate the injustice, vowing to share the "suffering and sacrifice" of Japanese Americans. Their goal was not just to alleviate the symptoms of this racial and religious harm, but to do what they could to remedy the problem.

Within two weeks of the attack on Pearl Harbor, the AFSC opened an office in Seattle, the first of several organized

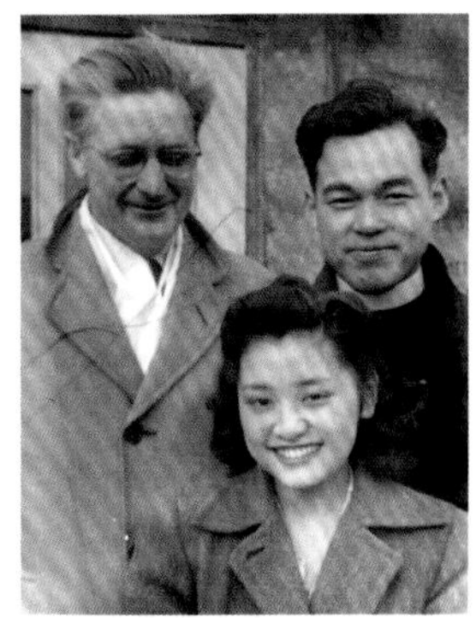

Above: Floyd Schmoe stands with Yoshi Asaba and Rev. Joseph Kitagawa while visiting the Minidoka concentration camp, Hunt, Idaho, ca. 1944.

specifically to lighten the burdens faced by Japanese Americans. Quakers from all backgrounds put their careers on hold to rectify the injustice. One, botany professor Floyd Schmoe, quit his job at the University of Washington to run the Seattle branch of the AFSC. Schmoe helped young Nisei avoid or leave the camps by finding universities to accept them and even hid students under blankets in the back seat of his car to drive them to the train station after curfew. As he later recalled, the "only crime" the students had committed "was that they had not been born white."

AFSC leaders continually questioned the ethics of collaborating with the US government on projects such as student relocation, even as they resolved to do whatever they could to help the innocent victims of this injustice. While some Quakers joined the AFSC like Schmoe, others took positions as teachers or administrators with the War Relocation Authority itself, reasoning that by doing so, they might be able to alleviate prejudice and unnecessary cruelty in the camps. Still others refused to offer any such aid. These Friends argued that caring for Japanese Americans would be doing what was in essence the government's job, so any support they might give would only serve to facilitate the injustice being perpetrated. Walking a fine line between these two perspectives, the AFSC stayed true to the Quaker commitment to open debate and individual discernment while remaining cautious to not do anything that could be construed as supporting the government's orders.

Below: Pamphlets published by Christian organizations advocating on behalf of incarcerated Japanese Americans, including during their resettlement outside of the camps.

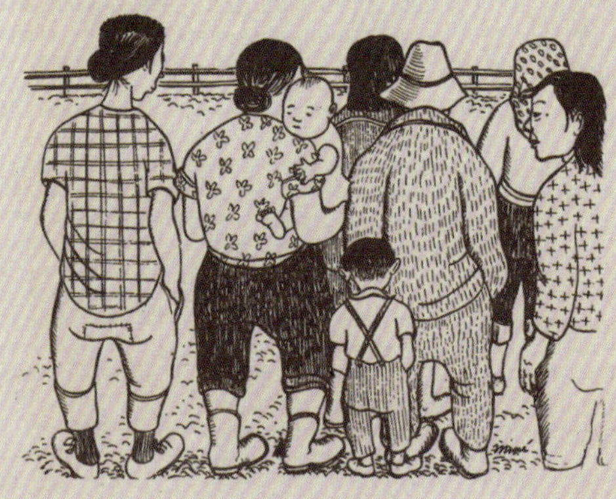

We Were So Alone,
Except for the Quakers

Karen Tei Yamashita

In the last years of her life, my mother Asako spoke more openly of the trauma of the war years and her incarceration at Topaz. She remembered how few people came to their aid, how few spoke out to protest that injustice. *We were so alone,* she said, *except for the Quakers.* And there was also the Fellowship of Reconciliation (FOR). I thought about this, about how a group of people under a spiritual and moral banner might come forward in a time of war hysteria, risking personal safety to act against the fury of public hatred, political manipulation, and unjust laws. What moral compass directs individuals to care beyond themselves for others? Was it, in the case of the Quakers and the FOR, their pacifism? In the story of war, what is pacifism and who is the pacifist? The deeper American history of these institutions is Christian and abolitionist, equal regard for all human life, connecting to the philosophy of Henry David Thoreau — the right to civil protest and nonviolent direct action. Pacifism: not passive denial, but an active choice of conscience. To arm oneself against an enemy, not with the gun but with the mind and the body.

I discovered in our family archive of correspondence and documents that our aunt Kay Yamashita was the pivot that connected our family to outside friendships with folks of conscience and kindness. Among seven family siblings, the youngest sister Kay was an unlikely pivot, in 1942, a recent graduate of Cal Berkeley, kid sister, naïve and idealistic. But by odd circumstances, when the entire population of Japanese Americans in the San Francisco Bay Area were imprisoned at Tanforan, on July 4, 1942, she was the lone "oriental" at a conference organized at Mills College by Caleb Foote of the Fellowship of Reconciliation. At this ten-day conference, convened to discuss, among many topics, Japanese American removal, Kay would meet, among many influential progressive folks, African American pastor Howard Thurman and Quakers Tom Bodine and Joe Conard. And in the following months, she also met and lived for a short time in Hidden Villa, ranch home of Quakers Josephine and Frank Duveneck.

The resonances of these connections are significant. Caleb Foote will go on to protest the racist injustice of Japanese American imprisonment, writing what is an astute legal dissent, with photographs by Dorothea Lange, in the pamphlet *Outcasts!* At the behest of FOR leader A.J. Muste, Howard Thurman and Alfred Fisk will found the multiracial Church for the Fellowship of All Peoples on Post Street in the emptied neighborhood of San Francisco Nihonmachi Japantown. And Quakers, Tom Bodine and Joe Conard with the help of the Duvenecks will organize the National Japanese American Student Relocation Council to help some 4,600 incarcerated students pursue higher education in over 600 institutions across the country. It could not be known then, but each of these actions held hope for the future.

Kay rejoined her imprisoned family at Tanforan and Topaz but was finally granted leave to work in Philadelphia, eventual headquarters for the Quaker project of nisei student relocation (NJASRC), under the leadership of John Nason. Thus Kay became engaged in meaningful work inspired by Quaker and FOR friends. In these war years, Kay and fellow staff workers communicated, in hundreds of letters back and forth, with young nisei students, working for their release from camps to secure placement in colleges and universities across the country. She also wrote to support, commiserate, cajole, and advise young people who'd left their families behind in prison camps to face a world of distrust and racial prejudice.

The practice of pacifism, of peacemaking, in what were the darkest times for Japanese Americans, was a gift of courage and light, upholding the right to protest, to seek justice, to face the future.

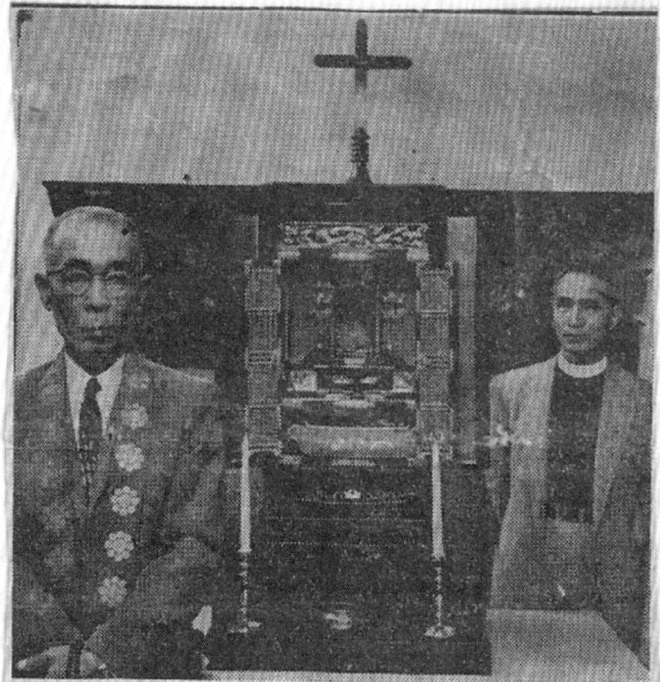

Buddhists and Christians worship in same room

★ ★ ★ ★ ★ ★ ★ ★ ★

TOLERANCE IN RELIGION

Buddhists, Christians Share Same Room

Buddhists and Christians of Japanese background worship in the same room at 2200 Blaisdell Av.

Their sharing of facilities in the Japanese-American Community center there is "very unique," according to the Rev. Andrew N. Otani, director.

The Twin Cities Buddhist association conducts a Sunday school — in English — at the center at 9:30 a.m. each Sunday.

It sponsors an adult service the second Saturday evening of the month—in Japanese. A Buddhist minister from Chicago comes here to conduct.

The Twin Cities' Japanese Christian church, of which Mr. Otani is pastor, has Japanese service at 11 a.m. each Sunday and prayer meeting at 7:30 p.m. each Wednesday.

When the Buddhist services are held, a portable Buddhist altar is brought in and placed below a fireplace mantel on which there is a permanent Christian cross.

The inter-denominational Christian congregation has its altar at the other end of the room. It is covered by folding doors when not in use.

The center is owned by the Protestant Episcopal diocese of Minnesota, which also pays part of the salary of Mr. Otani, an Episcopal priest.

It is supported by the community at large and is "open to anyone who wants to use," Mr. Otani said.

Some 250 families in the center's membership help finance its operation.

The center hopes to raise one-third of its $3,000 annual budget at its annual bazaar in the center Sept. 21. Scheduled from 12 noon to 6 p.m., the bazaar will feature Japanese foods (sukiyaki, tempura, sushi, rice cakes) and Japanese flower arrangements.

Besides the Buddhist and Christian churches, the center is also the headquarters of other organizations.

These include the American Indians, Inc.; the Rainbow club, a social group that includes Negroes, Orientals, Indians and Caucausians, and the United Citizens' league, a group concerned with the political education of the Nisei which also works against racial discrimination.

Religious Cooperation in Midwest Resettlement

Those who left camp during the war tended to end up in the Midwest where prejudices against Japanese American were not as severe. Those Japanese American Buddhists who managed to secure permission to leave camp were constricted by WRA policy that prohibited the formation of Japanese-only organizations. The practical effect of this was that, while Japanese American Christians were able to join non-Japanese congregations, Japanese American Buddhists who were intent on practicing their faith were forced to defy this policy. In some instances, when neither Christians nor Buddhists had sufficient members or resources to establish a new church or temple, they joined forces to create common interfaith worship spaces.

Interfaith Belonging for a Displaced Community
Todd Tsuchiya

The Japanese American Community Center (JACC) in Minneapolis was opened in 1949 by Reverend Daisuke Kitagawa with the financial support of the Episcopal Church. Reverend Kitagawa came to Minnesota in 1943 to serve as chaplain for the Nisei soldiers at Camp Savage and Fort Snelling in the Military Intelligence Service Language School (MISLS), where he remained after the war.

Sensitive to the challenges of assimilation faced by Japanese Americans settling in the Twin Cities after their release from camp, Reverend Kitagawa was eager to provide them with a welcoming space. The JACC's central location made for an ideal gathering place. Its main gathering hall held both Christian and Buddhist religious articles of worship; at the conclusion of the Buddhist service facing the *obutsudan* altar, those attending would turn their chairs to face a cross on the adjacent wall in preparation for the Christian service that followed. This inclusive approach was meant to ensure that religious affiliation was not a differentiating factor for those coming to the area. Reverend Kitagawa invited the Buddhist community along with other Japanese American organizations to use the Center as their home, and was instrumental in the formation of both the Twin Cities Buddhist Association and the Twin Cities Japanese Christian Union Church.

The JACC hosted many different kinds of social gatherings for Issei, Nisei, and Sansei, including Halloween parties, talent shows, and New Year celebrations—cultural events that remained important to this displaced community as it sought to forge a sense of belonging. Fond memories remain of searching for large blocks of ice with which to make shaved ice, and making sweetened *azuki* beans to pour over it for the summer bazaars. The large kitchen became a sanctuary for cooking delicious *sukiyaki* and preparing potluck food. Kids played in the basement, creating noise and chaos, while Issei ladies gathered to make *manju* together. Going to the center to see friends became the hub of family social life for children and grandparents alike.

The range of organizations allowed to use the JACC—which, besides the Twin Cities chapter of the JACL, Issei Kai, and the Young Buddhist Association, also included the American Indian Inc. and the Rainbow Club—helped to foster racial, cultural, and religious understanding. Each group that used the Center was assigned responsibilities to help care for it, ensuring that this community engagement was meaningful. The JACC in Minneapolis was truly a place of inclusion and community during a difficult time of resettlement.

Opposite: *Minneapolis Morning Tribune* newspaper article about the joint worship space of the Twin Cities Buddhist Association and the Twin Cities Christian Association at the Japanese American Community Center, circa late 1940s.

Returning to Pacific Coast Racism:
Religious Hostels as Temporary Shelters

The first stop for many Japanese Americans returning to the West Coast after they left camp at the end of the war were churches or temples that had been transformed into hostels. Often unable to rent or find jobs in their former neighborhoods due to lingering anti-Japanese sentiment, many families found themselves reliant upon the cheap housing being offered by these hostels, which also provided meals, religious services, and assistance in finding work and more permanent housing.

Sanctuary: A Room at the Hostel
Kristen Hayashi

As plans for the permanent closure of concentration camps by the War Relocation Authority (WRA) began to draw near, remaining incarcerees worried about what might come next. An acute housing shortage in the postwar period, combined with real estate covenants that excluded Japanese and other racial groups from home ownership throughout much of Los Angeles, made finding and securing permanent housing exceedingly difficult for former incarcerees. Hostels were a short-term answer to this problem.

The extreme fluidity of this type of accommodation was documented in weekly reports by the WRA's Los Angeles field office staff that included information on the number of hostels in operation as well as the number of residents living in them.

Despite not yet having secured housing or the promise of employment, Hisataro and Satsuyo Yanai decided that they would return to Los Angeles along with their four children, all of whom were under the age of five. Hisataro left Manzanar in late October 1945, right before the camp closed in November of that year, in the hopes of finding a hostel where his young family might be able to stay temporarily. Satsuyo and her children followed ten days later. WRA Welfare Unit records note that four months after their arrival in LA, the Yanai family remained unable to find employment or more permanent housing. Given their childcare needs, Hisataro and Satsuyo found it difficult to land jobs, which in turn made it impossible to afford housing. As a result, the Yanais remained at the Koyasan Hostel, a temporary housing facility operated out of the Koyasan Buddhist Temple at 342 East First Street in Los Angeles' Little Tokyo, surrounded by mostly single men.

Many of the hostels created for returning Japanese Americans were operated by religious or faith-based organizations. The Quaker-run American Friends Service Committee helped Reverend Sohei Kowta of the Little Tokyo-based Union Church open a hostel in nearby Boyle Heights. Charging $1 to $1.50 per day for a bed and two meals, this facility, the Evergreen Hostel, soon became the largest in the area.

At a time when Japanese Americans had been largely abandoned by the federal government, temple- and church-run hostels such as these helped to provide basic necessities to those needing help transitioning back into mainstream society.

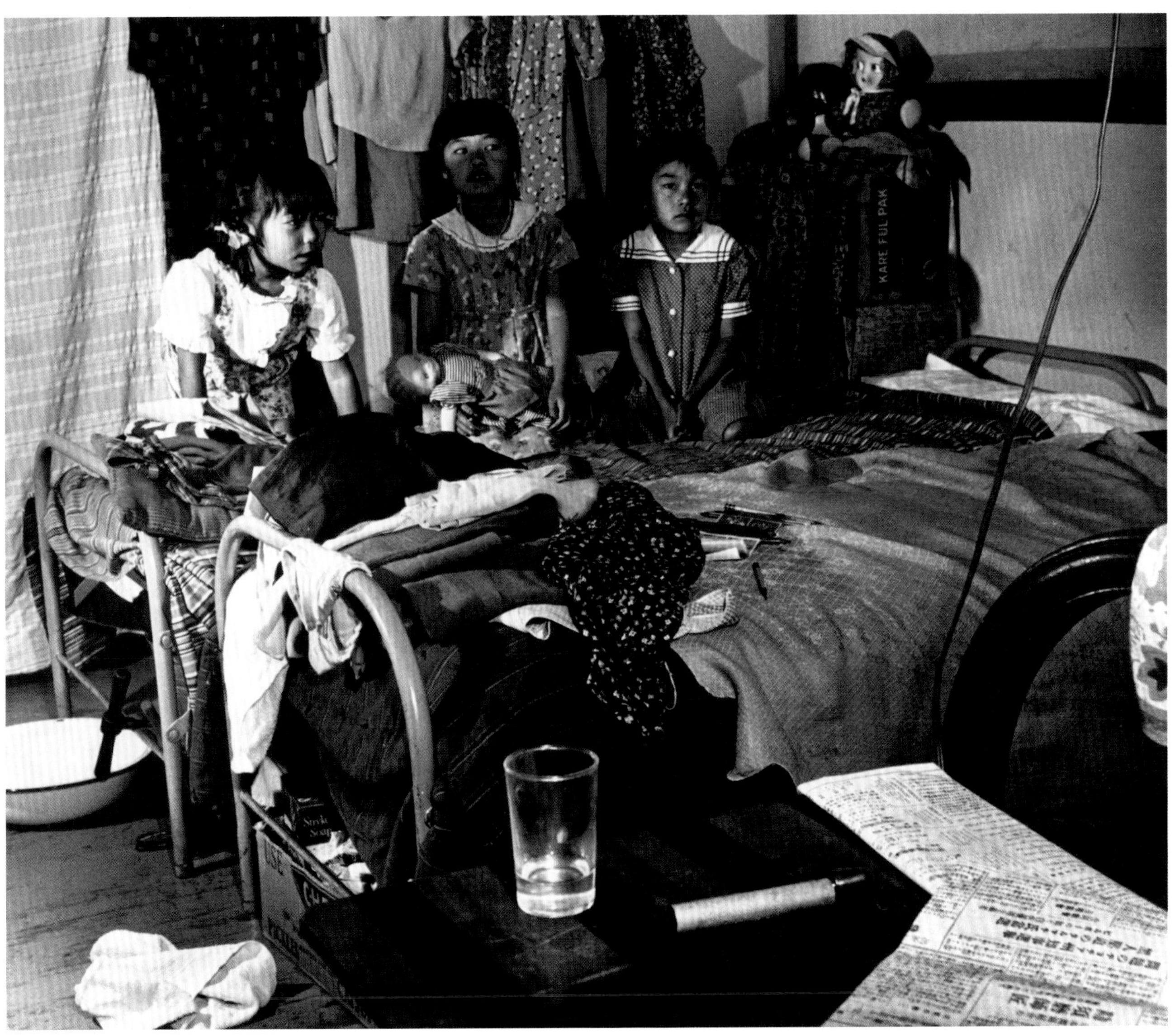

Below: Returning Japanese Americans at Evergreen Hostel, where up to four families shared one room, Los Angeles, California, ca. 1946. Photo by Marion Palfi.

As World War II labor shortages in the defense industry began to draw large numbers of African Americans from the South to California, many of the former Japanese American neighborhoods became predominantly African American. Some Black Christian churches and congregations enacted solidarity with the departed Japanese Americans by safeguarding their churches and the belongings that had been stored there — an act of kindness that was appreciated and reciprocated by the returning Japanese Americans.

Guardian Angels in the Midst of Incarceration
Rev. Mark M. Nakagawa

When more than 110,000 Japanese Americans were forcibly removed from their homes on the West Coast, strict limits on what they could take with them into the camps resulted in churches and temples becoming storage sites for their members. For members of the Centenary Methodist Episcopal Church (now known as Centenary United Methodist Church), this meant storing their belongings in the basement social hall of their church, which was at the corner of 35th Street and Normandie Avenue in South Los Angeles.

From 1942–1945, a small group of African American lay people who had been commuting to the east side of Los Angeles for worship began to organize a new Methodist church that would be able to serve the rapidly growing African American population on the west side of the city. This small congregation, who were members of Morgan Chapel at the time, worshipped in various places throughout the city, including Centenary, where they kept a watchful eye on the belongings left behind by Centenary members at the time of evacuation, ensuring they remained untouched.

The late Reverend Wesley Yamaka, whose Issei father (Reverend Yuzuru Yamaka) pastored Centenary at the time of evacuation and upon resettlement, recalled his father's gratitude and appreciation for this safeguarding of their belongings at a time when other churches and temples were being targeted by anti-Japanese opportunists and looters: "My father always said that when the Centenary members returned from the camps, all of the belongings they had stored at the church were in the exact same place where they had left them. He attributed this to the Morgan Chapel members, who kept watch over the belongings we had left there."

From 1945–1947, Centenary allowed the Morgan Chapel congregation to worship in their sanctuary on Sunday evenings, enabling them to grow and organize until they were eventually able to establish their own church near the corner of Adams Boulevard and Arlington Avenue in the West Adams area of Los Angeles. That small nucleus of a congregation would grow into what is now known as the Holman United Methodist Church. Its official history notes that "[d]uring the first two years, services were held in various locations, including a dance hall at the corner of Jefferson Boulevard and Normandie Avenue. Members also met in a vacated Japanese church until its congregants returned from the WWII internment camps."

Today, both Holman United Methodist Church and Centenary United Methodist Church are nationally known among their respective ethnic communities as well as the larger denominations of which they are a part. This story of how these two churches intersected and supported one another during critical periods of their histories is an enduring reminder of God's ability to provide hope and salvation when all else seems lost.

Senshin Buddhist Church Hostel

Rev. Masao Kodani

Buddhist interdependence is a fact, not an option. The Issei lost everything overnight; when they came back from the concentration camps to the West Coast, they had to start from scratch. Yet in just one generation—like the can't-fall-down Daruma doll of which it is said "*Nana korobi, ya oki—push it over seven times and it stands up eight times*"—they found a way to re-establish what they had lost. None of this would have been possible without the hard work and spiritual and practical assistance of a diverse group of advocates within and beyond the Japanese American community.

The hostel run in Los Angeles by the Senshin Buddhist Church in the immediate aftermath of the war is a case in point. By the time of the 1941 attack on Pearl Harbor, the mortgage for the construction of the Senshin Buddhist Church had already been fully paid off. It thus became one of many Japanese American places of worship used to store the belongings of members forcibly removed from their homes. Unlike many other such storage sites, however, Senshin could count amongst its clergy a non-Japanese convert, Reverend Julius Goldwater, who undertook the job of protecting the temple and the possessions stored there.

After the war, Reverend Goldwater—along with Reverends Kanmo Imamura and Arthur Takemoto, and later also Reverend Kyoshiro Tokunaga—also proved instrumental in helping to convert the Senshin Buddhist Church into a hostel for Japanese Americans returning to Los Angeles. The Senshin Hostel, which opened in 1945, was the first Buddhist hostel in the United States. Originally consisting of five rooms and a cellar space, the former temple space was divided up to accommodate a maximum of some fifty people. These temporary residents would stay at the hostel for up to a year and a half until they could find jobs and housing. When they left, the next group of families and individuals would move in.

The five- to six-year period immediately after the war was particularly difficult for returning Japanese Americans. Because nearby grocery stores refused to sell food to "the enemy," Reverend Goldwater and the not-yet-ordained Takemoto found themselves having to go to Chinatown to buy groceries, one of the few places where they would not be turned away.

Employment was another difficulty, since employers were often reluctant to hire recent returnees. One exception was an African American man, Roy Loggins, who ran a catering service for Hollywood movie productions. For many years, Loggins would hire Japanese Americans staying at the hostel to do part-time work for him, even taking them home to ensure they were safe from attack on the streets. Knowing how much the gesture would be appreciated, he would also stop by to drop off leftover food and ice sculptures from the parties he helped to cater. Unfortunately, our temple's later attempts to find him in order to recognize and thank him only succeeded some two weeks after his death.

Throughout this postwar period, as Senshin was also re-establishing itself as a temple, hostel staff worked hard to serve three meals a day to the residents. They also helped secure ration books for food and gas, provided car transportation when needed, and assisted in placing ads for jobs and housing. Meanwhile, Senshin members pitched in to help with services, family memorials, Sunday School, Japanese Language School, cultural classes, and religious conferences.

Without the efforts of a wide net of people such as Loggins, Goldwater, and the growing Senshin membership, the temple's rapid postwar growth would never have been possible. Bad times are only made worse by self-centeredness and attachment to permanence. Being in control only brings further grief. So when we ultimately consider this, we ironically find ourselves to be fundamentally okay.

Opposite: Los Angeles Japanese Methodist Church on the day Japanese Americans in this neighborhood were forcibly removed, Los Angeles, California, 1942.

Left: Koyasan Buddhist Temple, pictured in the background, was one of many religious institutions that were transformed into hostels, Los Angeles, California, 1945. Pictured in front are Gentaro Miyahara, hostel director; Carl Palmberg of the American Friends Service Committee; and Margaret Peterson and Jean Blair, assistants.

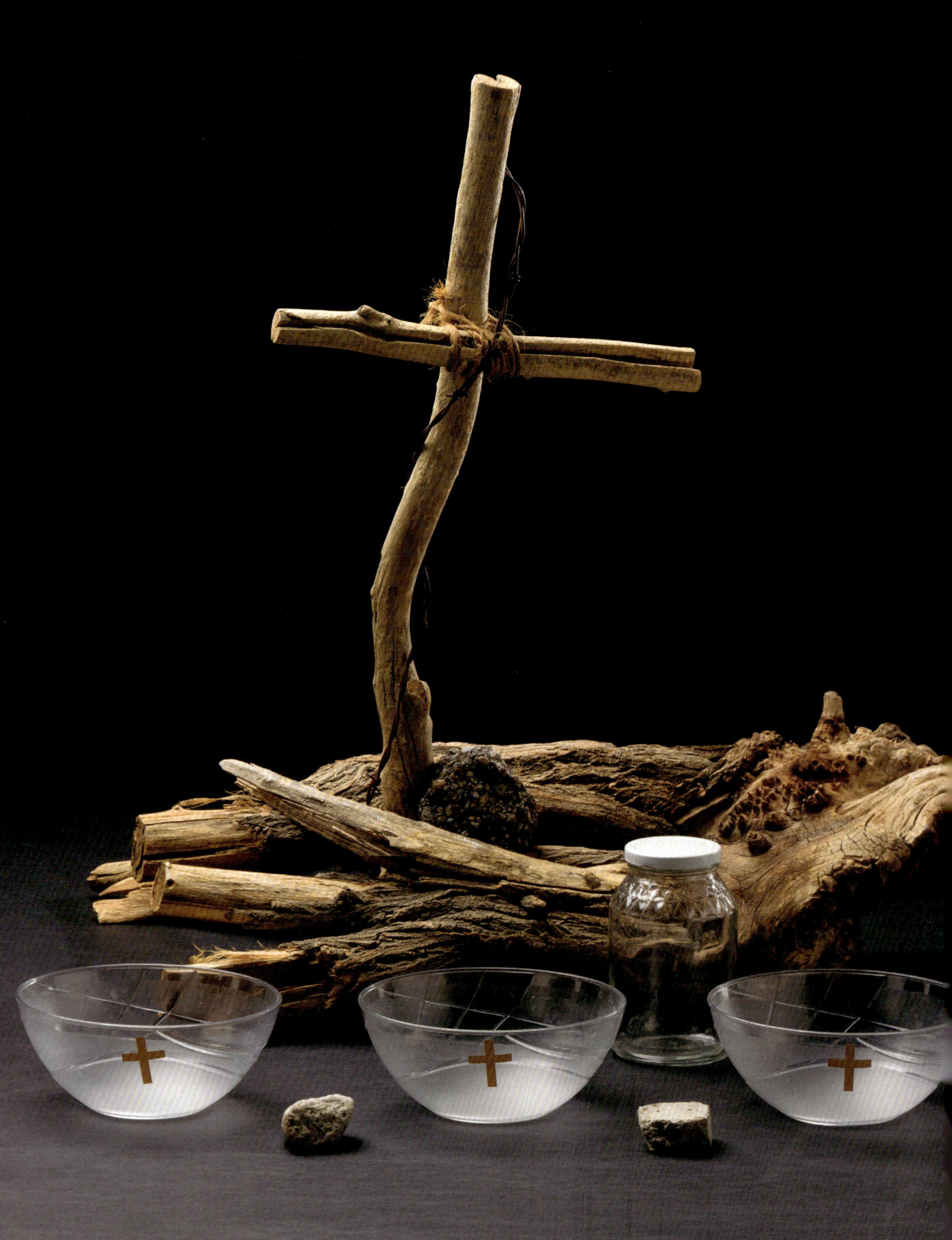

6

REPARATION

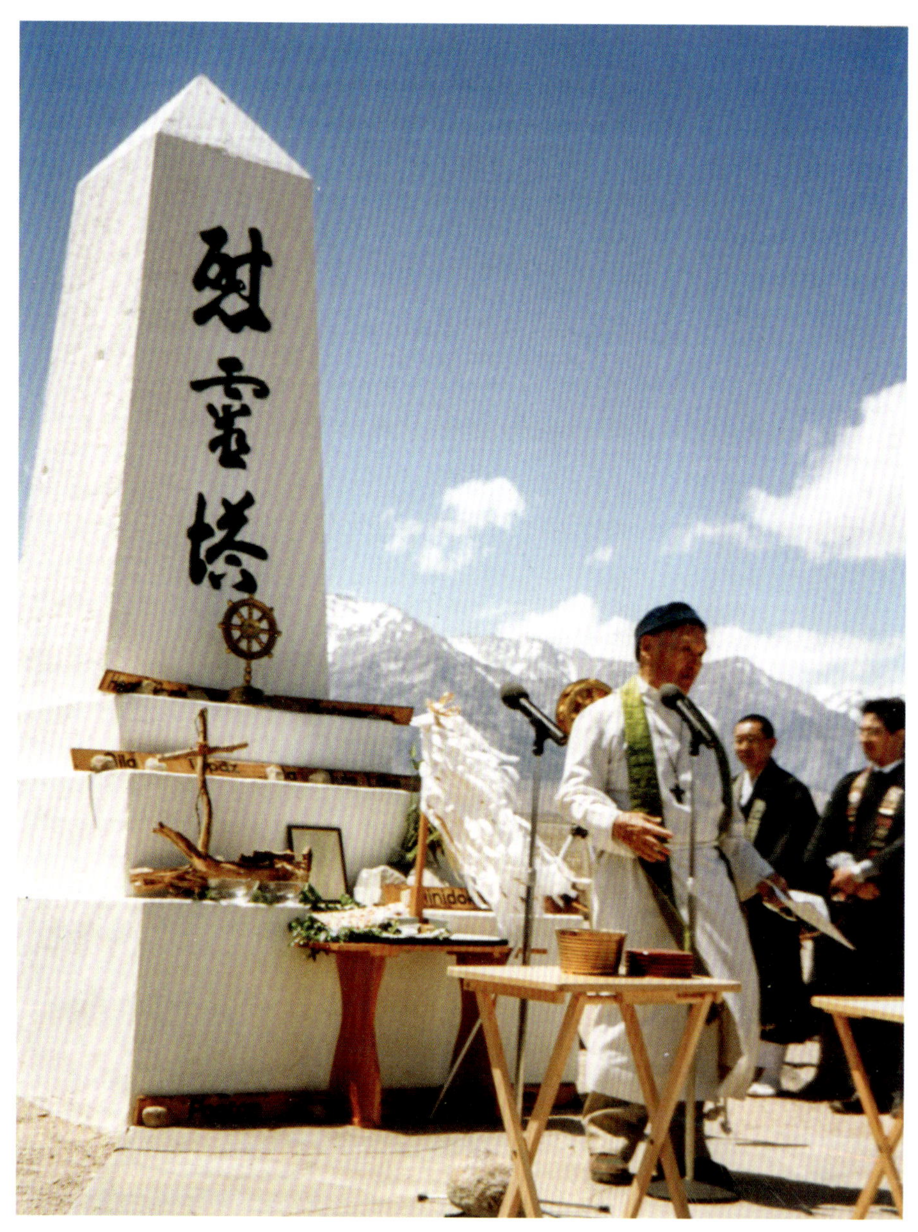

慰霊塔

Buddhist and Christian clergy played a central role in organizing the first pilgrimages to the concentration camps. Wanting to ensure that the cemeteries there were not abandoned, they felt an obligation to return. Soon, younger Japanese Americans had taken up the mantle of organizing these yearly pilgrimages to the camps, often continuing the practice of interfaith ceremonies as part of these gatherings. This, in turn, fed into the growing call for reparations that eventually resulted in the successful passage of the 1988 Civil Liberties Act, the first—and for the moment only—instance of the US government providing large-scale compensation for race-based injuries. "Reparations," a term originally derived from Roman Catholic rituals that seek to expiate original sin by honoring Christ, is most often associated with the search for justice for Black Americans. Theologically connected to the idea of atonement, this usage references slavery as America's original sin. Reparations from a spiritual vantage point is thus not simply about the passage of a piece of legislation. It demands a deep and lasting recompense for an injury that has incurred a moral debt.

For many Japanese Americans today, the long shadow cast across multiple generations by the hardships of incarceration and its aftermath means that the work of repair remains ongoing.

Opposite: Rev. Paul Nakamura of the Lutheran Oriental Church of Torrance, CA is accompanied by several Buddhist priests during an interfaith memorial service held at the Manzanar Ireito during the 2002 Manzanar Pilgrimage.

Page 138: The cross made by Rev. Paul Nakamura for the Manzanar pilgrimages.

Pilgrimage as Spiritual Repair

After the war, many Japanese Americans felt that the best way to restart their lives was to get as far away from the camps as possible. But a handful of religious clergy felt a deep sense of obligation to return to the camps to look after the cemeteries and offer their prayers to those buried there. These annual visits began immediately after the war when Reverend Shinjo Nagatomi and Reverend Sentoku Maeda, accompanied by Christian minister Reverend Shoichi Henry Wakahiro, returned to Manzanar, where they themselves had been incarcerated. They would make this trip every year until their own deaths.

By the late 1960s, younger Japanese Americans, eager to reframe the wartime incarceration as a gross violation of civil liberties rather than a source of shame, began coordinating similar pilgrimages. By then, most of the camps' physical structures had been dismantled or fallen into disrepair. Those attending the pilgrimages gravitated instead to the visually striking religious monuments that remained: the Ireito at Manzanar; the large cross built on a hill at Tule Lake; and the Ireihi at the cemetery in Rohwer.

Over the years, pilgrimages to the former concentration camps have become an important part of the effort to remember and reclaim the history of the mass incarceration. To this day, interfaith memorial services remain central to these occasions of healing and restoration, providing an opportunity for visitors to come together and recollect, mourn, and celebrate what has nonetheless survived.

Below: Stills from Janice Tanaka's 1976 film "Ohakamairi: A Visit to the Graves," featuring the Buddhist Rev. Sentoku Maeda and the Christian Rev. Shoichi Henry Wakahiro on one of their joint annual pilgrimages to Manzanar from the immediate postwar period onwards.

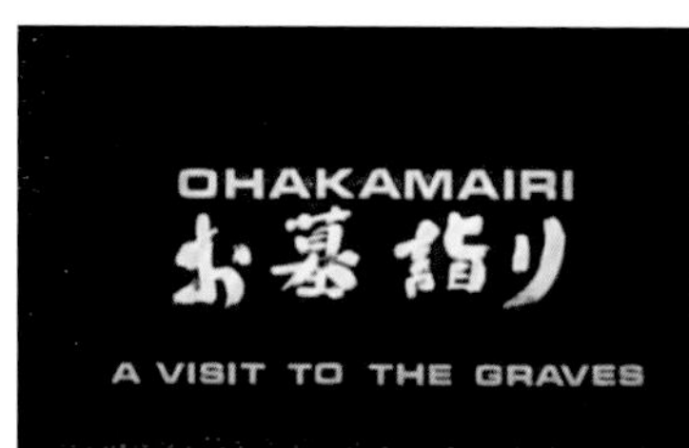

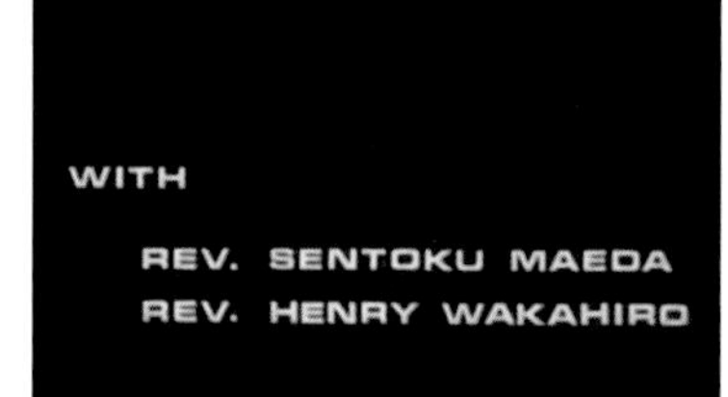

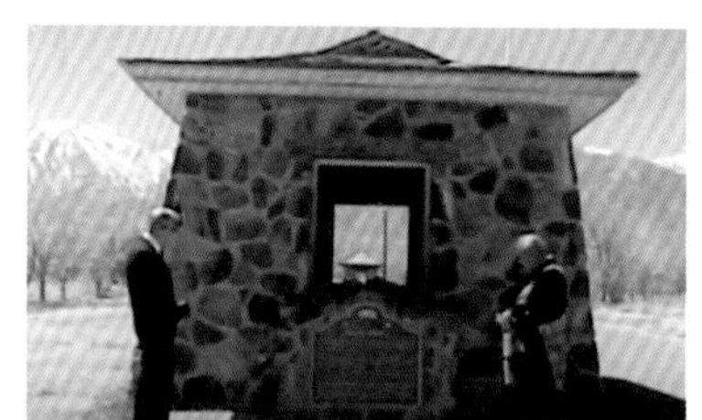

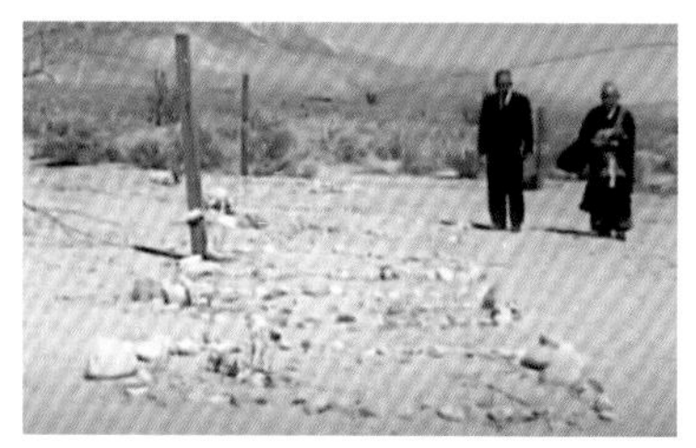

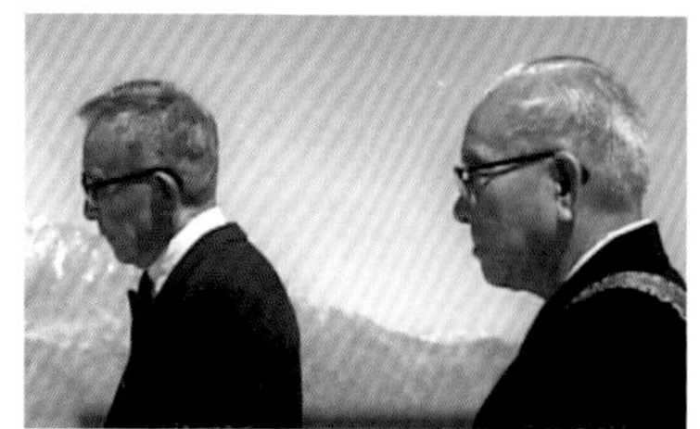

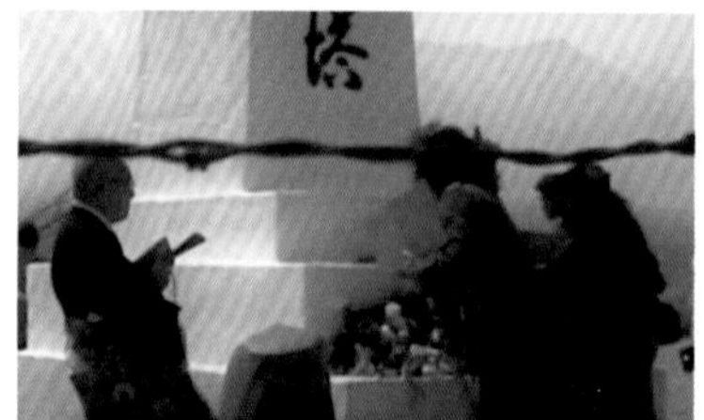

The Cross

Joanne Doi MM

The cross of our Christian faith insists on contemplating the mystery of God's grace in absence, in rupture, in betrayal and shock, in physical hardship, in psychological scars and denial. The cross is the site of suffering and hope. The memory of Jesus' suffering and death can hold within it all other memories of suffering. To walk the way of the cross is to take in our own losses: the chaos and threat of separation from family and community; the trauma of incarceration, harsh living conditions, illness, and death; betrayal by one's own country; internal divisions and suspicions. These forces of rupture would prefer that we forget about the infinite horizon of love in which we live.

Jesus' death is one of solidarity with suffering humanity. Thus our Christian *anamnesis*, our dangerous memory, returns us to the experience of love and mercy at the very moment we strive to bring about that love and mercy where it is absent. Our *memoria passionis* is also our *memoria resurrectionis* as we join with others in compassionate solidarity.

Listening to the wisdom of suffering must open us to others. As we allow difficult emotions to teach us what we need to know, we understand that to honor the full range of emotions available to us is an act of resistance rather than submission.

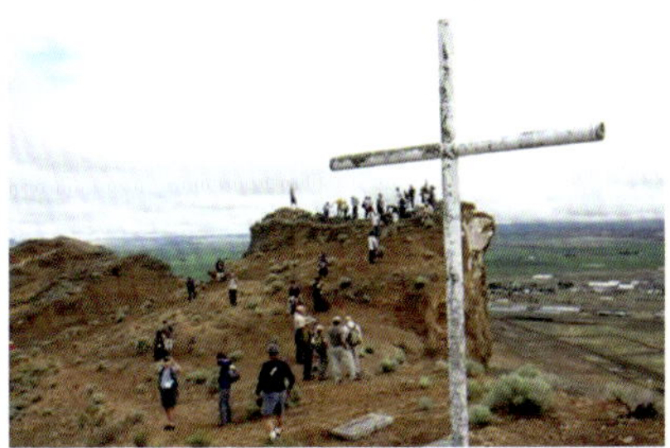

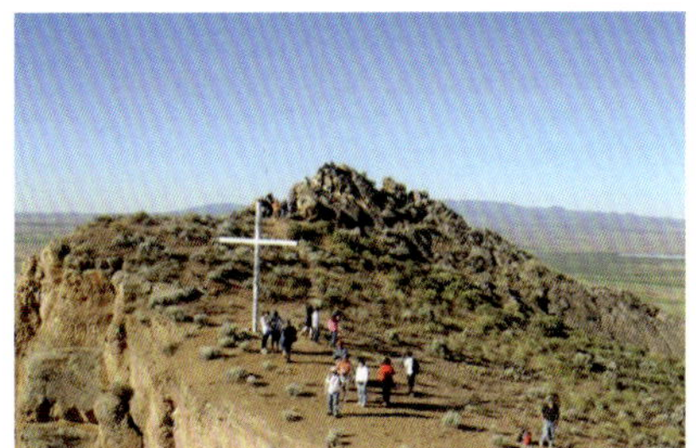

It is a wounded resurrection. The scars are still there, but they can become a source of healing. Entering into this process together provides an experience of vulnerability that paradoxically results in a sense of shared strength.

The solidarity of the cross can support us as we experience sadness and loss in the context of mercy, grace, and the infinite horizon of love, as we transform our loss into restored relationality and reciprocate in solidarity with others.

Above: A cross erected by former incarcerees at the top of Castle Rock next to the former Tule Lake Segregation Center is an important landmark and destination for pilgrimages. Photos from the 2016 Tule Lake Pilgrimage.

The Movement for Redress and Reparations

By the late 1960s, grassroots movements demanding some form of redress for the losses incurred by the mass incarceration of Japanese Americans during World War II began to emerge. Some groups advocated for litigating the wartime incarceration in courts, while others felt it would be more effective to push for legislation compelling a government investigation into what had occurred. In 1980, Congress established the Commission on Wartime Relocation and Internment of Civilians (CWRIC). The nine CWRIC commissioners traveled to ten cities across the nation and heard from over 750 witnesses. One of the commissioners assigned to the CWRIC, Jesuit priest Father Robert F. Drinan, was so moved by what he heard that he penned a newspaper editorial characterizing reparations as a form of atonement. These powerful testimonies led to the remarkable recommendation that the US government issue a formal apology and pay former incarcerees monetary reparations.

Among those who testified to the CWRIC commission were members of the religious clergy. Christian ministers such as Hideo Hashimoto, Paul Nagano, and Lloyd Wake recalled the profound feeling of loss and betrayal that they and their congregations felt upon learning that they were to be incarcerated; the deprivations they experienced while in camp; and the difficulties they faced while attempting to re-establish their interrupted lives after the war. Reverend Nagano noted how his Christian faith had helped him survive the camps: "I'm certain because of my faith in God, and my desire to keep up the morale of others, I was able to adjust to this shocking experience."

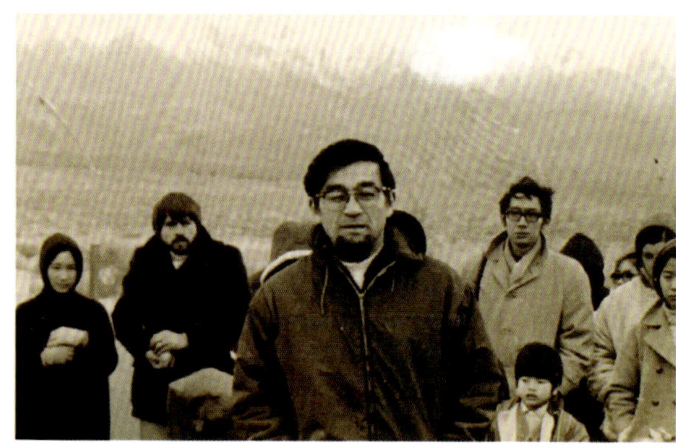

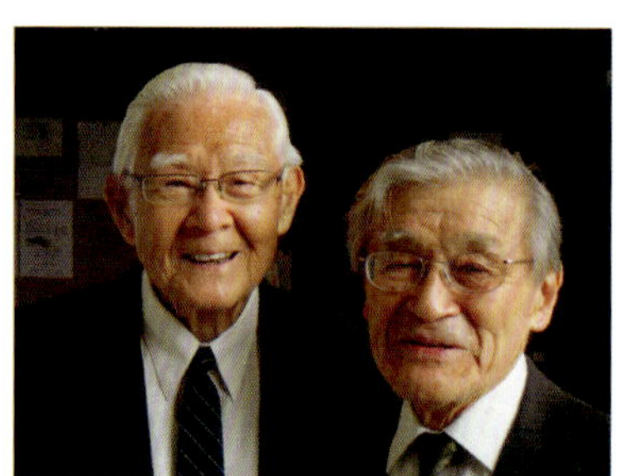

Right, top: Rev. Lloyd Wake attends the first official Manzanar Pilgrimage in 1969.

Right, bottom: Revs. Paul Nagano and Lloyd Wake, pictured here in 2014, both entered the ministry while they were incarcerated at the Poston concentration camp, and became important community leaders dedicated to justice. Both gave testimonies before the CWRIC commissioners.

Opposite: Rev. Hideo Hashimoto's CWRIC testimony given at the Portland, OR hearing on August 21, 1981. Hashimoto, who had been a minister with the Fresno Japanese Methodist Church when World War II broke out, gave his testimony in both Portland and Seattle, and shared excerpts from his sermon given before forced removal, as well as a letter that he wrote to supporters right after he entered the Fresno Assembly Center.

Hideo Hashimoto
8919 S.W. Ninth Drive
Portland, OR 97219

Written Testimony of Hideo Hashimoto to

Commission on Wartime Relocation and Internment of Civilians

August 21, 1981

My name is Hideo Hashimoto. I am Professor Emeritus of Religious Studies at Lewis and Clark College in Portland, Oregon. I am also a retired Methodist Minister. I am 70 years of age.

I was a 30 year old unmarried minister of the Fresno Japanese Methodist Church on May 15, 1942, when I was evacuated. I was appointed to the church in June, 1940, after my graduation from Union Theological Seminary in New York City. Much of my testimony based on articles and letters I wrote, mainly to outsiders, at the time of evacuation and relocation.

On April 18, 1942, I wrote to my friends scattered throughout the United States, practically all of them non-Japanese:

"In all these days, the heart warming and encouraging experiences in the midst of darkness have been your thoughtful letters and the sympathy and help of those Caucasian friends who have helped us unstintedly."

Since Pearl Harbor there had been little hostility expressed to the Japanese in Fresno area and a great deal of expression of friendship and support. Fair Play Committee was formed. Fellowship of Reconciliation was a moving core of the Committee. It was not until about February, 1942 when the professional anti-Japanese forces renewed their traditional activities and influenced politicians and military leaders. to agitate for wholesale evacuation of persons of Japanese descent.

". . .But to the people whom I serve these months have been time of uncertainty, fear, and heartbreaking disappointment. . . . The impact has been especially hard one for the Nisei, the American citizens of Japanese parentage. They were born in this country, were educated as Americans . . . and were thoroughly indoctrinated with the ideals of democracy and fair play. . . They have prized and have been proud of their citizenship . . . especially because their parents were denied the privileges of

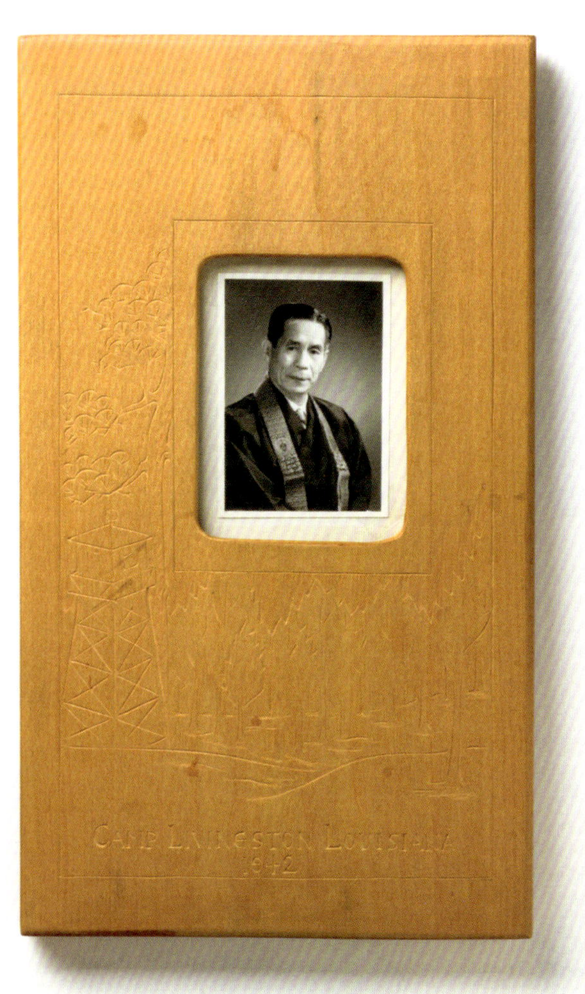

CAMP LIVINGSTON LOUISIANA
1942

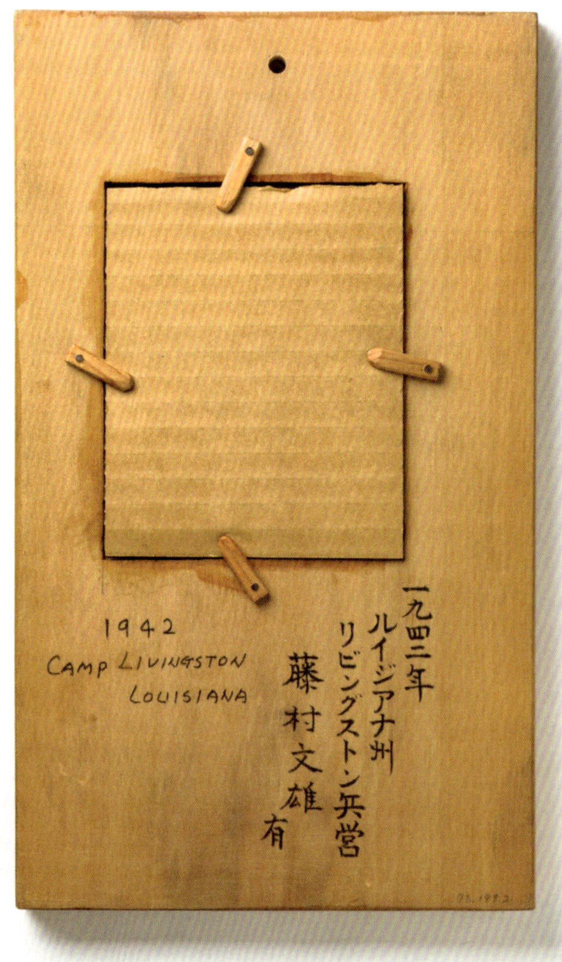

1942
CAMP LIVINGSTON
LOUISIANA
一九四二年
ルイジアナ州
リビングストン兵営
藤村文雄
有

Repairing the Racial Karma of a Nation

Buddhists priests also engaged in the reparations campaign, drawing on their tradition's approach to healing the harm that comes from race-based discrimination.

Bunyu Fujimura

Reverend Bunyu Fujimura, a Buddhist priest, gave testimony in Japanese at the Commission on Wartime Relocation and Internment of Civilians hearings in Los Angeles, highlighting the discrimination suffered by Buddhists in particular as a result of wartime hysteria. Reverend Fujimura—who ended up at four different internment camps run by the US Army and the Department of Justice: Fort Lincoln, Camp McCoy, Camp Livingston, and the Santa Fe Internment Camp—told the commissioners how humiliating it had been for him and other Buddhist priests to have their arrests reported by the media as if they were threats to national security. Recounting his experiences on the day after the Pearl Harbor attack, he also recalled how the chief of police in Salinas, CA, where he served as a Buddhist priest, ordered him to take down the large bell outside the temple where he served. Apparently, local citizens were worried that it might be used to aid the Japanese military should they try to enter the bay at Monterey. "How ridiculous to even think that its sound could be heard in Monterey, nineteen miles away," Reverend Fujimura said. "And how much more ridiculous to think that sounding it would be of any help to an invading army."

Kyoshiro Tokunaga

Another Buddhist priest, Reverend Kyoshiro Tokunaga, was the only litigant from the Department of Justice-run internment camps to participate in the effort by the National Council for Japanese American Redress (NCJAR) to sue the US government for reparations. Speaking to a reporter about his decision to do so, he told the story of how he had been befriended by an African American train porter while ill with a high fever during his long train journey to an internment camp in New Mexico. This porter helped nurse him through his illness, saying: "I can understand how you feel. We have been through this for hundreds of years." This link between the World War II Japanese American incarceration and the experiences of African Americans in the US prompted Reverend Tokunaga to reflect: "As a Buddhist I believe there is a karma for nations as well as people. The American karma is the actions and deeds of the past. It is something that we cannot escape."

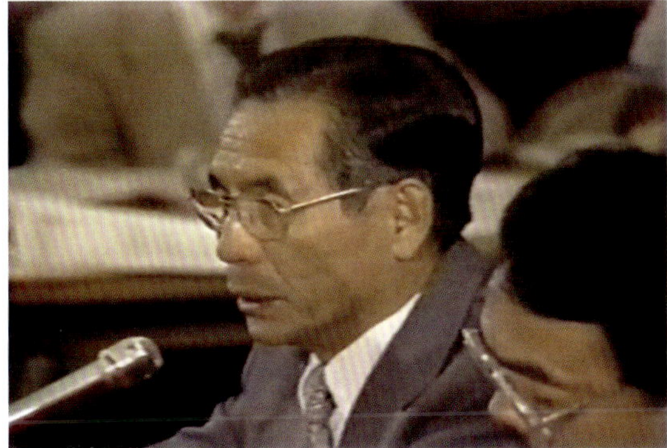

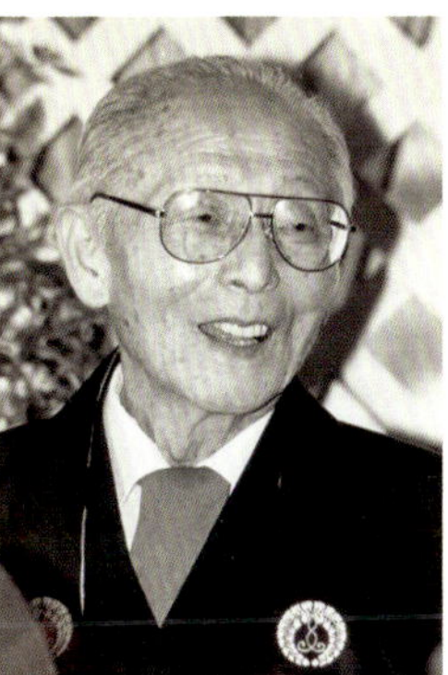

Opposite: Framed photo of Rev. Bunyu Fujimura made by Takae Hamada in the Camp Livingston Internment Camp, Louisiana, 1942.

Far left: Rev. Bunyu Fujimura giving his Commission on Wartime Relocation and Internment of Civilians testimony at the Los Angeles hearing on August 6, 1981.

Left: Rev. Kyoshiro Tokunaga served the San Jose Buddhist Temple after the war.

Interlinked Histories and the Ongoing Work of Repair

Many Japanese Americans have come to feel that the passage of legislation resulting in a letter of apology and redress checks cannot be the end of the story. For them, the true work of repairing the harm done by the wartime incarceration can only happen by uprooting the racial and religious animus that led to that incarceration in the first place. This has led them to connect their own experiences and histories with ongoing struggles against forced removal, family separation, unjust deportation, racist violence, religious intolerance, and the many other ways in which exclusion and supremacy manifest themselves. This deep spiritual work, framed by Buddhists as the alleviation of karmic suffering and by Christians as atonement for sin, has prompted solidarity with the many other communities that have been discriminated against based on race and religion from the United States' founding to the present day.

Solidarity as Spiritual Practice
Satsuki Ina

Solidarity, in the deepest sense, is a spiritual practice. It is a way of acting, perceiving, and being that connects us with our wholeness. When acts of inhumanity are perpetrated, or the denial of our humanness dismissed, a fractured psyche results, dividing one's sense of self, obliterating one's connection to others.

When WWII began, my family, along with thousands of others', was cast out from the American mainstream, stigmatized and abandoned, banished to isolated areas of the country and imprisoned by barbed wire barriers and armed guards. Oppression of this kind, and racism more specifically, results in the fracturing of our sense of interconnectedness. To survive this trauma, we often compensate by closing ranks, choosing sides, silo-ing our lives and our understanding of others. Our human capacity for empathy becomes limited to our identified "tribe," and exclusion becomes a protective strategy to justify and maintain some sense of power and control. Yet the fractures thus created never fully heal: the true source of the problem is never resolved, the longing never quite satisfied.

Solidarity is a spiritual practice because it heals the wounds of human trauma. It uplifts and makes possible what is for the common good. In solidarity, we reach out beyond our "tribe," beyond our comfort zone, to welcome and invite others who are different from ourselves into our daily lives, into our way of seeing the world, into our dreams. In this way we expand our separate selves and experience the richness of diversity and the fulfillment of wholeness. We heal our self-protective boundaries and walls, grow our capacity for empathy, reimagine ourselves and our possibilities. No longer clinging to rigidly fixed yet fractured selves, we can become multidimensional, we can mend when we claim others as our family.

Eighty years later, those of us who were children in those prison camps gathered to protest the incarceration of thousands of innocent children and families, mostly from Central America, being held behind barbed wire. We called ourselves Tsuru for Solidarity. Because of our own long-buried wounds of imprisonment, family separation, and community fracture, we were drawn, almost driven, to protest, to show up, to stand with those being targeted for exclusion. As we chanted and beat our taiko drums in protest, I experienced an extraordinary sense of being alive. I felt the presence of my parents and grandparents and a deep love for all who had joined in this act of solidarity. We hung colorful paper cranes on the barbed wire fence in the hopes that the children could see us and know that someone outside cared. In solidarity, we were sending hope. In so doing, we were healing the child inside each of us.

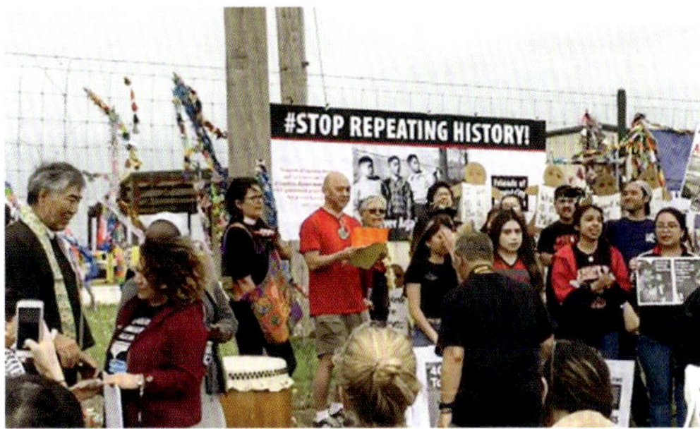

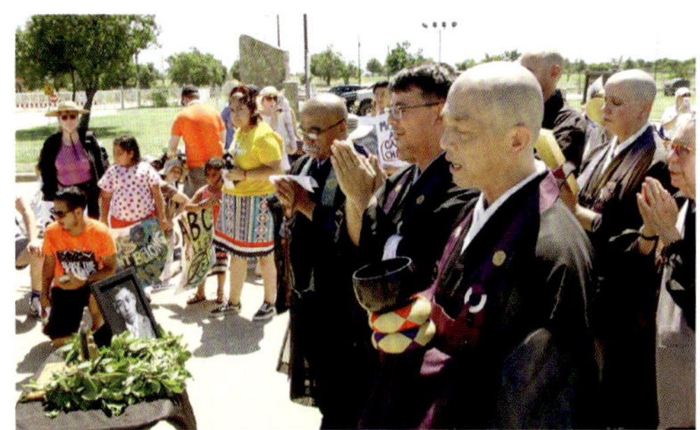

"Stop Repeating History!"
Ron Kobata

When I was invited by Tsuru for Solidarity to travel to the former site of the Department of Justice camp in Crystal City, Texas, it was in my capacity as a Buddhist priest: I had been asked to conduct a memorial service for three girls of Japanese descent who had died in a drowning accident while interned there with their families during World War II. Now, eight decades later, children were again being detained, this time at the ICE-run South Texas Family Residential Center in nearby Dilley.

For most people, the notion of protest is associated with being against some issue or situation. But I saw my participation in the vigil at Crystal City as an opportunity to repair, from a Buddhist perspective, some of the harm that had been perpetrated upon the Japanese American community eight decades earlier by linking that experience to the federal government's policy of locking up and separating children from their families.

The spiritual intent of Buddhist rituals—the chanting of sutras and burning of incense—is to transform ignorance to enlightenment, suffering to joy, conflicts to peace, dissatisfaction to gratitude. The Crystal City vigil began with speeches by those who had spent their childhood in the camps and by public officials. Following a drumming ceremony presented by a member from the local Carrizo Comecrudo tribe, I offered an opening chant, affirming the spiritual basis for coming together to protest the harm being perpetrated on children separated from their families and placed in cages. As I took part in these activities, I recalled how the first people arrested by the FBI following the attack on Pearl Harbor were Buddhist priests and reflected upon the role they must have played in bringing a sense of spiritual grounding to the families in the camps.

The slogan "Stop Repeating History" brings to mind the Buddhist view that understands *samara*, the aimless cycle of birth and death, as being rooted in self-centered ignorance that divides the world into the isolation of me and you, us and them. The confusion and frustration that arises out of the fixated mind repeating the same delusions over and over without realizing why can be countered by the Buddha's insight that we are all living within a dynamic, interdependent system of life.

Breaking out of the cycles of delusions that make us believe our lives are not interconnected is to stop repeating a history of harm and exclusion that affects ourselves as much as it does others. Protesting for peace is a way of giving comfort, a prayer for healing and harmony and respect that connects the past and the present and us to one another.

Above, left: Rev. Ron Kobata (left) at the Tsuru for Solidarity Protest at the South Texas Family Residential Center, March 2019.

Above, right: Revs. Shumyo Kojima, Duncan Ryuken Williams, and William Briones officiating a memorial ceremony at the Fort Sill Army Base for Kanesaburo Oshima, shot by guards in 1942 at the Fort Sill Internment Camp. At a protest in July 2019, organized by Tsuru for Solidarity and United We Dream, against the use of Fort Sill to detain migrant children separated from their families.

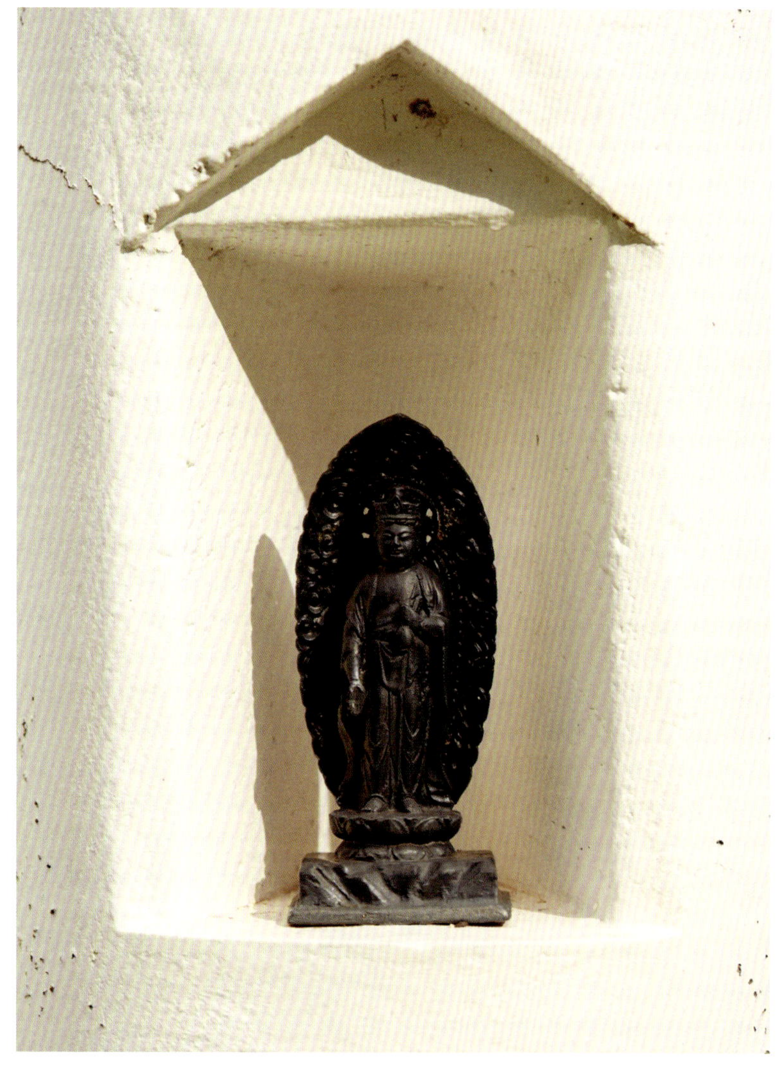

Detail of Waimea Shingon
Mission War Memorial.

My Plea

Oh God, I pray that someday every race
May stand on equal plane
And prejudice will find no dwelling place
In a peace that all may gain.

— Mary Matsuzawa, in *Cactus Blossoms,* 1945:
    Poems by students of Butte High School

In a Buddhist Forest

Even if you're not a Buddhist,
even if you couldn't care less,
or don't know beans about Buddhism

with its various practices and paths,
even if you've never even been
knowingly near a Buddhist temple

or a Buddhist, much less
observed the gathering at "E" and Kern
outside West Fresno's Buddhist Temple,

even though you never ascended the steps
to attend a service in the main hall
of guided shrines and bells and incense,

even if you don't know lacquer
from plastic, dinosaurs from dragons,
or have never heard chanting

or listened much to pigeons in eaves,
children reciting in a basement,
families being ceremonious in an annex,

yes, even though you may even be
anti-Buddhist, whatever that is,
I would guess that you've never the less

been a distance on a path of your own,
given and received respect,
let a few things be, a few things pass,

realized that results of deeds
"good" or "bad," had occasional
flashes of compassion and impermanence,

and even if you've never ever considered
becoming a Buddhist, whatever that is,
wherever that is, well, not to worry:

Your Buddhist Self proceeds accordingly—
In a Buddhist City, in a Buddhist Forest...

— Lawson Fusao Inada, 1997

LET NOT
YOUR HEART
BE TROUBLED
JOHN 14:1

Acknowledgments

This companion book to the exhibit "Sutra and Bible: Faith and the Japanese American World War II Incarceration," co-presented by the Japanese American National Museum and the USC Shinso Ito Center for Japanese Religions and Culture, would not have been possible without the help and generosity of numerous people and institutions.

As the co-editors, we must start by thanking the three people who stuck with us over the course of many months from conceptualization to the finalization of this volume. First, Sunyoung Lee of Kaya Press provided the highest level of editorial assistance to improve the quality of writing in this volume. She pushed us to write, and therefore think, more deeply about the significance of the artifacts in this exhibit and why religion matters. Second, Sean Deyoe, the book's designer, transformed the mass of text and images into one of the most compelling exhibit catalogs we have seen. Third, Jhani Randhawa was our project manager, who somehow coordinated the hugely complex task of pulling us together while sticking to a schedule.

We must acknowledge the hard working team of the two co-presenting organizations—JANM and the USC Shinso Ito Center for Japanese Religions and Culture—for the production of the exhibit, with special thanks to JANM President Ann Burroughs. Other staff include Shannon Takushi, Higino Abrajano, Erin Aoyama, Thomas Gallatin, Clement Hanami, Kristen Hayashi, Jamie Henricks, Shawn Iwaoka, Coffee Kang, Evan Kodani, Rick Noguchi, Mia Russell, John Tonai, Doug Van Kirk, and Rosie Yasukochi.

We were very fortunate to have the guidance of two advisory committees of scholars and community members, who kindly devoted time to reviewing materials and connecting us to artifacts from around the country. They include: Michihiro Ama, Anne M. Blankenship, Tommy Dyo, Janis Hirohama, Beth Shalom Hessel, Mitch Homma, Naomi Hirahara, Jane Naomi, Iwamura, Tetsuden Kashima, Peter Manseau, Dexter Mar, Michael Masatsugu, Eiko Masuyama, Brian Niiya, Gail Y. Okawa, Dakota Russell, George Tanabe, Todd Tsuchiya, Nancy Ukai, Mark Unno, Jonathan van Harmelen, and Patricia Wakida.

We must also thank Kaoru "Kay" Ueda, the Stanford Hoover Institution's Japanese Diaspora Initiative, and the members of the extensive Kitaji family—in particular Laura (Kitaji) Dominguez-Yon—for allowing us to feature the Kitaji Bibles. Other community members and scholars who were so helpful include: Patty Arra, Gil Asakawa, Patricia Biggs, Ken Fong, Norman Furuta, Nate Gyotoku, Kyle Iwanaga, Japanese Cultural Center of Hawai'i (JCCH), the Joonji-Shibata Family, Shokai Kanai, Shumyo Kojima, Alisa Lynch, Rika Marubashi, Rose Masters, Eric L. Muller, Kay and Frank Murakami, Audrey Muromoto, Jiko Nakade, Rev. Mark M. Nakagawa, Lynn Nomura, Nancy Kyoko Oda, Janice Tanaka, Mary Urashima, Bill Watanabe, and Karen Yonemoto.

Kaya Press offers special thanks to the Choi Chang Soo Foundation and Stephen CuUnjieng for their support. Additional funding was provided by generous contributions from: Lydia Arbizo, Manibha Banerjee, Partha Banerjee, Lily & Tom Beischer, Jamel Brinkley, Sonali Chanchani, Jade Chang, Wah-Ming Chang, Samantha Chanse, Anelise Chen, Anita Chen, Lisa Chen, Floyd Cheung, Jayne Cho, Judy Miyoung Choi, Katelin Chow, Agnes Chu, Elizabeth Clemants, Susannah Donahue, Irving Eng, Matthew Fargo, Sesshu Foster, Thea Gray, Kimiko Hahn, Paul Heck, Jean Ho, Jonathan Hugo, Ann Holler, Huy Hong, Andrew Kebo, Vandana Khanna, Joonie and Jungin Kim, Kyung Kim, Karen Koh, Sabrina Ko, Juliana Koo & Paul Smith, Kien Lam, Catherine Lee, Cathy Lee, Ed Lin, Helen Kim Lee, Whakyung Lee in memory of Sonya Choi Lee, Andrew Leong, Nancy Leong, Keesoo Huh, Abir Majumdar, Shikha Malaviya, Gregory McKnight, Samhita Mukhopadhyay, Jean Naylor, Minkyung and Yun Oh, Minya Oh, Julia Oh, Chez Bryan Ong, Eric Ong, Josephine Park, Amarnath Ravva, Yutaka Sato, nitasha sawhney, Roch Smith, Jungmi Son, Nancy Starbuck, Robin Sukhadia, Tait Sye, Joyce Talley, Alanna Taylor, Patricia Wakida, Esme Wang, Aviva Weiner, Heather Werber, Duncan Ryuken Williams, William Wong, Amelia Wu & Sachin Adarkar, Anita Wu & James Spicer, Yoojin Grace Wuertz, Nancy Yap, Max Yeh, Stan Yogi, Shinae Yoon, Mikoto Yoshida, Jenny Tinghui Zhang, and many others.

Credits

Page 1: Brian Suda Photography, Courtesy of Nichiren Mission of Hawaii

Page 2: Courtesy of the Kitaji Family/Hoover Institution Library & Archives

Introductory Photo Essay: Densho, Frank Kuno Collection, ddr-densho-128-48; Courtesy of Kyle Iwanaga; Courtesy of Homma and Wada Families; Densho, Frank Kuno Collection, ddr-densho-128-49; Gift in Memory of Mrs. Tome Yoshida (91.90.170), JANM; Courtesy of Homma and Wada Families; Densho, Bainbridge Island Japanese American Community, the Hayashida Family Collection, ddr-densho-34-49; Used with permission, Utah State Historical Society; Gift of Terminal Islanders Club (96.276.64), JANM; Courtesy of the Tenrikyo Mission Headquarters (2000.231.8), JANM; Gift of Al M. Nakamura (92.89.13), JANM; Courtesy of the Tri-State Denver Buddhist Temple; Densho, Courtesy of the Natsuhara Family Collection, ddr-densho-18-48; Courtesy of the New York Japanese American United Church

Prologue: Courtesy of Zenshuji Soto Mission; Courtesy of Ray T. Akazawa (92.101.1), JANM; Courtesy of St. Francis Xavier Church/Maryknoll; Densho, Seattle Buddhist Temple Archives, the Matsuzari Family Collection, ddr-densho-38-27

The Second Dislocation: Library of Congress (LC-USZ62-91831); Brian Suda Photography, Courtesy of Bishop Eric Matsumoto; JIR Files, Folder 272, University Archives & Manuscripts Department, University of Hawai'i at Manoa Library; Gift of Jane Sachiko Kodama, in Memory of Takenori and Matsuko Kodama (2004.96.4), JANM; Gift of Jack

Opposite: End papers of the first Kitaji Bible.

and Peggie Iwata (93.102.102), JANM; Gift of Susan K. Mochizuki and Ann K. Uyeda (2006.133.5), JANM; Courtesy of the Dyo/Fukui Families; Gift of the American Friends Service Committee (94.122.4I), JANM; Collection of JANM; Buddhist Churches of America (BCA) Archives, Courtesy of UCLA Library Special Collections; Gift of Jim Hirabayashi (98.345.1), JANM; Gift of Susan K. Mochizuki and Ann K. Uyeda (2006.133.35), JANM; Densho, Dorothea Lange Collection, ddr-densho-151-311

Resilience: Courtesy of Wisdom Publications; Library of Congress (LC-DIG-ppprs-00333); Courtesy of Homma and Wada Families; Courtesy of Heart Mountain Foundation; Courtesy of St. Francis Xavier Church/Maryknoll; Gift of Walter Muramoto Family (97.293.5), JANM; Gift of June Hoshida Honma, Sandra Hoshida and Carole Hoshida Kanada (97.106.1DC), JANM; Gift of Isamu Sam Kayano (91.146.16), JANM; Gift of Michiko Otaya (94.8.2), JANM; Courtesy of Shirley Nagatomi Okabe Collection, Manzanar National Historic Site; Brian Suda Photography, Courtesy of Nichiren Mission of Hawaii; WRA photo (no. B-898); Gift of Michiko Otaya (94.8.3), JANM; Gift of June Hoshida Honma, Sandra Hoshida and Carole Hoshida Kanada (97.106.1K), JANM; Courtesy of Bill Manbo and Eric Mueller; Gift of Miyoko (Takeuchi) Eshita (96.491.3), JANM; Gift of Dr. and Mrs. Masy Masuoka (92.109.51), JANM; Gift of the American Friends Service Committee (94.122.4AC); Gift of Tamotsu Ikemoto (93.104.6), JANM; Gift of Masy A. Masuoka, O.D. (91.124.15), JANM; Gift of Mine Okubo Estate (2007.62.180), JANM; Kango Takamura paintings (Collection 433), Special Collections Library, Charles E. Young Research Library, UCLA; Courtesy of Maureen Poon Fear; Ruth Strout McCandless Collection on Nyogen Senzaki (Collection 2296), Library Special Collections, Charles E. Young Research Library, UCLA; Brian Suda Photography, Courtesy of Japanese Cultural Center of Hawai'i; Gift of Diane Hara (88.20.4), JANM; Brian Suda Photography, Courtesy of Kona Daifukuji Soto Mission; Gift of June Hoshida Honma, Sandra Hoshida and Carole Hoshida Kanada (97.106.2AU), JANM; Courtesy of Gail Y. Okawa; Gift of the Gilroy Buddhist Community Hall (2001.392.1-9), JANM; Courtesy of the Nishiura Family Collection; Photo by Rebecca Goldschmidt, Courtesy of the Joonji-Shibata Family; Densho, National Archives and Records Administration Collection, ddr-densho-37-536; Courtesy of Nancy Kyoko Oda; Gift of Kinuko Matsumura and Family (95.205.1), JANM; Gift of Madeleine Sugimoto and Naomi Tagawa (92.97.9), JANM

Sutra and Bible: Gift of Les and Nora Bovee (94.158.1), JANM; Courtesy of the Kitaji Family/Hoover Institution Library & Archives; JANM (94.195.29N); Courtesy of Cal State Dominguez Hills, California State University Japanese American Digitization Project, Satoru Maeda Album; JANM (95.194.25C); Mary Griggs Burke Collection, Gift of the Mary and Jackson Burke Foundation, 2015, Metropolitan Museum of Art; Photo by and Courtesy of Nancy Ukai; Gift of Church Divinity School of the Pacific (2000.102.1), JANM; Gift of Sumi Maruyama (2001.180.1), JANM; Gift in

Memory of Tetsuzo and Chizuko Taguchi (96.136.1), JANM; Courtesy of Homma and Wada Families; Gift of the Kubo and Ichihara Families (91.93.108), JANM; Gift of Don Okubo (2005.153.9), JANM; Courtesy of Kyle Iwanaga; Courtesy of Furuta Family; Courtesy of Kyle Iwanaga; Courtesy of the Kitaji Family/Hoover Institution Library & Archives

Remembrance: Brian Suda Photography; Densho, War Relocation Authority, Minidoka Collection, ddr-fom-1-92; Courtesy of Shirley Nagatomi Okabe Collection, Manzanar National Historic Site; Courtesy of Manzanar Historic Site, Nagatomi Collection; Gift of the Walter Muramoto Family (97.292.15G); 93.113.9, 2001.184.2, 2001.184.3, 2007.70.3, 96.93.1, 94.94.1, JANM; Gift of the Walter Muramoto Family (97.293.8), JANM, Courtesy of Homma and Wada Families; Brian Suda Photography; Gift of Florence Izumi (95.198.42), JANM; Brian Suda Photography, Courtesy of Liliha Shingon Mission; Courtesy of the United States Army Signal Corps; Gift of Bob McCallagh (93.156.8), JANM; Gift of Mary Saito Tominaga (94.6.9, 68, 69), JANM; Brian Suda Photography, Courtesy of Nichiren Mission of Hawaii

Solidarity: Gift of Elizabeth Y. Yamada (93.75.10, .20), JANM; Courtesy of Jonathan van Harmelen; Azalia Emma Peet Papers, 7043, Smith College Special Collections; Courtesy of the Tacoma Public Library 80/8891; Courtesy of the Shirley Nagatomi Okabe Collection, Manzanar National Historic Site; Courtesy of St. Francis Xavier Church/Maryknoll; Courtesy of Brooks Andrews; Densho, Mamiya Collection, ddr-densho-13-45; Gift of T. Yata Collection (95.189.6), JANM; Gift of the American Friends Service Committee (94.122.4V), JANM; Courtesy of Todd Tsuchiya; Collection Center for Creative Photography, Copyright Center for Creative Photography, Arizona Board of Regents; Library of Congress (LC-USZ62-127883); WRA photo (no. K-288); WRA photo (no. I-966)

Reparation: Courtesy of the Manzanar Historic Site; Collection of Emily Anderson; Courtesy of Janice Tanaka; Courtesy of Hiroshi Shimizu; Courtesy of Stephen Nagano; Gift of Hideo Hashimoto (95.60.14), JANM; Courtesy of Visual Communications/NCRR; Gift of Reverend Bunyu Fujimura (93.198.2), JANM; Photo by Stefan Finsterle and Courtesy of the Tokunaga-Wan Family Collection; Courtesy of Nancy Ukai; Courtesy of United We Dream; "In a Buddhist Forest" reprinted with permission from Lizzie Davis at Coffee House Press

Photo essay: California State University, Sacramento, Gerth Special Collections and University Archives; Courtesy of St. Francis Xavier Church/Maryknoll; Anaheim Public Library; Gift of Elizabeth Shigekawa (2000.199.13), JANM; Gift of Nichiren Buddhist Temple of Los Angeles (2002.111.2), JANM; Courtesy of Japanese Evangelical Mission Society; Courtesy of Jon Ido; Courtesy of Homma and Wada Families; Photo by and Courtesy of Marilyn Torres; Courtesy of Gen Fujitani; Courtesy Lily Harumi Baba (2001.223.1), JANM; Courtesy of George Tanabe; Gift of Ruth Tsuchiyama (98.378.9), JANM

Below: Heart Mountain sutra stone with the character for "path" or "way."

Page 156, top: Obon at Sacramento Buddhist Church, 1952.

Page 156, middle: First gathering of St. Francis Xavier Catholic Church after World War II, Los Angeles, California, 1945.

Page 156, bottom: Taiko drummers perform at Obon celebration at Orange County Buddhist Church, Anaheim, California, 1993.

Page 157, top: Gathering of Nisei Christian leaders that led to the establishment of the Japanese Evangelical Missionary Society (JEMS), Mt. Hermon, California, 1950.

Page 157, bottom: Rev. Shokai Kanai leads members of the Los Angeles Nichiren Buddhist Temple as they process through the Boyle Heights neighborhood for a ceremony commemorating the founder of Nichiren Buddhism on the anniversary of his death, Los Angeles, California, 1999.

Page 158, top: A summer camp for special needs youth by JEMS, held at Mt. Hermon, California, 1995.

Page 158, bottom left: Yuriko Warden helps at a Christmas party at the North Shore Baptist Church, Chicago, Illinois, ca. 1962.

Page 158, upper right: Seattle Japanese Baptist Church congregation gathers to celebrate the 120th anniversary of the church's founding, Seattle, Washington, 2019.

Page 158, lower right: Salt Lake Buddhist Temple during the annual Nihon Matsuri, or Japan Festival, Salt Lake City, Utah, 2018.

Page 159, top: Dancers celebrate Obon at Honpa Hongwanji Betsuin of Hawaii, Honolulu, Hawai'i, 2016.

Page 159, bottom: Soka Gakkai International (SGI) members gather in front of their newly constructed headquarters in Los Angeles, ca. 1965.

Page 160, top: Toro Nagashi, or lantern floating ceremony, held in conjunction with the Obon festivities at Haleiwa Jodo Mission, Hawai'i, 2009.

Page 160, bottom: Members of the Los Angeles Japanese Baptist Church gather in front of their sanctuary in Los Angeles, California, 1964.

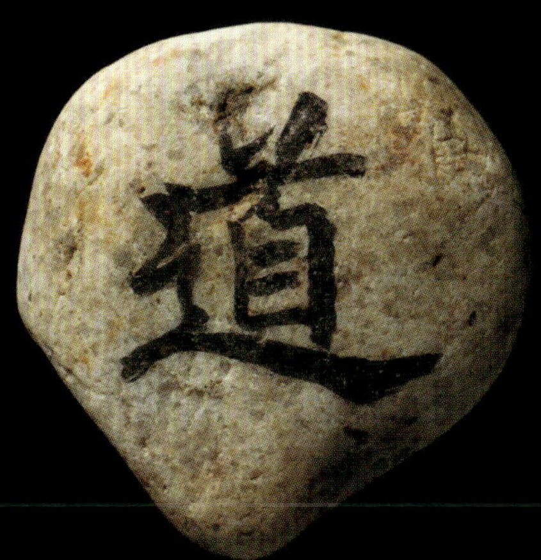

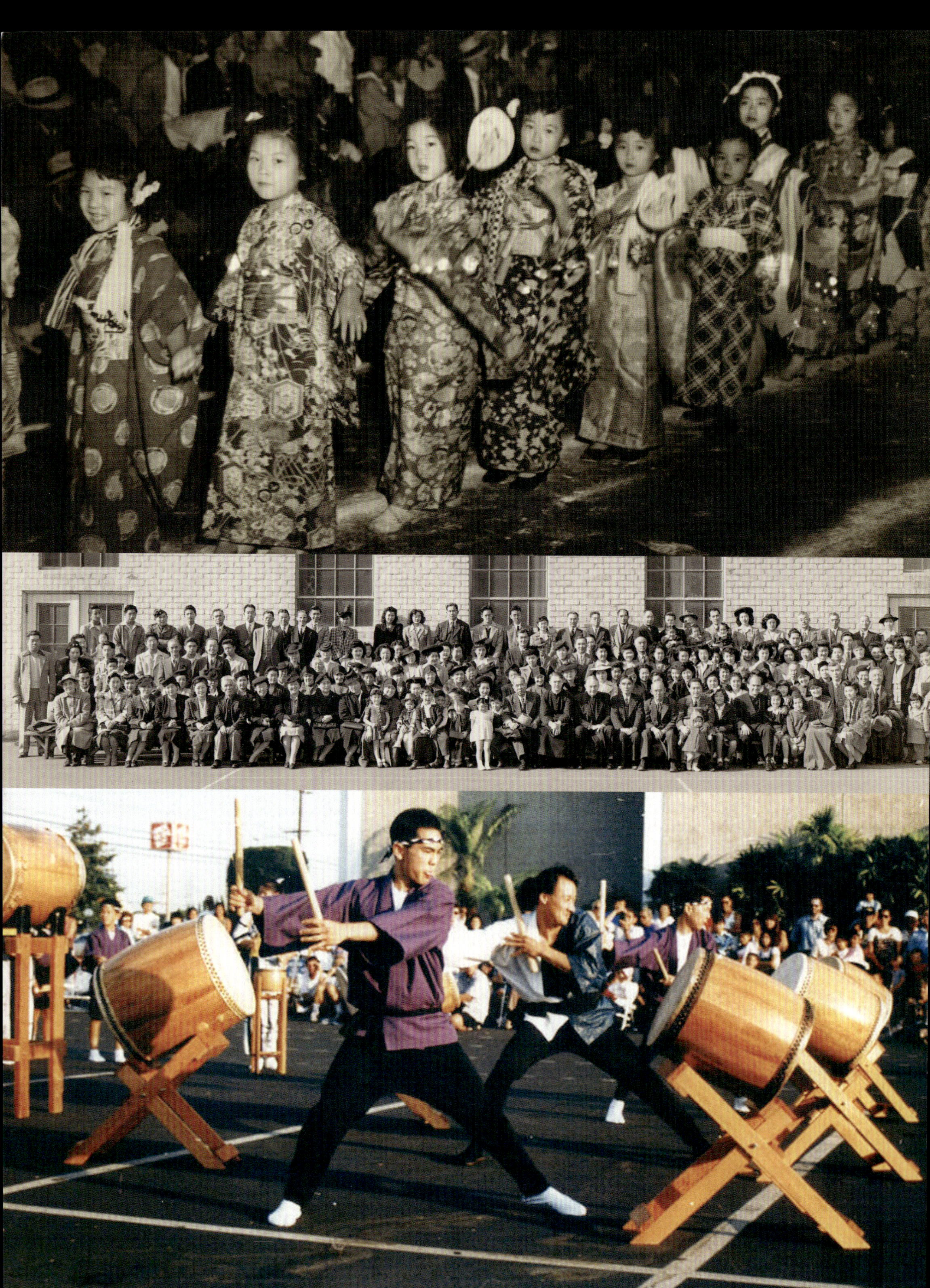

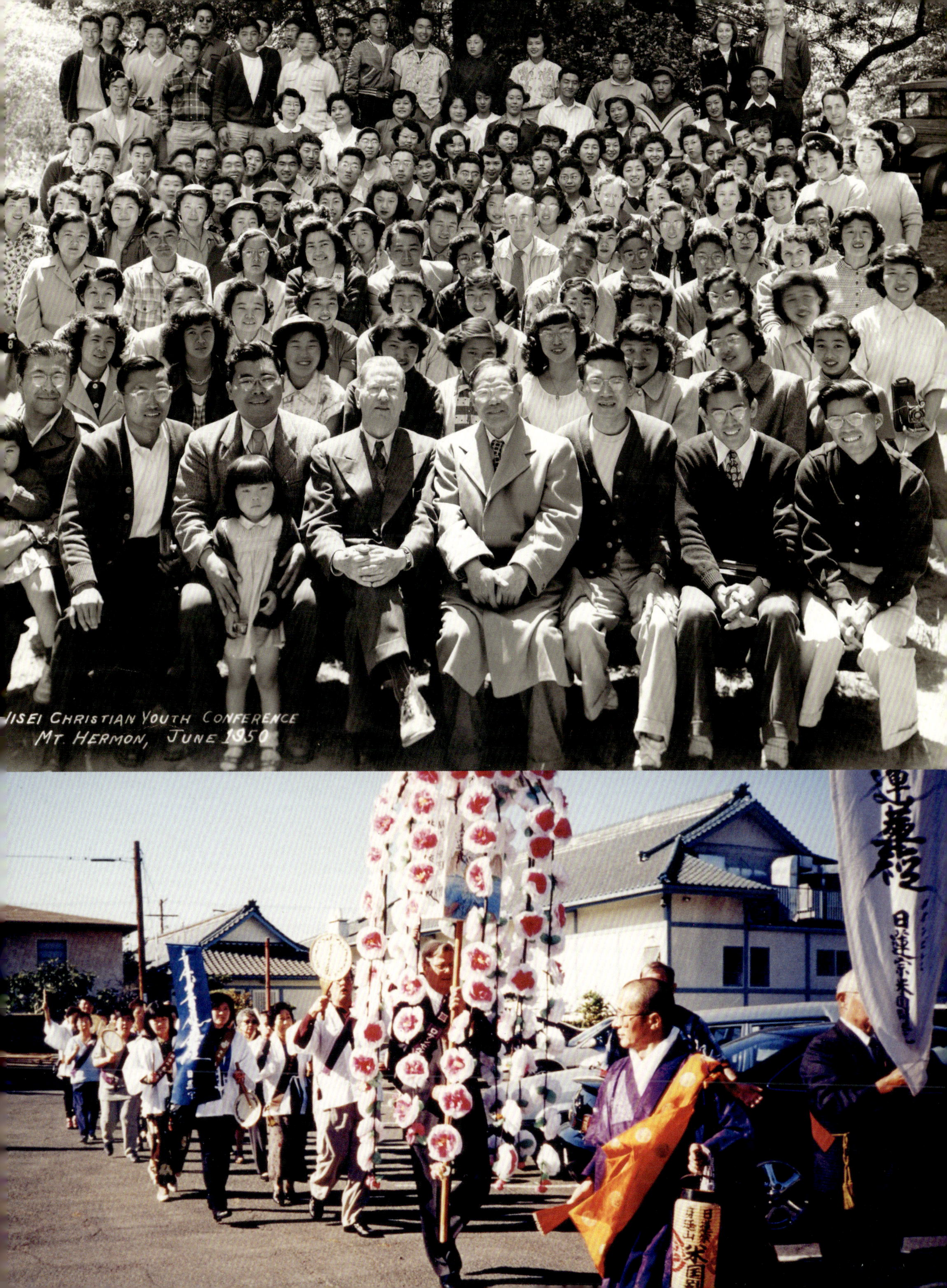

NISEI CHRISTIAN YOUTH CONFERENCE
MT. HERMON, JUNE 1950

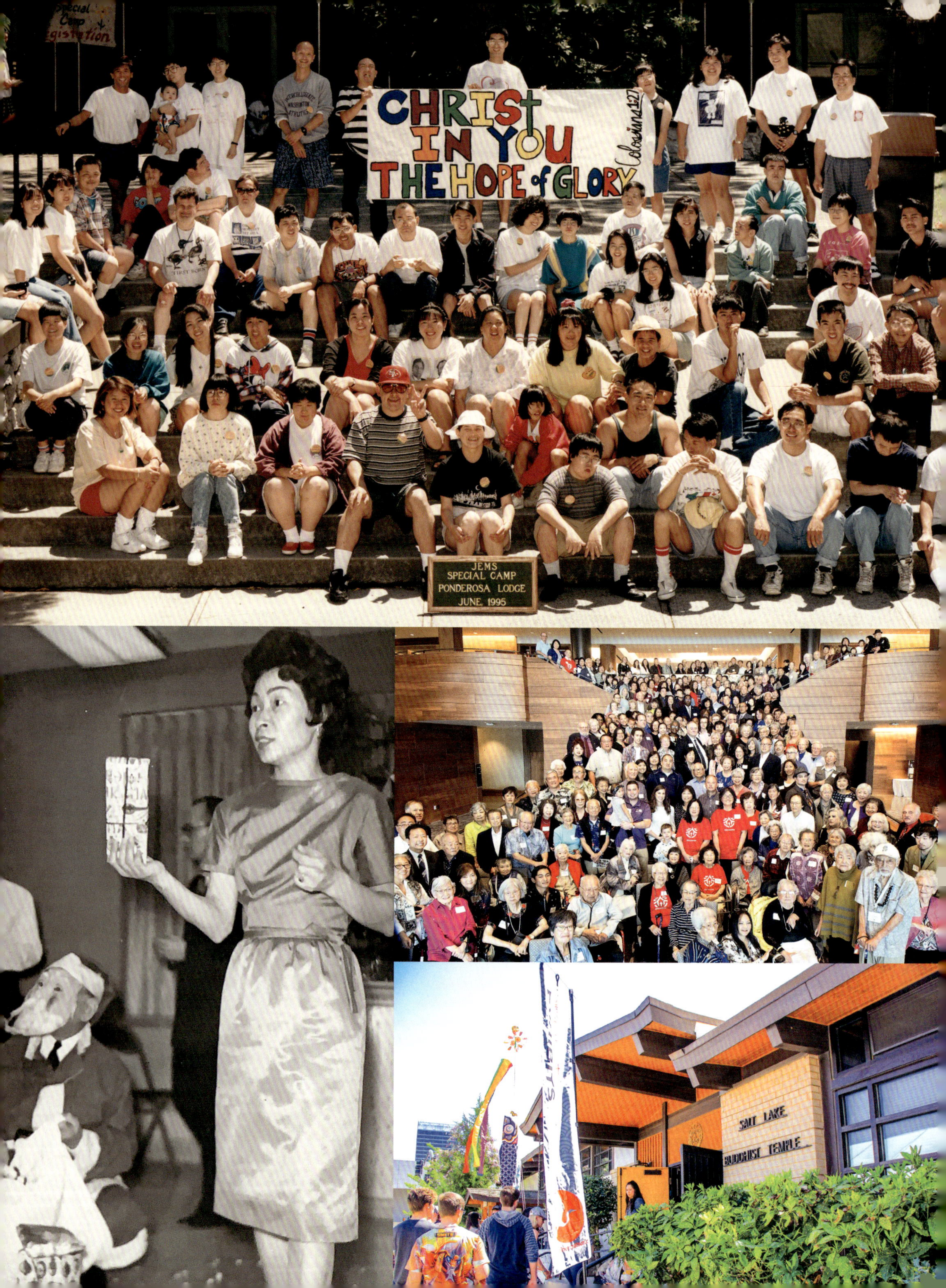
CHRIST
IN YOU
THE HOPE of GLORY
Colossians 1:27
JEMS
SPECIAL CAMP
PONDEROSA LODGE
JUNE, 1995
SALT LAKE
BUDDHIST TEMPLE

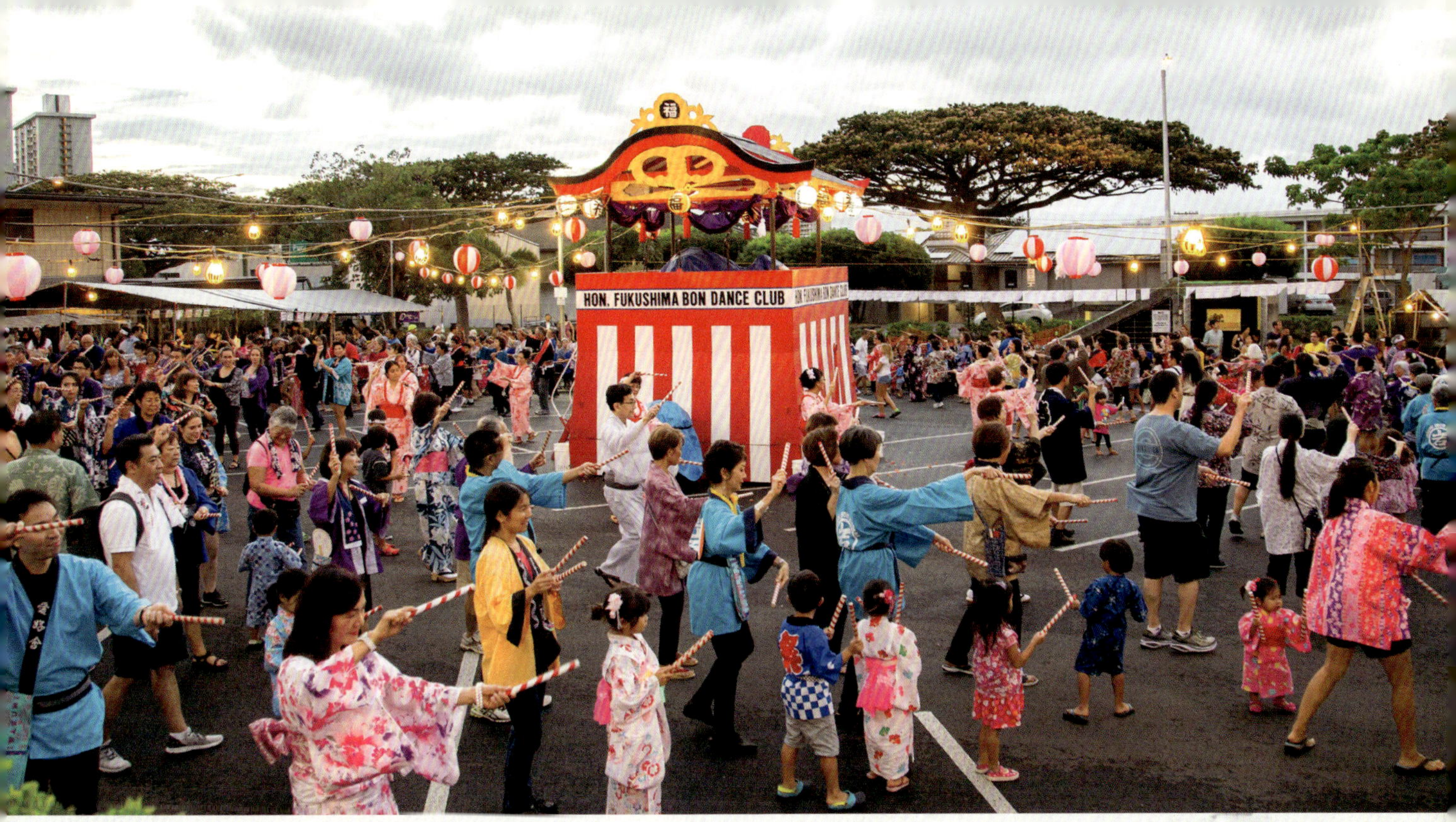

HON. FUKUSHIMA BON DANCE CLUB

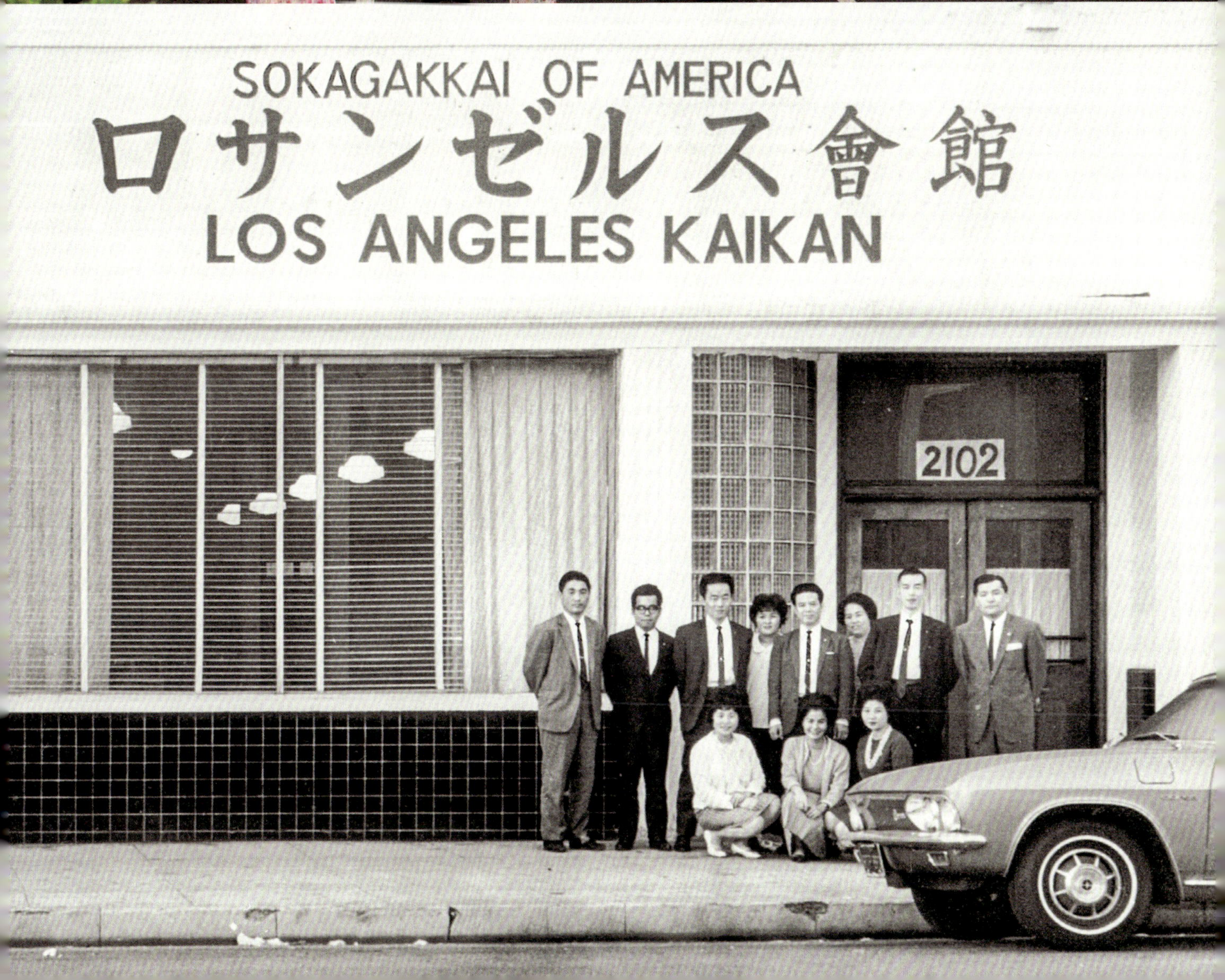

SOKAGAKKAI OF AMERICA
ロサンゼルス會館
LOS ANGELES KAIKAN
2102

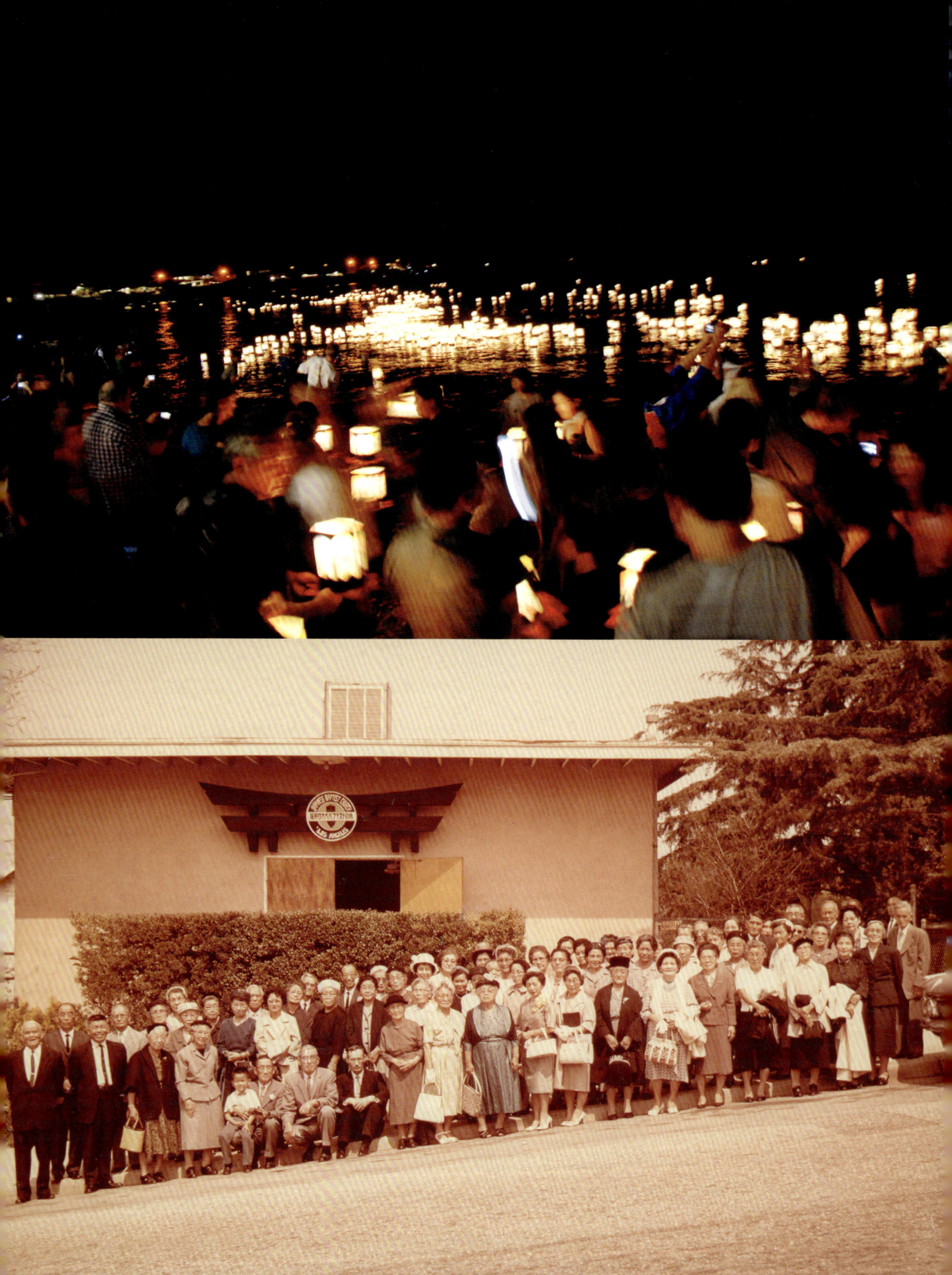